the book of

Celtic Magic

WWW.BOBJONESMEDIA.COM

About the Author

Kristoffer Hughes is a native Welsh speaker, born to a Welsh family in the mountains of Snowdonia in 1971. He lives on the Island of Anglesey, Wales, the ancestral seat of the British Druids. His love of Celtic literature and traditions guided his path into the exploration and practice of Celtic Paganism. He is the founder and head of the Anglesey Druid Order and studies with the Order of Bards, Ovates and Druids. In 2012 he was awarded the Mount Haemus Scholarship for original research in Druidism and related subjects. Kristoffer frequently presents workshops and lectures throughout the United Kingdom. His love of Celtic heritage and culture inspired him to pen his first book, *Natural Druidry*, in 2007.

Videos, sound bites, and contact information for the author can be found here:

WWW.KRISTOFFERHUGHES.CO.UK

WWW.ANGLESEYDRUIDORDER.CO.UK

Kristoffer Hughes

the book of Celtic Magic

Transformative Teachings from the Cauldron of Awen

Llewellyn Publications
Woodbury, Minnesota

FIRST EDITION
Third Printing, 2015

Book design and edit by Rebecca Zins
Cover design by Kevin R. Brown
Cover illustration by John Blumen
Interior bird illustration from *1167 Decorative Cuts CD-ROM and Book* (Dover Publications, 2007);
page 283 glyph illustration © Taryn Shrigley;
all other illustrations by the Llewellyn Art Department

Library of Congress Cataloging-in-Publication Data
Hughes, Kristoffer, 1971–
The book of celtic magic : transformative teachings from the cauldron of awen / Kristoffer Hughes.—First edition.
pages cm
Includes bibliographical references and index.
ISBN 978-0-7387-3705-8
1. Mythology, Celtic—Wales. 2. Magic, Celtic. 3. Celts—Religion. I. Title.
BL980.G7H835 2014
299'.166—dc23

2014011644

Llewellyn Publications
A Division of Llewellyn Worldwide Ltd.
2143 Wooddale Drive
Woodbury, MN 55125-2989
www.llewellyn.com

Printed in the United States of America

FOR

Barrie and Kristal Jenks

AND

Christopher and Susan Hickman

in honor of your friendship

Contents

Acknowledgments

I am indebted to so many kind, wise, and patient folk who helped in the writing of this book, whether through advice, information, or just as long-suffering ears to my woes. Ian Gibbs for his constant support and help even at times when his patience must be stretched to the limits. Penny Billington for her wit, sharp intellect, and the wonderful long telephone calls. Barrie Jenks who constantly surprises me with his knowledge, sagacity, and inspiration; you are a ray of Awen. Christopher Hickman, who rushes to my aid whenever I am in fear of a melodramatic breakdown: you are a joy and a font of advice and wisdom; I praise the gods for your friendship. All the other members of the Anglesey Druid Order, you are all rather fabulous. Jonathan Holland and Michael Howell, who endured hours of my ramblings without (seemingly) losing the plot and were of immense help with the properties of herbs. To all the Pagans out there who devote themselves and their practice in honor of the spirit of Celtica. Last but by no means least, to my ever-patient editorial team at Llewellyn Worldwide, Elysia Gallo and Rebecca Zins, thank you.

Introduction

This is primarily a book about sacred relationships—of connecting and aligning oneself to the archetypes, trees, plants, and animals of the Celtic traditions. Celtic magic may be intimately linked with your own sense of ancestry as an ethereal web connecting you to a culture that continues to thrive to this day. Your reasons for choosing to purchase this book may well mirror my reasons for wanting to write it: to connect to the powerful undercurrent of the Celtic spirit.

Celtic magic transforms the magician; I was transformed by the process of aligning myself with this magical current—a current that spans 3,000 years, from the dawning of the Iron Age through the coming of the Romans and to the height of the Medieval renaissance. It is this current of magic that I present to you in the pages that follow—true magic experienced by a magician of the Celtic tradition. The magic is tried and tested. I do not offer a random series of magical practices but true practical magic born from the cauldron of the Celts. It has worked for me and for a number of others over the years, and it will work for you.

The magical discourse presented in this book has not arisen from the need to "pad out" a book, and I hope that you will sense that as you read. In a manner, this is my own Book of Shadows or grimoire; a collection of magic that I have used over the years, it is a reflection of my understanding of what magic is and how and why we use it. But there is more to this book than a presentation of magical actions. My hope is that this book and the magic it contains will transform you—will move you closer to the continuum of the Celts and cause you to become a practical Celtic magician. My hope is to offer you insights into my practice so that you may glean the importance of being in close relationship with the powerful forces of Celtica.

◆ ◆ ◆

Vocationally my path is that of Druidry, but contrary to popular belief, Druids also practice magic. My training is steeped in both Druidry and what the English-speaking world would classify as Witchcraft; my spirituality combines the cultural philosophy and worldview of Druidry with the practical aspects of folk magic and Witchcraft. With that in mind, this book is suitable for witches, Wiccans, Druids, and Pagans alike. While the rituals presented here are different from common Pagan practice, they are not included just to appear different or quirky; they are actual rituals utilized by several groups of people and have been formulated to evoke the Celtic worldview.

Celtic Defined

The term *Celtic* refers to a cultural tribal group defined by their use of language who spanned parts of Northern Europe and in particular the regions of Gaul (modern-day France and Belgium), the British Isles, and Ireland—where they continue to exist to this day. Identified by their use of art, social organization, and mythology, their influence has been long lasting and a subject of study for centuries. There are two primary streams of Celtic culture, each defined by its use of language. The first is designated the term *Q Celtic* and refers to the Goidelic or Gaelic languages—Scots Gaelic, Irish Gaelic, and Manx. The second stream is designated the term *P Celtic* and refers to the Brythonic or Brittonic languages, which survive in the form of Breton, Cornish, and Welsh.

It is important to note that the term *Celtic* does not refer to a bloodline but rather to a cultural line; it is this freedom of movement that enables the Celtic spirit to migrate and settle in other lands. The Celtic culture seems to have condensed in the island regions of northwest Europe, which are also the regions most replete with Celtic myth and lore. This may well indicate that the Celtic culture imprinted itself on earlier traditions, where the designers of the stone monuments and their priests evolved to become the Druids of the Celtic era.

To many the Celts are a people of long ago, lost to us by the chasm of time. But the Celts are still here: they exist as the people and descendants of the six primary Celtic nations of Brittany, Cornwall, Wales, the Isle of Man, Scotland, and Ireland. Celtic *identity*, however, is a fluid affair whereby millions of individuals worldwide identify themselves or aspects of their ancestry, whether genetically or spiritually, as being inherently Celtic.

I use the term *Celtica* throughout this book to refer to the connective spirit and the commonality of mythology and traditions that glue the current six Celtic nations to each other and to the people who align themselves with it. I suggest that Celtic magic is mythocentric, which is the defining factor that sets it apart from other magical systems. This mythocentric quality brings to Celtic magic a pantheon of gods and goddesses, demigods and demigoddesses, and their mysteries.

The pantheon, myths, and magic that I present in this book are rooted in the British Celtic tradition as preserved in the Welsh. This may be new to you, for the majority of books that focus on Celtic magic and spirituality tend to concentrate on the Irish material. While that tradition bears a striking semblance to the British mythological sagas, and many of its deities share similar names and legends, it is outside my area of expertise. It is for this reason that this book will not feature or discuss Irish Celtic, with the exception of the discourse on the ogam divination system.

Myth and legend speak of deep mystery and the secret teachings of an ancient priesthood. Celtic magic gives us the privilege of skimming its surface of mythology if we so wish, touching the fronds of its power and swimming with it for a while, or we may choose to dive into the depths of its cauldron of wisdom and become fully immersed in a magical tradition that spans thousands of years, where we may become priests in service to Celtica. The beauty of Celtic magic lies in its flexibility and its vibrant river of continuation that streams from the past, carving a channel into the future.

The Tree of Tradition: Branches of the Mabinogi

Magic was commonplace in the mythologies of the Celts; the majority of deities and other characters we meet in the chronicles either possessed magical abilities and attributions or frequently used magic for a specific purpose. Spellcasting, conjuration, invocation, and the use of magical tools and paraphernalia are common themes within Celtic mythology and lore.

These traits can be seen demonstrated in the Celtic legendary collection known commonly as the Mabinogi or the Mabinogion. These tales will feature heavily throughout this work, for in it we find references to the pantheon of Celtic deities. We are introduced to the semi-divine children of the gods and goddesses, and we capture a glimpse of pre-Christian belief structures within them. The Mabinogi collection is presented as complete tales in the White Book of Rhydderch (1325) and the Red Book of Hergest (1375); fragments of the tales occur in earlier manuscripts, and it is generally accepted that they contain themes that are significantly older.[1] Aspects of the Mabinogi saga are mentioned in the works of Taliesin, which are set in the time of King Maelgwn of Gwynedd in the sixth century and recorded by Gildas in his *De Excidio Britanniae*.

While the latest manuscripts are medieval, academic studies suggest that the tales existed in the vernacular for centuries prior to their being penned by the medieval scribes.[2] To paraphrase the medievalist Will Parker, it is a truism that more or less every single aspect and theme within the Mabinogi has its roots in the pre-Christian past.[3] The Mabinogi collection contains eleven native tales that have been recorded by the Welsh; however, only four are identified as containing the term *Mabinogi*. These are called the four branches of the Mabinogi. These important, multilayered tales can be used as keys to access the profound mysteries of the Celts.

This book will serve to guide you into the tumultuous currents of the Mabinogi and offer you a clarity of practice that can accentuate and color

1 Ford, *The Mabinogi*, 2.

2 Haycock, *Legendary Poems from the Book of Taliesin*, 9–13.

3 Parker, *The Four Branches of the Mabinogi*, 653.

your own traditions. I will examine many of the archetypes that I have met along my own journey into the heart of Celtica and on sojourns to the Celtic otherworld. I do this by means of introduction to enable you to sense the magic that hides beneath the words of the Mabinogi, which the Celtic scholar Dr. Brynley Roberts describes as

> remnants of the Brythonic mythology and the beliefs of the Britons in the otherworld—Annwn—and they are concerned with gods and men; they consist of characters from the pantheon of Celtic Britain who form the heroes of the four branches.[4]

In order for much that follows to be of benefit to you, the Mabinogi should be essential reading. Online versions are plentiful, and there are dozens of printed editions available at most booksellers. My hope is that this book will provide you with a launch pad to facilitate your own dive into the depths of the Celtic mysteries. While some of these tales may seem overly complicated or nonsensical, do not lose heart; this book will serve to guide you in seeing the clues to mystery that swim between the lines.

A Challenge

In the late nineties I happened across a book by the late Celticist Alexei Kondratiev, and within its pages I found myself faced with a challenge:

> The six Celtic languages are still alive, if not well. In them are stored, as on a disk, several millennia of a people's unique experience, waiting to be given a new dynamic expression by that generation who will dare to break the colonial shackles of fear and self-doubt.... We must, as they did, have the imagination to give flesh to life-giving myth, and the will to work its pattern into our existence. Every one of us who has felt the beauty of the Celtic world vision must act, each in our individual ways, now before it is too late. Do something![5]

What you hold in your hands is my attempt to do as Kondratiev asked—to ride the waves of his challenge and express my connection to the power

4 Translated by me from the Welsh forward to *Y Mabinogion* (Ifans, xiii).

5 Kondratiev, *Celtic Rituals*, 52.

of Celtic magic. By doing this, I hope you also will take the challenge to step into the crystal-clear waters of the Celtic cultural continuum and emerge, radiant with Awen, to inspire the world.

How to Use This Book

This book represents a personal journey, a magical memoir of exploration, practice, and ritual. Central to the tenet of Celtic magical belief is the importance of Awen, the divine spirit of inspiration, and one of the functions of the magician is to inspire. My hope is that these thoughts and explorations of the archetypes, deities, and magic of the Celts will inspire your own practice. Scattered throughout the book you will find numerous contemplative exercises; these are essential for the digestion and assimilation of the information presented to you. I suggest that you find yourself a little notebook or journal to be used exclusively in conjunction with this book. Periodically I will ask you to jot or note some of your thoughts and visions from the contemplation exercises and, of course, to record your magic when you perform it. It is important for you to do these exercises, for they assimilate the words into meaningful patterns in your mind. Essentially they will help you make sense of the information I offer you.

While this is my journey, many others have walked this path with me. My mentors and teachers guided me to the cauldron's edge and encouraged me to peer through the steam. I offer you a similar guiding hand through the forest of Celtic magic and into relationship with Celtica.

Kristoffer Hughes
Isle of Anglesey, Wales
WINTER 2013

PART I

Weaving the Web of Celtic Magic

1

Understanding Celtic Magic

Magic may be defined as the energetic undercurrent of the universe that is accessible from the edges of the human psyche as a force that is used to cause or create change. Natural forces are inherent within everything that exists in our universe, and that includes you; what you do, think, say, and feel has a direct and sympathetic effect on the world around you. It affects the underlying motion of the universe, if you like. Imagine a spider's web of glistening silver that stretches beyond this world and connects all other worlds to it. This web permeates the visible and invisible worlds, existing everywhere simultaneously, and is a metaphor for the underlying current, or energy matrix, of the universe; everything is connected. The magician knows this wisdom and consequently manipulates the web at will. Using magic, we tug at one strand of the web, causing vibrations to ripple from its source to affect the whole. The will of the magician travels along that conduit, or path, and initiates change to occur in accordance with his or her will.

Celtic Magic and Witchcraft

The culture of the ancient Celts was one where magic was commonplace; the word *witch* did not exist, at least not with its anglicized meaning. The common people and the Druids practiced what we would identify today as Witchcraft, this being the practical aspect of natural manipulation and transformation by supernatural means; being religious was not required for this magic to be effective. Today, Druidry in Wales continues to be a magical tradition. As a Druid I use spellcasting, conjuration, incantations, and amulets to express the connection I have to the natural world and the Divine—traits that are normally associated with Witchcraft. Druidry is my religion, but it is one that embraces and practices *swyn*, an ancient Welsh word that can be translated to mean "charm or incantation; magic." However, the practice of *swyn* is not defined by a religious affiliation. *Swyn* is the functional aspect of magical practice, and it has survived despite the Reformation and the later Christian revivals of nineteenth-century Wales. It survived, for the people could not be without it. Its function was essential for the well-being of the people; with few medical doctors at hand, the *swyn* (or *swyngyfaredd*, the wise women and men who used the Old Ways to heal) were assets that communities valued. While the persecution of witches and Witchcraft ravaged England, Wales—in stark contrast—was relatively untouched by the witch-hunting fever. The Welsh had no point of reference that referred to the vulgar character of the witch hysteria, as *swyn* was a vital component of Welsh society.

When the witch craze eventually impinged on Welsh society, attitudes changed, and the innocents who faced the judges were identified as *wits*, which is a clear borrowing of the English word *witch*. This demonstrates that the Welsh were, in fact, borrowing the term *witch* from the English together with its new associations rather than perpetuating a long-held mistrust of magic and Witchcraft. The *swyn*, however, continued to practice their arts with little recourse or reprimand because they did not fit the stereotypical witch figure popularized by the prejudice of the witch hunters and the church.

The Druids came and went, the elite magicians, wizards, and astrologers came and went, but the *swyn*—the folkloric practitioners of magic—survived. This magic is rich in heritage and ancestry, but it does not denote the survival of an intact system of Witchcraft or Paganism; it simply denotes a practice that utilized a conduit of supernatural power to activate it. It is truly of the land. The historian Richard Suggett suggests it is likely that the attitude towards Witchcraft in Wales was influenced by the predominance of the Celts and their ancient priests, the Druids, to be practitioners of magic.[6] Wales was and continues to be a land saturated in magical practice that cannot be defined by tradition or religion. *Swyn* exists despite them; it, like magic, is neutral, and yet its practice can be incorporated into any religious system, as it invariably was. There are examples of *swyn* charms and incantations that contain references to Jesus and the Holy Spirit and others that are wholly animistic and focused on the earth.[7] It is this old magic that sings from the pages of this book. It is this old magic that forms the practical aspect of my spirituality.

Englynion: The Power of Words

An *englyn* (plural *englynion*), or song-spell, is the strict metering of poetic verse that often appears hand in hand with acts of magic, implying that these metered, rhyming verses had a power beyond that of simple words. Elements of this continue to be perpetuated in the construction of rhyming verses in modern spellcraft. Bards of the Celtic nations were magicians in their own rights who used words to transform, inspire, satirize, create, and also destroy. Creating *englynion* for our own ceremonies and acts of magic are powerful methods of accessing the subtle realms while simultaneously connecting to the Celtic spirit.

The casting of spells (which can be defined as the utilization of words that have power to transform its target) and the use of incantations that, when used with due ritual, produced magical results were attributes of ancient

6 Suggett, *A History of Magic and Witchcraft in Wales*, 8–13.

7 Ibid., 29.

Druidic practice. An element of this can be seen in the numerous *englynion* that are recorded within the Mabinogi collection and other tales. These rhyme verses are replete with occult symbology and mystery and seem to be the outward expression of the magician's intent. The vocal repetition of an *englyn* effectively acts as a mantra, stilling the noise of the mind and focusing the magician's intent on the act at hand.

The poetic verses that appear throughout this book are *englynion*. Instructions for the performing of a particular spell or rite may appear in verse; take note of these. Words that appear in italics are intended to be spoken out loud. The "ng" sound in *englyn* is pronounced exactly as the "ng" sound in *song*. Therefore, utter a short "e" (as in the "e" in *elephant*), followed immediately by the "ng" sound, and conclude it with "lyn," pronounced exactly as you would say the name *Lynne*. Do not pause on any sound; it's quick, precise: *ENG-lyn*. Its plural, *englynion*, is pronounced *eng-LUN-eeon*.

Defining Celtic Magic

Celtic magic is the practice of a cultural strand of magic without the necessity for a religious framework. For example, Wicca is a religious practice that embraces magic and Witchcraft across a wide range of cultures, although it is heavily influenced by the Celtic tradition. Druidry is a religious practice which arises from the Celtic culture; Celtic magic naturally is a facet of that, but I emphasize that one does not need to be a practicing Druid to connect to and practice Celtic magic; it appeals to Wiccans, Druids, hedge witches, and ritual magicians alike. There are many solitary practitioners who identify themselves as Celtic Pagans, i.e., their entire frame of reference stems from the Celtic cultural continuum; it is what informs their practice.

Culturally Celtic magic connects us to the tribal spirit of the ancient Celts of northern Europe and the British Isles. Its roots sink deep into the soft green earth, and its voice sings from the heights of mountains. Woods and forests, streams and rivers carry the whispers of magic from one place to another. Blood is thicker than water, but ancestry is thicker still. It is this connection by means of culture and heritage that connects practitioners to the magic of the Celts. Therefore Celtic magic can be defined as what connects the practitioner to the streams of the Celtic cultural continuum.

The Celtic cultural continuum is not a bloodline; a gene does not exist that defines a person as being Celtic. The fact that its identification is one of culture provides it with a delicious fluidity. Although it epitomizes a group of people who identify themselves as Celtic through means of language, locality, or heritage, it is predominantly a spirit, and one that has continuously evolved and adapted to the needs of the people who align themselves to it and to the arbitrary forces that affect it. Blood may be thicker than water, but the spirit is what sings from the connection of blood with the land; it is stronger and thicker than genetics. The ethereal quality of the Celtic spirit has enabled people the world over to *feel* Celtic; something within their being sings out to that culture and calls them to it.

EXERCISE
THE CELTIC CULTURAL CONTINUUM

Stop for a minute or two—take a breath with the land beneath you, breathe in the sky above you, and deeply breathe with the rhythm of the seas that surround the shores of your land. Close your eyes and imagine a river, its crystal-clear waters smoothing the stones of its bed, water-loving plants waving their green fingers at you from the depths. It is begging for you to enter it, to taste it, to feel its coolness against your skin. Now imagine stepping into this river and watching its flow ahead of you, following its course into the distance until it turns a corner and vanishes into mystery. With a slow breath, imagine turning round and looking upstream; the river reaches far back into the mountains, back through soil and rock, and back even further through the corridors of time. The river contains the water from rainfall that may have showered the land a hundred years ago or perhaps a thousand years or more. You stand in this place bathed in the water of culture and heritage; you are a part of it. It is not as tangible or traceable as blood, for it is mystery. Sense the currents of the past flowing from the ancestral landscape, coursing through your body and resuming its never-ending path into the future. You are this river; you are the continuum. Sigh heavily with the river's flow, and open your eyes. Record your thoughts and visions in your journal.

◆ ◆ ◆

The Celtic cultural continuum can be perceived in the analogy of this river; it is a stream that runs from the past, through the present, and into the future. At any point along its course you may step into its current; by doing so, you are participating in something immensely sacred and magical. You are immersing yourself in the memory of the Celtic culture, its myths and magic. It survives for your survival; its current flows by means of the rivers of your life.

The Rules of Celtic Magic

Integrity is a word that every practitioner of magic should have tattooed on their body, together with a positive morality and the ability to honor yourself, others, and the world around you as much as is humanly possible, and to take your ethics seriously and judge well; never judge others harshly. The rules of Celtic magic are painfully simple: do not take advantage, and be careful of your intent.

When we practice magic, we must be perfectly clear of what we are doing, why we are doing it, to whom we are doing it, and what the consequences will be. Whatever you cast into the ocean will always return, transformed, on the tide. You may not like what comes back, but it's yours and you are going to have to put up with it. So the best way is to make sure that whatever you do cast into the tides of magic has enough integrity and stamina to survive its tumultuous journey across the vastness of the universe and return altered but not hideously so, and not to anyone's detriment.

Think: that is the keyword for any form of magic. I tend to be one of those magical practitioners who makes lists. I draw a good thick line vertically down a blank page and write the word FOR above one column and

AGAINST over the other. Okay, I hear you, this may come across as me being so anally retentive that I cannot sit down for fear of sucking up the furniture—but I can assure you that's not the case. If you are going to be the cause of change in the universe, it's rather sensible to think about it long and hard first. What will the consequences be, not just to yourself but to anyone else who could possibly be smacked in the face, however inadvertently, by your magical endeavors? Cause and effect, a standard rule; things always come back on the tide.

The Art of Magic

Manifestation swims at the heart of Celtic magic. The creation of something that previously was not there is potential and the materialization of that potential. When we take something from nothing and give it shape and form and meaning, we partake of the sacred ritual of creation; we become creators.

Practical art is no different. The very act of art is the magical process of creation through the manifestation of artistic inspiration. The artist is faced with a blank canvas or page; there is nothing there but pure potential. By reaching through the void and connecting to the streams of creativity, the artist invokes her inspiration from memory, experience, culture, etc. She then brings forth that inspiration and, by means of evocation, creates something that was previously unmanifest. A few seconds later, that potentiality is materializing itself on canvas, on paper, on the strumming of fingers over strings, in the movement of dance. It may appear as the writing of an author or the lyrics of a songwriter. All these things are manifestation. They are evoked from the body and mind of the artist and given shape and form.

Betwixt and Between: The Power of Liminality

Liminality—from the Greek *limen*, meaning "threshold"—brings a subtle power to magic by utilizing the subtle forces that linger between the seen and unseen, apparent and unapparent. Liminal places, times, and spaces are effective tools that ready the mind for magic and serve as a conduit for the projection of will and desire. When we move into liminal space or time, the world may feel slightly different—and, most importantly, so will the magician.

Using liminal time is essential for practical, effective magic, for it utilizes the natural energies of the world around us. Think of the certain times within a normal twenty-four-hour cycle where liminality can be found—a time that is betwixt and between. Subtly it is the point between darkness and dawn—the false dawn, if you like, where we are neither in night nor day. The other will be its opposite: at dusk, that peculiar light where it's not quite dark enough to warrant switching on the lights and yet it's too gloomy to do practical stuff like reading. In our material, time-driven world, liminality can be at the stroke of midnight, the witching hour, when we are between days; midday is that point where morning gives way to afternoon and we find ourselves in a peculiar state of enforced limbo. These examples serve to demonstrate that liminality is both a natural and an induced state. Dusk and dawn are quite natural, whereas our concepts of midnight and midday are constructs that humankind has created, yet they have become imbued with a power—with magic.

The seasons also have a liminal aspect, for they are dependent on several factors that may be vastly different from one area to another. Beltane, the great festival of virility, fertility, and growth in the Celtic calendar, is the point where spring gives way to summer, but the magic lies in its liminal quality of being between seasons. Beltane may occur in the south of England in mid-April, whereas in the Highlands of Scotland it may be a full month later. Liminality is fluid; it flows like the river of the Celtic consciousness, it is powerful and brings substance and great energy to magical practice.

EXERCISE
THE MAGIC OF LIMINALITY

Stop for a minute or two—take a breath with the land beneath you, breathe in the sky above you, and deeply breathe with the rhythm of the seas that surround the shores of your land. Imagine a bridge that crosses a stream or a river; this is the epitome of liminal space, neither on ground nor in the air, not on earth nor water. It is betwixt and between. In your vision it is midnight; sense a silence that sings of magic. Feel the particles of water that rise from the river below, and glance down at its inky blackness, flickers of starlight glittering on its surface. What does it mean to be liminal? Why is this essential for magic? Standing at the center of the bridge, look to your right; this is the world of ordinariness, of work and cars, obligations and bills. Now glance to the left; soft grass and the whispers of aspen sing the songs of the lands of magic. The expanse between is crossed by the bridge of liminality. Feel, sense, and be here now. With a deep breath and a loud sigh, arise from your vision and record your thoughts in your journal.

◆ ◆ ◆

Make the effort to find the liminal places and spaces within your own locality. Note how they make you feel and how they may benefit your magic. Stiles, estuaries, bridges, moorlands—all these places possess a betwixt quality that can color and clothe your magic with mystery and power. They may be of this world, but they act as a bridge for the mind that crosses the great divide between the apparent and the subtle worlds. By tapping into liminality, we are accessing another resource that affects and effects one's magic.

Part 1

Living Magically

Service is essential to the living of a magical life and the ability to listen intently to the wonders and mysteries of our universe. It is by serving the gods of tradition and mystery and lending our ear to those who may need us to listen that we inspire the world. Through our magic we cause change, and the primary change must be what occurs to the magician. And this occurs because of servitude, by working our magic for the benefit of our communities, our tribes, be these family and friends, work colleagues, or far-flung people on distant shores.

Magic teaches us to listen to the subtle forces of the universe. And it is by listening to our communities and reaching out when people are in need that we swim with deep honor and integrity.

Living a magical life is a frame of mind; it is seeing the potential in all things and being able to act on that. It is the subtle yet powerful ability to observe the natural world and see signs and omens in places that few others do. It is taking responsibility for your own actions and having the ability to respond to that when things do not go quite as planned. A magician is, above all else, humble and wonderfully inspirational.

A magical life is a life that lives with magic, seeing it in all places, not just in times of great need.

◆ 2 ◆

Awen: The Spirit of Celtic Magic

Within the Celtic cultural continuum there is a unique and fundamental force or power referred to as Awen in Britain and as Imbas in Ireland. This chapter will explore the magic and wonder of this force and its importance to the practice of Celtic magic. By aligning oneself to the power of Awen, we move into the energetic stream of Celtica and its wisdom. Here we will explore Awen's origins and the archetypes that represent it together with rituals that will introduce you or deepend your connection to Awen. Ultimately this chapter seeks to inspire you to integrate Awen into your practice, moving you closer to a relationship with the subtle forces that activate Celtic magic.

◆ ◆ ◆

Awen is the underlying current of the universe that is available to us right now. The magic of Awen can be seen emulated in quantum science as the vacuum state also known as the Zero Point Field; in a magical sense I like to refer to it as the A-field. It is the bridge that connects all things; it is the web of existence and experience that knots the wisdom of the universe together. Nothing is separate; everything is connected by the river of Awen. When we consider this, we can sense how our magic works and actually observe its workings through Awen's flowing streams. We step into these streams to activate the will and bring about change—magic.

When uttered correctly, Awen almost sounds like a sigh—it is pronounced quickly and consists of two syllables, "ah" and "when" (pronounced exactly as the English word *when*). Awen is a feminine noun, and although it cannot truly be translated into English, it can be taken to mean "flowing spirit." However, Awen is not to be confused with divinity or deity; if it had a voice, it would say this: "Before the gods and goddesses were created, I am." The word itself is ancient and can be found in various Celtic manuscripts dating from the ninth and possibly sixth centuries.[8] No doubt it was a word that was used in the oral traditions of the Celts for a significant amount of time prior to its recording on paper. Awen—two syllables that make a small word that packs quite a punch.

The Three Rays of Light

Awen is symbolized by three columns, or rays. Known as "the three Rays of Light" or "the three Pillars of Wisdom,"[9] they articulate the magic and wonder of Awen and express it in a symbol that can be drawn thus:

8 Haycock, *Legendary Poems from the Book of Taliesin*, 12.

9 Nichols, *The Book of Druidry*, 123.

There is no evidence to suggest that the symbol was used in antiquity, though the word itself was certainly in use, and although there are several sigils and carvings that appear similar to Awen, ranging from Britain to ancient Egypt, there is no conclusive evidence that it represents the same concept. Realistically we can only trace the symbol with certainty to the end of the eighteenth century.

In 1792 an eccentric and outspoken character from south Wales by the name of Iolo Morganwg was to revolutionize the Celtic revivalist movement. He initiated the popularity of Druidism and Celtic studies, and although he is accused of forgery, it cannot be disputed that he was also a poetic genius. Many of his theories have been adopted by cultural and Celtic revivalist and reconstructive groups. It is to him that the symbol is attributed, which appeared posthumously in his collected work known as *Barddas*.

According to Morganwg, the three columns of light represent the holy name of God, the origin of letters, and the stations of the sun, which he describes as follows:

> The first sign is a small cutting or line inclining with the sun at eventide, thus /; the second is another cutting, in the form of a perpendicular upright post, thus |; and the third is a cutting of the same amount of inclination as the first, but in the opposite direction, that is against the sun, thus \; and the three placed together, thus / | \.[10]

The Bard William Evans offers further insight into the symbol's solar associations:

> The three shafts of light represent in an abstract form the three stations of the sun at the four calends of the year, or ancient times of holidays. The angles formed by the arms of the divine symbol are those subtended by the apparent positions of the sun at a point of observation on the earth at these given times.[11]

Thanks to the efforts of Iolo Morganwg, Awen has a symbol, one that subsequently has been adopted by the current Pagan and Bardic movements.

10 Ab Ithel, *The Barddas of Iolo Morganwg*, 21.

11 Evans, *The Bards of the Isle of Britain*, 70.

The symbol evolved to the needs and beliefs of those who fell in love with it and has evolved uniquely to the needs of modern Paganism with the inclusion of the three dots and three circles that surround the symbol. These additions are not present in the original Iolo Morganwg manuscripts.

The three dots above it represent the three blessed drops of Awen that arose from Cerridwen's cauldron to transform the prototypic initiate, Gwion Bach, who was subsequently reborn as the prophet magician Taliesin. The circles that surround it represent the three Celtic realms of land, sea, and sky.

In early Celtic lore, Awen represents the universe becoming aware of itself; to the Christian societies of Wales and Cornwall, it was seen to represent the Holy Spirit and the name of God. When the universe became aware of itself, an explosion occurred that caused the springing forth of light and vitality and all the living things in the universe. All things burst forth in praise of the universe's conscious awareness of itself. From one came two, the universe's consciousness and matter; from the two came a third, which is the relationship between the two; this is the essential component for the activation of magic. This is the realm of Awen, the betweenness. The universe burst into the song of creation, each aspect carrying the spark of the initial explosion of awareness. With this it is said that every voice, every hearing, all life and being, sight, and seeing are one and united with the universe.

Iolo Morganwg took an ancient concept, breathed new life and meaning into it, and offered it shape and form in the guise of the three rays of light. Each ray is attributed a vowel—three vowels that contain the song of the universe, the song of inspiration and transformation. These vowels are believed to contain the origin of every form and sign and voice, every sound and name and condition in the entire universe. These vowels are O, I, and W and correspond to each of the three pillars of light / | \.

From left to right, the first vowel, O, is pronounced as a long *oh* sound. It arises and resonates from the top of the lungs and the lower throat. It is attributed one of the three primary functions of Awen: to understand the truth.

The second vowel is I and is pronounced as a long *ee* sound. It arises and resonates high in the throat and at the back of the mouth. It is attributed the second primary function of Awen: to love the truth.

The third vowel is W and is pronounced as the *oo* sound in "zoo." It resonates at the mid and front sections of the mouth, then transfers through the pallet into the nasal region. It is attributed the third primary function of Awen: to maintain truth.

EXERCISE
SINGING AWEN

Stop for a minute or two—take a breath with the land beneath you, breathe in the sky above you, and deeply breathe with the rhythm of the seas that surround the shores of your land. Stand with your feet shoulder-width apart and your hands extended at about a 45-degree angle from the side of your body, palms facing outwards. Breathe in deeply and audibly, imagining the landscape around you seeping through the breath and into your lungs. Voice the first vowel, O, for as long as your breath will last. As you intone, feel the earth and sense your place in nature. Where does the vowel resonate the most for you; how does it feel? Continue to intone the vowel for as long as is comfortable and in multiples of three. Consider the nature of your truth and your understanding of it.

Take another deep and audible breath and breathe in the moistness of sea and water; sense the seas, oceans, lakes, and rivers reaching into your body on the currents of your breath. Exhale and intone the second vowel, I, and maintain it for as long as your breath will last. Imagine the water of your own body being carried by the breath and connecting to the spirit of sea and water; see it joining, swimming, and moving as your water flows with the waters of the world. Where does this resonate? Continue to intone the vowel in multiples of three. Consider what it means to love your truth.

Take another deep breath, sucking the sky down and into your body. Cloud and thunder, lightning and mist flow from the regions above to be joined in the denseness of your body. Exhale and intone the final vowel, W, and maintain it for the duration of one breath. Sense your spirit rise to meet the sky gods as they, too, sing in unison with you. Where does this vowel resonate the most; how does it make your body feel? Continue in multiples of three until you sense it is right to stop. Consider the manner in which you maintain your truth.

Record your experience in your journal.

◆ ◆ ◆

The magic of Awen lies in the fact that it has transcended time and change. It has twisted and shaped its form to be relevant for any time and for any group of people.

The Function of Awen

People rarely see what is right in front of their noses. Too often folks will seek to find Awen in the depth of vision, believing it to be some amorphous silver stream of energy that is somehow out there—untouchable, distant, and mysterious—whereas in truth it is the complete opposite. Awen is everywhere at all times, and we are never separate from it; it is only our awareness of it that causes us to feel that it is "other." We swim within its currents, and it can be seen everywhere, for everything is a reflection of the universe's ability to create, and it does so for one reason: to express, to be, to experience.

Awen activates the magic of Celtica. It is its driving force, the singular spark from the dawn of creation that flows through the known and unknown universe. It is by means of Awen and swimming in its flow that we are effectively able to sense the course of our magic and also its consequences, and we do this by being aware of its flow and our direction within it. Guides and allies exist that help us connect to the power of Awen—gods and goddesses, prophets and magicians who claim to know it, who summoned it from the depths of the cauldron of existence.

The primary deity of Awen is the witch goddess Cerridwen. This enigmatic figure is the epitome of witchdom—the original Celtic witch, if you like—a figure that has evolved to become the witch goddess, the mother of all witches. Before a full description of Cerridwen is given a little later, it is sufficient for now to give you a flavor of her position in Celtic magic, for she acts as a catalyst for the imbuing of Awen. She is the original witch who took to the hidden arts to brew a potion of Awen so powerful that it would imbue the one who would ingest it with all the wonders and sciences of all the worlds. In her cauldron she brewed a potion that concentrated the streams of Awen into a single location. This resulted in three blessed drops, each one an attribute of Awen itself.

Awen and the Cauldron

There is a non-human archetype present in Cerridwen's tale: the cauldron, which exists as more than simply a tool or vessel. It is the embodiment of potentiality, inspiration, and transformation; it brewed the prototypic potion of Awen for the transformation and teaching of an archetypal initiate of Celtic magic and mystery. As a consequence, all subsequent cauldrons—particularly those used for ritualistic and magical purposes—are sympathetically linked to the vessel of the witch goddess.

In my book *From the Cauldron Born: Exploring the Magic of Welsh Legend and Lore*, I explore in depth the function of the cauldron as a magical vessel and its essentialness in the practice of Celtic magic. The cauldron is not passive; it is an active aspect of the teachings of Celtic magic that swim in the streams of Awen—it is its point of entry, if you like, the initial station from where we perceive its expression in the physical realm. Except in vision we never see the streams of Awen; we only see its expression by means of the subtle and creative arts. The cauldron acts as a doorway, a tool that activates our visions, thus enabling us to visualize its currents and its streams flowing from the invisible realms between and betwixt to affect the world and our place within it—and, of course, our magic.

EXERCISE
APPROACHING THE CAULDRON

Stop for a minute or two—take a breath with the land beneath you, breathe in the sky above you, and deeply breathe with the rhythm of the seas that surround the shores of your land. Imagine you are standing on the banks of a wide river. The water is flowing fast, and its voice rises to caress the trees that lean lazily towards its moistness. It is a relaxing and calming sound. To your right is a wooden bridge that leads to a small island in the center of the river. The island is green and lush.

Imagine that you approach the bridge and feel it creak under your feet as you walk its boards towards the island. As you step barefooted onto the moist green grass of the island, you see before you a large cast-iron cauldron. It sits above a small fire of oak wood and is suspended by three chains that reach into the sky and vanish from sight.

You approach the cauldron and place both your hands against its rim; your palms caress the tactile pearls that decorate its edge. Suddenly your feet feel glued to the ground, your body stiffens, and you are unable to move a muscle; only your eyes move as you glance over the edge of the cauldron and into its depths. A swirling vortex of vapor spirals within, explosions like miniature stars gleam from the darkness, and you know that there is mystery here. Within the cauldron you are seeing the birth of galaxies, the death of stars, and the wonder of creation. All potentiality lies within this symbol.

You note movement ahead of you. Your eyes lift, yet your body remains glued to the spot. A woman in grey stands opposite you, and behind her the shadowy form of eight other women; her hands are held over the cauldron's mouth. Her eyes are pitch black; her smile, reassuring.

"The cauldron will not boil the food of a coward," she says.

You are suddenly released from your paralysis, and the lady is gone.

Allow the vision to dissolve and return to the present moment. What mystery did you see and sense in the belly of the cauldron? Record your experience in your journal.

Guardians of the Cauldron

Numerous guardians and protectors of the Celtic cauldron challenge the seeker and teach us that those who seek Awen and the mysteries of the cauldron must be in possession of certain qualities. Bravery, courage, and stamina are among the most essential. We are continuously informed through the myths of the Celts that the cauldron will not tolerate cowardice, indifference, or foolhardiness. The seeker who quests for the magical arts must be strong of will, determined, disciplined, and, above all, of good intent. This does not imply that the cauldron punishes or reprimands; it just will not reciprocate. "It will not boil the food of a coward,"[12] we are told; its function is useless, pointless to those who approach with cowardice or ulterior motives.

The opposite qualities of cowardice are demanded by the cauldron and its guardians. Magicians train their minds and bodies; they are learned folk who study hard and work harder, honing their skills to become the most adept practitioners they can be. They are ready to face responsibility and the consequences of their actions. This strength of spirit comes from knowing one's craft; when one approaches the cauldron and its guardians, one does so with a brave and courageous heart, determined and strong of will. With these qualities come humility, honor, and a positive morality, attributes that swim in the deep belly of the cauldron and in the flowing streams of Awen.

In Celtic myth the cauldron is guarded, protected, or owned by female priestesses who challenge those who approach it, as if readying the querent for the experience of Awen. To know it conceptually is one thing; to experience it is quite another.

The cauldron and Awen go hand in hand; it is as much an ally to the practitioner as any other archetype. It is the cauldron that sits in a central position in the triskelion ritual in chapter 5. Contemplate and examine the cauldron and your relationship to it and Awen by focusing on the following questions:

12 "*Preiddeu Annwn*" (The Spoils of Annwn) in the Book of Taliesin.

- Do you use a cauldron in your daily devotions and rituals? If so, why?
- Are you familiar with the cauldron in Celtic myth and legend?
- Can you identify and retell a Celtic legend that contains a cauldron?
- What do the myths teach us about the nature of the cauldron?
- Do you identify the cauldron with a particular deity? If so, why?
- What do you believe are the inherent qualities of the cauldron?
- Do you perceive the cauldron as a material tool or a portal to other realms?

Record your thoughts in your journal.

EXERCISE
PRIESTESSES OF THE CAULDRON RITUAL

The shadowy figures you encountered in the previous contemplative exercise are representative of the nine maidens who guard and kindle the cauldron that lies in the depth of Annwn—the indigenous Celtic underworld. In the poem "The Spoils of Annwn" (given in full in chapter 30), Taliesin informs us that "my first words were spoken concerning the cauldron, which is kindled by the breath of nine maidens."

To acquaint yourself with the cauldron and its guardians, perform the following ritual, preferably on the sixth day of the new moon and at night, with all lights extinguished except for one small candle placed at the farthest end of your ritual space. You will need a cauldron or other large potlike vessel and nine candles of any variety positioned in a wide circle approximately 2 to 3 feet from the cauldron's edge. Burn strongly scented incense within the cauldron or, if it's not safe to do so, place an appropriate incense burner within the cauldron.

To begin, take yourself between the worlds; with eyes closed, imagine a fort. It revolves around a central platform, its four walls grinding against stone as they turn. A heavy mist obscures the center of the fort, but you can just make out a large black cauldron standing atop glowing blue flames.

You walk towards it. As you do, your path is blocked by the form of a woman who steps from the mist to prevent your passing. You feel your feet leave the ground, and you rise several feet into the air; from this point you can see the cauldron clearly. Pearls glisten around its edge; swirling clouds of darkness swim within its depths. Surrounding it are the shadowy figures of nine maidens.

You send them a greeting and project your intent: to know the cauldron and its nature.

With a deep breath, return to your ritual space and open your eyes.

Burn more incense in the central cauldron and with your hands outstretched, palms down, say the following:

My words shall be spoken of the cauldron,
kindled by the breath of maidens nine,
I come to this place and call to the maidens,
their virtues forth to shine.

Pick up the nearest candle to you, light it, and hold it at arm's length. Repeat the following:

Guardian of the cauldron, keeper of the flame,
bring forth your gifts of wisdom; let me approach the cauldron.

Recall the image of one of the maidens from the previous journey and project your intent towards her. With a nod of your head, place the lit candle upon the ground. Proceed to the next candle and repeat the process with these words:

Guardian of the cauldron, keeper of the flame,
bring forth your gift of innocence; let me approach the cauldron.

Guardian of the cauldron, keeper of the flame,
bring forth your gift of humility; let me approach the cauldron.

Guardian of the cauldron, keeper of the flame,
bring forth your gift of courage; let me approach the cauldron.

Guardian of the cauldron, keeper of the flame,
bring forth your gift of generosity; let me approach the cauldron.

Guardian of the cauldron, keeper of the flame,
bring forth your gift of trust; let me approach the cauldron.

Guardian of the cauldron, keeper of the flame,
bring forth your gift of self-knowledge; let me approach the cauldron.

Guardian of the cauldron, keeper of the flame,
bring forth your gift of friendship; let me approach the cauldron.

Guardian of the cauldron, keeper of the flame,
bring forth your gift of integrity; let me approach the cauldron.

After the final candle has been positioned, turn once more to face the cauldron with your hands outstretched above it. Sense the presence of the nine maidens around you and the virtues they represent.

Sit and be still within this space, and contemplate the virtues and their applicability in your life. How do you express these virtues, and are they of good stead to allow the cauldron to boil?

Consider that the primary function of the maidens is to ensure that the qualities of the seeker are befitting of the cauldron's mystery. Each maiden is representative of a quality essential for accessing the cauldron, but there are two sides to these attributes, and meeting the priestesses will highlight any weakness—the kink in the chain of your virtues. Therefore, in the silence, consider the opposite qualities of the virtues and how they affect your life and your ability to pass the maidens and approach the cauldron unhindered and with integrity.

Wisdom	Foolishness
Innocence	Corruption
Humility	Arrogance
Courage	Cowardice
Generosity	Selfishness
Trust	Distrust
Self-Knowledge	Ignorance
Friendship	Enmity
Integrity	Dishonesty

Examine these qualities and how best you might address them in the silence at the cauldron's edge with the nine maidens surrounding you.

As you sense the ritual nearing its end—as the energies of the maidens dissipate—thank them one by one by lifting each candle in turn and blowing out the flame. Repeat the following:

Breath of my breath, warm thy breath;
breath of your breath breathe in me.
May the virtues of wisdom, innocence, humility, courage, generosity,
trust, self-knowledge, friendship, and integrity be mine.

When all the candles are extinguished, return to your everyday business, sleep, and on the morrow awake and contemplate the virtues and functions of the nine maidens.

Getting to Know Awen

Recall the Celtic cultural continuum exercise on page 7. The same metaphor can be utilized to feel and understand the flowing movement of Awen, which is often described as a river. There is much mystery here, and Taliesin, in one of his poems, teaches us about the nature of Awen—what it does and how it affects the practitioner who swims in its currents:

Awen I sing, from the deep I bring it.
It is a river that flows
I know its might
I know how it ebbs
And I know how it flows
I know its course
I know how it retreats
I know the creatures which are under the sea
I know the nature of each one in the shoal.[13]

The above demonstrates that Taliesin is not just aware of the concept of Awen, he is intimately connected to it, and by proxy of this connection he is aware of things beyond the perceived limitations of the human senses. Note that he does not use the word *believe*—he does not *believe* he knows, he *knows*, and there is a great teaching here. It is this knowing that Taliesin speaks of as a consequence of his conscious connection to Awen. By aligning himself with its river, the course of which he fully understands, he is aware of all things that exist in the sea.

The sea itself acts as an analogy for interconnection. There is only one sea; it is the same body of water that we step into around the British Isles as it is around the shores of Thailand. It is the epitome of interconnection. Taliesin knows everything, for Awen is everything, by standing in it—by being immersed in its power, we are accessing the hard drive of the universe, where everything is known. This is the power of Awen. It streams from the past through the present and into the future with no beginning and no end.

Awen allows you to access the wisdom of a culture steeped in mystery and magic. It brings another depth of knowing to your practice by means of ancestral connection. By working with it, you perpetuate this teaching and make it applicable to you and your life; by proxy you will inspire a new generation of magical practitioners to stand in the flowing river of inspiration and be the shining, radiant rays of Awen.

13 "*Angar Kyfundawt,*" the Book of Taliesin; my translation.

EXERCISE
BECOMING AWEN

Contemplate the magic of interconnection that Awen represents and the manner by which it permeates the universe and activates our magic.

Place a small lit candle in a cauldron or similar vessel. Position yourself so that when you sit before it, you see only the glow of candlelight but not the flame. Extinguish all other lights. Stare intently at the glowing cauldron, and allow your breath to rise and fall steadily. Allow all distractions and input from the outside world to fade into the background.

Imagine that the light in the cauldron comes from a source that is beyond the solid base of the vessel—it reaches into the worlds between and betwixt. It is the light of Awen that flickers from the cauldron's belly.

Allow your eyes to fall gently shut and focus on the center of your being, the void, the nothing that is full of potential. As you breathe in, visualize the pulsing beat of the darkness; as you breathe out, see the illumination of Awen bursting through the void, propelling your inspiration and creativity into the world. Keep breathing and imagining darkness into light, light into darkness, manifest and unmanifest.

Know that you are all things and have been all things; you carry the wisdom and experience of the universe within you. As Awen courses through you, as you swim in its depths, you can access the storehouses of wisdom, the universal records, and the wisdom of sages.

Open your eyes, blur your focus so that the light and the cauldron merge as one, and repeat these words from ancient times:

> *A'm swynwys sywyt sywydon kyn byt*[14]—
> *(AM sue-UN-wiz sow-it sow-WID-on kin bit)*
> *The wisdom of sages created me before the world was made.*

Repeat the above sentence nine times. With each vocalization, see the path of ancestors behind you reaching back through the mists of time.

---

14 From *"Kat Godeu"* (The Battle of the Trees), the Book of Taliesin.

Memorize the following or have it written down and placed between yourself and the cauldron:

I have been a multitude of shapes
Before I attained this form.
I was a slender sword,
I was a droplet in the air,
I was the light of distant stars.
I was a word in writing,
I was a book in my prime.
I was the light of a lantern.
I was a path,
I was an eagle,
I was a coracle on the sea,
I was effervescence in drink,
I was a raindrop in a shower.[15]

Read each one aloud three times, and with each vocalization imagine being what is described. This is no easy task, for none of them are human in nature, but according to the poem that contains this riddle, you have been all these things and more before you assumed your current form. You can access all these states by the connective river that links them: Awen.

Now take one line from the above and express it in the physical world. Place yourself in its experience and paint, write, sculpt, sing—whatever it takes to express the inherent nature and quality of that thing.

◆ ◆ ◆

Now that we are armed with the knowledge and experience of Awen and the mystery of its primary symbol, the cauldron, we can implement its use in ritual.

15 Adapted by me from "*Kat Godeu*" (The Battle of the Trees), the Book of Taliesin.

◆ 3 ◆

Celtic Magic Ritual

Ritual is a system of transitory symbols and gestures formed in a liminal space to transition a person from an ordinary to an extraordinary state. This chapter will offer you a ritual system that is rooted in Celtic mythology and thought. Its function is not to replace your current ritualistic practice but to offer you a system that is not wholly reliant on the common Gardnerian-influenced rituals of modern Paganism. The function of this type of ritual is to offer you a portal that accesses the storehouse of Celtic wisdom by utilizing words, symbols, and energies that are indicative of Celtica. By performing these rituals you will be aligning yourself with a system that is rooted in the Celtic tradition. They will serve to enhance your practice and deepen your connection and relationship with the spirit of Celtica.

◆ ◆ ◆

Ritual is essential for effective magic in that it provides a space wherein we straddle the worlds—we leave behind the humdrum of ordinary reality and assume a magical reality. The symbols and gestures that we use take on many forms: they can be the particular use of language and words that may be presented in verse, the use of various tools and clothing, and the utilization of liminality—all of these things tell the mind that something extraordinary is about to happen.

Ritual is about preparation, and its focus is to cause the magician to enter a state that is betwixt and between the worlds, without preferring one over the other. Ritual induces a state that is conducive for magic, and that is why we use it.

Our reality is dense and material, and we are products of this reality, stuck within the solidity of our bodies and the world upon which we live. When we practice magic, the restrictions of the physical dimension become irrelevant; it is by the effective use of ritual that we learn to leave the limitations of the physical world and access the storehouse of magic that is just beyond the edge of reason.

Ritual acts as a bridge that connects the finite mind to the infinite mind; it serves to inform us that we are about to participate in something extraordinary. Effective magicians see, sense, and feel more than is apparent in the visible world, and it is ritual that is utilized as a conduit for this to happen. In order to sense the magical world, the ordinary senses must be temporarily disabled to allow for the subtle senses to be given voice, but they are normally overwhelmed by our tremendously sensory, vivid world. So we must quieten the noise of the ordinary to enable the subtle senses to rise and do their work. Without preparation, magic is ineffective. Ritual is the classroom of the magician, the place where the subtle senses are nurtured and the spirit is given a voice.

Generally we live busy lives. How often do we get an opportunity in our schedules to stop, unwind, and relax—to have some quality leisure time to ourselves or to spend with friends and family? Magicians are busy people; not only do they have jobs and families to contend with, they also have to make time for study and practice. Ritual facilitates this; it causes the temporary stopping of all that business. We rush here and there in our tasks, lost in the simple act of living, and yet magic asks for us to use our subtle senses, but how can we when we are so damned busy?

Ritual is the key. It provides the space that we need to breathe a little, to step out of humdrum and out of the rush of life and step into the magical persona that hides just beneath the veneer of ordinary. It's always there; we just have to give it the space it needs to leave the shadows and become a part of our life. This is part of the discipline of magic; we must have ritual in order to become the sensing beings that we must become in order to be effective magicians. It causes us to listen.

Intent

At the heart of any magical act there must be firm and solid intent, and that intention must be grounded in integrity. If it isn't, and things go horribly wrong or not quite in accordance with your desires, then you will have only yourself to blame. Magic comes with great responsibility, and the key to that is your ability to respond to all the variables. So to ensure that everything is taken into consideration, meticulously plan your magic ahead of time. Using oracles and systems of divination may, on the surface, seem a little excessive, but on the contrary, the utilization of such skills is vital to a magician's continuous development.

Plan, plan, and plan, and when you think you have planned sufficiently, look at it again, make lists for and against, the pros and the cons. Evaluate, see the woods for the trees, keep your actions as honorable as humanly possible, and ensure that you can justify working the magic in the first place.

When it comes to intent, keep in mind these three words: clarify, state, and maintain.

Clarify your intent by examining it closely and asking yourself important questions relating to the issue at hand. What are your motives for doing this? What will the possible outcomes be? What are the variables—the unforeseen things that initially may not be apparent? What do the oracles say? Question, examine, and clarify the issue so that it is perfectly clear in your mind.

State your intention within the ritual and during the act of magic. This sends a powerful message to the gods, goddesses, and the universe that you are being grown-up about it all; you are taking responsibility, and you are willing to face the consequences of your actions.

Maintain that intent throughout the ritual. Do not flounder; you are a magician of the Celtic traditions. Maintain your confidence and intent. Carry the intent beyond the ritual in the quiet parts of your spirit, that place that knows all things. Maintain that magic; keep it close to you. Do not speak your intent to anyone who is beyond the ritual space.

The Tools of Ritual

The beauty of Celtic magic is that you won't need a whole repertoire of tools, where you are faced with the anxiety of having to get them and finding the money to buy them. All you will require is a wand and a cauldron (or something that vaguely looks like a cauldron, as long as it's watertight and can take some heat). The function and purpose of the wand will be fully explored later, but suffice to say that, for now, this is the tool which functions as your bridge to the natural world; it is an extension of your will. It will act in a similar function to the way wands are used in other magical traditions; the only difference here is that preferably you will have created your own and will already be in relationship with it. Full instructions and advice on wand-making will be given a little later. Your wand also will be representative of directional energy and creativity.

The cauldron will sit at the center of your ritual space. Its function is to act as the vessel of crossing; it is symbolic of the bubbling of inspiration and magic that seeps into our world from the fabric of the cosmos. This is a portal to the otherworlds and will serve as the heart of your ritual space. It is via this portal that the energies you will be using will be summoned, and it is through this portal that you will focus your intent and will.

Whatever arbitrary tools you may wish to have present in your rituals are entirely your own choosing. You may wish to decorate the space with lanterns or candle holders that have significance to you; you may choose to delineate the space with stones from a sacred river, lake, or beach. You may wish to have a special plate or dish to hold the incense prior to casting it onto the coals. Celtic magic gives you the freedom to decorate your magic with whatever you see fit. The primary symbols are simple, easy to understand and connect to, and they are all that are truly necessary. Anything else is fine—use your inspiration and intuition, go by hunch and gut feeling. The triskelion ritual in chapter 5, although complete, is also a clotheshorse that you may adorn with your own attire, colors, and style.

Protection

Attitude goes a long way in magic—a good attitude; that is, one based on the intent that you are bringing to the ritual and the integrity that you carry with you. The powers of nature have no ulterior motive to kick your ass just because they want to, and in Celtic magic there is no concept of absolute evil. Spirits of the otherworld may challenge you, but they do not pose you great threat; however, a good dash of magical health and hygiene is recommended. Depending on your own magical background, you may choose to enclose your ritual space in a magic circle, a sphere of energy that keeps what you are doing in and possible negativity out. In Celtic magic it is the ability of the magician and his or her own power that protects the space and the work from any interfering influence.

Later you will discover the value of summoning and invoking powerful allies to assist you in your magic. These act as a buffer, deflecting or neutralizing any negative influences that may affect your magic, as will the spirits of the three realms, which will be explored just a little later. Protection—in the sense that something is out there and if you don't look out, it's gonna get you—is a somewhat disempowering concept. In Celtic magic one uses common sense, ensuring we know what we are doing, what the influences are, and that what we are about to do has integrity. If you feel in any way threatened during a ritual, then you must ask yourself why; what is causing you to feel like that? You are a magician; take to your oracles and systems of divination. If anything feels a miss, then seek out an answer. Be well versed in issues of psychic health and hygiene: read up on the matter, study, and learn.[16] However, if you do feel the need to protect yourself, try this meditation before and after ritual work.

MEDITATION
THE LIGHT SHIELD

Stop for a minute or two—take a breath with the land beneath you, breathe in the sky above you, and deeply breathe with the rhythm of the seas that surround the shores of your land. Draw up a surge of emotional energy from the core of your being and focus on the center of your body—the area known as the solar plexus. Pull your emotions into this place; you will feel a flutter like butterflies in the stomach. Keep doing this in multiples of three. With every breath you take, hold that breath, pull raw emotional energy, and direct it to this place. Imagine that a circle is drawn around you only a few feet from your body; it may be tubular or you may visualize it as a sphere. See the emotional energy seething in your midriff. It begins to glow; keep directing energy into this place. When you sense it is at its optimum, send it out in a flash of light, exactly as you would imagine the flash from a camera. Exhale as you see this light, this shield of energy, erupt from your solar plexus and form a shimmering shield at the edge of the circle. Look at it with your subtle eyes—it appears like the waves of heat that rise from hot tarmac. Know that it is there. Sit with it for a few minutes, and then draw it back to yourself, a reverse flash that implodes into your body.

Become aware of your surroundings, and record your visions and thoughts in your journal.

16 I highly recommend you read Dion Fortune's *Psychic Self-Defence* and Ellen Dugan's *Practical Protection Magick*.

◆ 4 ◆

Constructing Celtic Rituals

Celtic ritual as presented in this book is culturally specific to the Celtic cultural continuum; it is to that stream of consciousness you will be connecting. This system is not dependant on the classical style of ritual that was formulated and popularized by the late Gerald Gardner. Almost all Neo-pagan rituals that cast a circle and call to the four classical elements and the God and Goddess as duality can be traced back to Gardner and the Golden Dawn, who influenced his magical practice. What you will find here is the suggestion of a culture-specific ritual that invokes the spirit of Celtica in a fresh and original format while being respectful of tradition and evocative of past wisdom.

The Components of Celtic Ritual

Traditional elements are not present in the mythologies of the Celts; what is evident is their veneration of three realms—those of land, sea, and sky. The common four elements of earth, air, fire, and water, and their placements at the cardinal directions of a magic circle, come from classical Greece. Within the Mabinogi and other chronicles of the Celts you will see frequent mention of the three realms, particularly in the tale of Cerridwen and Taliesin.

There is great mystery within the concept of the three realms, and although hardened Pagans may be screaming that I cannot leave fire out of the equation, I ask you to bear with me. This ritual format is based wholly on the principles of land, sea, and sky, but not simply as elements; they are more than the sum total of their elemental correspondences, and this is what makes a Celtic magic ritual different from that of other Pagan traditions. In Celtic magic and philosophy fire is not considered one of the realms, nor is it considered an element; instead, it is perceived as what transforms or brings action to the other three.[17] The beauty of it is, even if you belong to a group, grove, or coven that has established working practices, this ritual can be incorporated into it. It will not denigrate or antagonize any current system you may be using.

The primary ritual, called the triskelion ritual, has at its center a triskele; the entire space is created around the arms of the triskele, which spiral outward from a central point. The triskele symbol is pre-Celtic in origin and can be found adorning the tombs and chambered cairns of Britain, Ireland, and Brittany, and was adopted as a component of Celtic art and symbolism. The triskelion ritual honors and connects to the three realms of land, sea, and sky. These can be perceived and visualized as the three spiral points of the triskele, which is drawn thus:

17 Markale, *The Druids*, 151–158.

Surrounding the triskele is a circle. This contains the experience of the ritual. In an open ritual or when several people may be present, it is represented as the space in which they stand and form the edges of the circle. The triskele is a deeply sacred symbol of the Celts and epitomizes their connection to tripartite structure, the sacredness of triplication, where they perceived the sacred and its mysteries in sequences of three.

The triskele spins out from emptiness, from the great void; this is indicative of the soul of the universe, Awen, the sheer potential that underlies the physical realm and all other worlds beside it. From this place of nothingness, three arms reach out; they become aware of themselves and of their connection to the source, and each one expresses that connection in its own unique way. It is the significance of these attributions that causes the symbol to be a valid component of Celtic ritual.

The Spiral of Land

The arm that represents land is initially indicative of the ground beneath your feet; it is symbolic of your locality, your homeland, and it represents the comforts of home, security, and nourishment. This is the place that your ancestors inhabited, and as you look beyond what is beneath your feet, you see the land stretching away from your known world. Land is more than the element of earth, though it contains it and its attributions, but this concept of land extends beyond this world to represent all the worlds that our eyes can see as stars in the night sky. In our sacred space it is the microcosm, an attribute that emulates the universe in its entirety. Within this point lies the potential and possibility of physicality. It is here that the gods and goddesses of the land and of planets and moons and suns can be sensed and invoked. The first sacred sound of Awen is equated to land, the *O* vowel—it comes from the mouth, our place of expression, and its vibrations resonate within the center of your face.

Meditation
THE LANGUAGE OF LAND

Stop for a minute or two—take a breath with the land beneath you, breathe in the sky above you, and deeply breathe with the rhythm of the seas that surround the shores of your land. What is land? What does it represent? Is it more than the sum of what you can see? Is it more than the earth itself? The physical elements that make your body come from magic: a star died—dense matter collapsing, imploding—and in that immense heat, with gravitational forces that tear atoms apart, the carbon in your body was created. Transformed by heat, your body was forged in the material of stars. Land exists beyond this earth; it is the living expression of the universe. Think on the creation of the material within your body. Closer to home, what creatures inhabit the land nearby—the plants, animals, rocks, and hills? What is their nature? What does land actually represent? Who are the gods of your land?

Return to the present, and record your thoughts in your journal.

The Spiral of Sea

The next arm of the triskele sweeps from the center and represents the sea. This is the representation of the universal soul; it is what connects everything else to itself. As a microcosm it is the point symbolizing that you are intricately connected to everything that exists, and it is connected to you. The message of the sea aspect is that you are not and cannot ever be truly alone. By the web of soul and the magic of interconnectivity, you are the universe singing in praise of itself. When you stand at this point and call to the powers of the sea, you call to the source of all things, to the great soul of the universe. The soul, in turn, is the house of the spirit. This is a place of feeling and emulates the emotional connotations of water as found in other Pagan ritual systems. At this point we call to the fluid gods of the sea and those deities who represent interconnection. The second sacred sound of Awen is equated to the sea, the *I* vowel; this sound is lower than the center of the face and comes from the lower throat and the upper chest.

MEDITATION
THE SEA, SEAT OF THE SOUL

Stop for a minute or two—take a breath with the land beneath you, breathe in the sky above you, and deeply breathe with the rhythm of the seas that surround the shores of your land. Where is the sea in relation to your home; can you visit it in your mind? What does it smell like? What does the salt taste like on the edges of your tongue? What is the name of this sea; is it not the same body of water that laps at distant shores? In Old English the word *saouel* (soul) means "from the sea." It is everywhere; it is omnipresent. What does this mean, this interconnectivity? *Sea* is more than the sum total of our planet's seas; it is a symbol for the sea of soul that connects the universe to itself. It is the source, the place of origin. Even humankind is believed to have come out of the primordial seas. What does this mean to you? What visions come from contemplating the sea?

Breathe deeply and return to your ordinary state. Record your visions and thoughts in your journal.

The Spiral of Sky

Moving to the third arm of the triskele, we stand at the point of sky. Our eyes are naturally drawn skyward to the vast space of the world above. With a breath, we take in its substance and the molecules that make up our earthly atmosphere; this is breath and vitality and the place of the spirit. From the Latin *spiritus* meaning "vital breath" and related to the Latin *spirare* meaning "to breathe,"[18] the spirit breathes life and animation into this experience of living. It is a spark of the soul that is immersed in the experience of living and life, an ethereal substance that dances in and out of the physical realm. The sky is the rainbow bridge that spans the chasm between spirit and soul. This is the point of inspiration, of creativity and vitality; the gods of the high places are here as the gods and goddesses and the sun and moon, for we perceive them as being a part of our skies. The sky deities are ethereal and

18 *Chambers Dictionary of Etymology*, 1047.

move like the wind; it is from here that we call them to our place of ritual. The third sacred sound of Awen is equated to the realm of sky; the *W* sound resonates high up in the head, above the level of the nose.

MEDITATION

SKY, SPIRIT, AND SOUL

Stop for a minute or two—take a breath with the land beneath you, breathe in the sky above you, and deeply breathe with the rhythm of the seas that surround the shores of your land. Breathe down the sky; sense it coursing through your lungs, the molecules of air that ride on the back of blood cells nourishing, sustaining. This is vital breath. Our spirit is breath, the breath of the soul. The sky is the bridge between the matter and ether; it is the manifestation of Awen.

Where is your spirit; does it sit within your body? Maybe this is not an easy task, for where is the air of sky? We believe it to be above, but it is not. It exists within and without. Sky is in all places except for the vacuum of space. But even here, as it is caught in the gravity of stars, it comes into being.

Spirit—why is it different from soul?

Return. Become aware of your surroundings and your sojourn into sky. Record your visions and thoughts in your journal.

Setting the Scene

At the center of the triskele, which will form the central point of your ritual space, stands the cauldron; this, in turn, symbolizes the deep, the Awen, the portal to the unseen. It is the point of entry and exit.

Delineating or marking out the ritual space may be done in advance. If you have a permanent space such as a grove, room, or garden to use, then you will substantially mark the area with items that will not be removed at the ritual conclusion. Delineation may also take place during the rite; either option is fine, and the technique is the same for both options. The actual charging or empowering of the space takes place during the actual ritual.

Items Required

Essential:

- cauldron
- wand

Nonessential:

- candles
- physical representations of land, sea, and sky
- incense and charcoal blocks

Begin by placing the cauldron in its allocated space. It may sit directly on the ground or you may construct or find a small table for it to sit upon; the choice is entirely your own. The size of you ritual space will be determined by the amount of participants; if it's just yourself, then keep it small and contained. However, if thirty people are present, then it will need to be a great deal larger. Naturally the space itself is delineated by a circle, and the reasons for this are twofold. Firstly, human beings will naturally gather in a circle, and it represents nature as cyclic. Secondly, it is a symbol that most Pagans are familiar with and can easily visualize at the edge of the ritual space. The diameter of your ritual space should be marked in multiples of three—6 feet, 9 feet, 12 feet, and so forth.

Stand directly next your cauldron, close your eyes, and visualize a bird's-eye view of the ritual space. Imagine the triskele taking shape, its spirals curling to a point a short distance from the edge of the ritual space. Open your eyes, move to the terminal points of the triskele you visualized, and mark those points with a candle or something that is symbolic of land, sea, and sky. Be imaginative; create. You may also choose to have nothing present at the terminus of the triskele.

If you wish to mark the circle that contains the triskele, then do so with whatever material you feel is appropriate. Stand your wand point down against the edge of the cauldron until you are ready to begin.

Preparation Summary

- predetermine size and edge of circle / ritual space; mark if necessary
- place cauldron at center
- visualize the triskele; mark the point of triskele arms if you like
- decorate the space according to your own preference

With preparations in place, the main body of the ritual can be performed.

5

The Triskelion Ritual

I have included some words in Middle Welsh within this ritual; I suggest you use them to connect to the Celtic continuum through the power of words. A phonetic version is given to make life a little easier; practice them if you can. I also give the English translation; by all means use them interchangeably.

To avoid the tediousness of multiple outlines, the ritual that follows is suitable for a solitary or group setting. In a group context, for example, you may designate three individuals to call the attributes of land, sea, and sky. Obviously in a solitary setting you will be doing everything yourself. The designation of active parts within a group will form aspects of your ritual preparation and planning.

This is a detailed breakdown of the ritual; do not be daunted by its length. I have ensured that all bases are covered and that nothing is left to assumption. A summary of the ritual will be found at the conclusion of the ritual description.

◆ ◆ ◆

Prepare yourself for the ritual in advance and dress appropriately.

Approach your ritual space and walk directly to the center. Stand with feet shoulder-width apart and arms extended slightly from your body with palms facing outwards. Allow your eyes to close. Take one deep and audible breath with the land beneath your feet, and draw the energies of the earth up your feet to pulsate through your body. Hold that breath for a few seconds and sense the land within you. Exhale fully and audibly.

Take a second deep and audible breath with the seas and oceans that surround your nation; draw this energy into you and feel the tides of your being moving with the seas. Hold your breath for a few seconds, sensing the sea within you ebbing and flowing. Exhale fully and audibly.

Take a third deep, audible breath with the sky above you, and pull that energy down through your mouth and nose, deep into the core of your being. Feel the moistness of the sky as it sinks further into your body. Hold your breath for a few seconds, sensing the power of the sky within you. Exhale fully and audibly.

Say these opening words out loud:

> *It is not of mother and father that I am made. I am the creation of nine forms, from the fruits of beginning, from the blossoms of trees, from the earth and the water of the ninth wave. The wisdom of sages fashioned me; I had being before this world was made.*[19]

Take an additional three breaths with land, sea, and sky. Reach for your wand and hold it in your active, or power, hand.

Take your wand and walk consciously, with awareness of each footfall, to the point of the triskele that you have designated as "land." Stand with your feet shoulder-width apart. Stretch your arm and point your wand towards the ground/land at an angle of approximately 45 degrees. Keep your other

19 Adapted and translated by me from "*Kat Godeu*" (The Battle of the Trees), the Book of Taliesin.

arm next to your body with your hand extended so that your palm is facing the ground.

Repeat these words or similar with power and conviction, evoking the visualization and the emotions you encountered in the meditation dedicated to land. When you speak of the gods, these words must arise naturally from your connection and devotion to them; because of that, only one line appears in this example in relation to them:

> *Songs of the land, I call to thee; come by memory of ancestors to this place. By tree and sod, by rock and mountain, I summon the powers of the firmament. Come by molten stone and iron core, hearken to these words I speak. Moon of earth, now hear my call; come by rays of silver light. Material realms both near and far, stir now to this call. Gods and goddesses of the land, O mighty ones, [insert names], I call you; bring to this space your wisdom and guidance; come by means of plant and tree, arise from hill and mound. Spirits of the land, arise—stir now to these words. Powers of the land, be here now.*

Take a deep, audible breath with the land as you draw your wand back towards your body, pointing straight down to the ground at all times and held close to the body; this is the wand's neutral position as you transition from one point of the triskele to another. Sense the land's power and what it represents spiralling at the terminus of the triskele arm. Slowly, being conscious of every footfall, turn around and walk back towards the center and then immediately to the point of the triskele that you have designated to represent the sea.

Stand with your feet shoulder-width apart. Stretch your power arm and point your wand directly at the horizon. Hold your free arm close to your body and bend your forearm up; your hand should be just in front of your shoulder with your palm facing the horizon.

Repeat these words or similar with power and conviction, evoking the visualization and the emotions you encountered in the meditation dedicated to sea.

Songs of the sea, I call to thee; hearken to this call. Come by powers of the ninth wave to this place. Songs of ocean ebb and flow, come and greet thy caller; lunar lover and currents wide pull against thy tide. Creatures of the depths of time, stir and hear my cries; trenches deep that encompass mine, abyss of nothingness shine. Realm of mystery and currents long, come now to this place. From depths of earth to unknown worlds, I call you to this space. Mighty ones, gods and goddesses of the seas within and those without, [insert names], come by wave and tide. Be here now!

Take a deep, audible breath with the powers of the sea as you draw your wand back towards your body; hold it in its neutral position as you move on. Sense the sea's power and what it represents spiralling at the terminus of the triskele arm. Slowly, being conscious of every footfall, turn around and walk back towards the center and then immediately to the point of the triskele that you have designated to represent the sky.

Stand with your feet shoulder-width apart. Stretch your power arm upwards so that it is vertically above your head and point your wand directly at the sky. Position your free arm horizontally to the side, with your palm turned to face the sky.

Repeat these words or similar with power and conviction, evoking the visualization and the emotions you encountered in the meditation dedicated to sky:

Songs of the sky, I call to thee; hearken to this call. Lofty place of spirits, come by breath of Awen to this place. Songs of dawn and twilight of vitality and inspiration, hear this call; come be in this space. Winged ones seen and unseen, and those who dwell between, listen to this cry. Place of apparition and bridge of spirit and soul, starlit skies and breath within, I draw one to the other. Gods and goddesses of the skies, O mighty ones, [insert names], come by sigh and song. Be here now!

Take a deep, audible breath with the powers of the sky as you draw your wand back towards your body; hold it in its neutral position as you move on.

Sense the sky's power and what it represents spiralling at the terminus of the triskele arm. Slowly and conscious of every footfall turn around and walk directly to the cauldron at the center.

State your intention. Hold your arms out horizontally, with your wand held aloft, and state the intention of the ritual. For example:

> *I come to this place where land, sea, and sky are present and in the company of [insert deity/deities' name/s]. I state that I come with no malice and that my intention is to cause healing for [name]. Be you witness and protectors of this rite.*

Keep your arms outstretched and cast your energy shield to the edges of the space; like the flash of a camera, sense it erupting from you instantanously. See its shimmering edges and know that no malice can cross it. Say these words:

> *May those who come with honor be honored; may those who come with dishonor be dishonored.*

Sense the spirals of the triskele pulsing to the powers of land, sea, and sky. Now focus your attention on what enables these things. Deep within the cauldron, the portal to the otherworlds, swims the power that brings meaning and action to the three points of the triskele. From its depths bubbles the current of the universe, Awen; all potential is here. You now summon this force from the depth of meaning.

Hold both your hands over the cauldron, angled so that your wand is pointing directly into its belly. And here comes the tricky bit—a splash of real Celticism. Do not be daunted. Words have power—throw yourself into the moment! Close your eyes and imagine a seething torrent of energy cascading from the cauldron to envelop everything around you. See it permeating everything.

Speak these words with power and conviction; repeat them in multiples of three until you feel Awen bubbling within you, its currents pulling your atoms and molecules to itself. Know that these ancient words are connecting you by sound and intent back through the mists of time; you speak the words of the ancestors. All the powers of Celtica arise with the uttering of these words:

Yr Awen a ganaf—or dwfn y dygaf.[20]
(Urr ah-when a GAN-av—oh-rr dOO-vun uh DUG-av.)

If all that is too much for you, then repeat them in English or alternate both Middle Welsh and English; the choice is entirely yours. It's the connection that matters.

The Awen I sing—from the deep I bring it.[21]

As you feel the currents move through you, raise both your arms up to form a wide *V* shape, hands to the skies, wand held aloft, and chant the three sacred vowels of Awen:

O, I, W.

Allow all three vowels to cascade, one after the other, in a single breath. Breathe in and repeat in multiples of three. Your body now forms an inverted Awen symbol—\ | /—and the intention is that you are projecting that force outwards. Having sung it from the deep, calling it to move with you, you now sing it outwardly, inspiring the world.

Breathe deeply at the conclusion of the chant.

Next you will perform the body of the ritual itself; this may be a celebration of the cycle of moon and sun, the seasons, a work of healing, magic, divination, or a rite of passage; having set the scene, you are now ready to begin.

Conclusion

When the main focus of your ritual reaches its conclusion, it is time to close the space and end the ritual.

None of the components that you called will be dismissed, as they are powers that are continuously present. To believe we are able to dismiss them

20 *"Angar Kyfundawt,"* the Book of Taliesin.
21 Ibid., my translation.

would be foolhardy. Concluding the ritual will be a system of acknowledgement and honoring.

Place your hands over the cauldron, wand aloft in your power hand. Close your eyes and intone the three sacred vowels, again in multiples of three:

O, I, W.

See the bubbling essence of the flowing spirit within the cauldron. Imagine your intent sinking into the ever-flowing course of Awen, working its magic, affecting and changing. When you are ready, repeat these words:

Yr Awen a ganaf, afon cyt beryt.
Gogwn y gwrhyt. Gogwn pan dyleinw.
Awen, Awen, Awen.[22]
(Urr Ah-wen a GAN-av, AH-von KIT BER-it.
GOG-oon uh GOO-rit. GOG-oon PAN DULL-aeenoo.
Ah-when, Ah-when, Ah-when.)
The Awen I sing, a connected river which flows.
I know its might. I know its flow.
Awen, Awen, Awen.[23]

Take three deep breaths and acknowledge the power of Awen within you.

Walk firmly to the point representing sky, assume the position you did when calling it, and say:

Powers of sky, gods/goddesses [name them] of the lofty places, hear these words. Long may you inspire and bring meaning; long may you serve as a bridge between spirit and soul. I give you thanks, sky within and skies without. Blessings to the realm of sky.

Walk swiftly by means of the center to the point of sea; assume the same position, wand pointed to the horizon, and say:

---

22 "*Angar Kyfundawt*," the Book of Taliesin.

23 Translated and adapted by me from "*Angar Kyfundawt*," the Book of Taliesin.

Powers of the sea, gods/goddesses [name them] of the deep, hear these words. Sing your songs of unity and current; long may you serve as the flow of the soul. I give you thanks, sea within and seas without. Blessings to the realm of sea.

Return to the center and move swiftly onto the final position, wand pointed towards the ground, and say:

Powers of the land, gods/goddesses [name them] of the firmament, hear these words. May you stand firm and your songs forever sing in the smallest parts of being. May you serve to remind us of our place of our origin. I give thanks to the land within and the lands without. Blessings to the realm of land.

Return to the center and, with a sharp intake of breath, see the shield that you extended to the edges of the ritual space shrink. It does so almost like a bubble bursting and returns in a split second to the core of your being.

The ritual is complete.

Grounding

It is important that you return fully to the ordinary world lest a part of you becomes lost in the between places, which leaves one feeling somewhat beside oneself. Dizziness and a sense of not quite being present are symptoms of not having fully grounded. Therefore, ensure that you eat something satisfying and have a drink; if you are with friends, laugh and enjoy being with each other. Forget about the ritual—it is done; it happened between the worlds. It does not need further discussion; leave it in the surety that it is doing its thing. Later, participate in something mundanely human: wash the dishes, do some laundry, clean something, watch TV—anything that will bring you fully back to earth.

Summary

- approach, prepare, settle
- opening words
- call to the land, sea, and sky
- state intention
- extend shield
- cauldron, calling Awen
- vowel chant
- the work
- acknowledge Awen
- vowel chant
- give thanks to land, sea, and sky
- ground

◆ ◆ ◆

So there we have it, a step-by-step guide to the creating of Celtic ritual. The actual workings of it will be decorated by yourself; other words and associations will naturally occur as you move into relationship with the three realms and your magical allies, which we explore next. All these things become the accoutrements that bejewel your rituals and make them personal to you and the people you practice them with.

PART 2

The Companions of Celtic Magic

6

Magical Allies

In every walk of life there are experts, specialists in their field, who have been trained and educated to help those who seek their particular form of speciality. This may apply to a man who lays carpet, a doctor, a plumber, a librarian, or a teacher. There are times when we need to consult or seek the assistance of someone who will help us or bring about a required result. The same can be said for magic. Within magic we are not alone; there is absolutely no need to be stumbling along in the dark, unaware of what is around the corners, bumping into furniture, crying out in pain and frustration simply because we don't know what on earth is going on or what we should be doing.

This is the point where an effective magician will turn to a team of magical allies: supernatural entities, gods, goddesses, genius loci, demigods, and ancestral spirits that the magician has aligned with in order to make his or her magic most effective. This provides the magician with a greater advantage and makes for better practice. Reaching out for assistance is a humble and sensible action; it is not something that belittles the skills or adeptness of the magician. It is no different from employing folk who are specialists in the ordinary world.

I have categorized magical allies into three distinct groups, each with its own set of allies with unique functions and attributions. I classify them as

- gods and goddesses
- demigods/goddesses (half deity/half mortal)
- genius loci, or spirits of place (including ancestors)

In the following chapters each will be described fully with an exploration of how we connect and form relationships with them, what their functions are, and how best to engage with them.

By utilizing magical allies we are accessing an ancient storehouse of wisdom and knowledge that has survived in various guises for over 2,000 years. The allies that I present to you in the following chapters have been essential components of the Celtic spirit and culture for centuries; they express a people's connection to their land and the manner by which they made sense of life and its trials, its joys, and the passage of time. They provided a glimpse into the world of the spirit and the origin of the soul; to some extent, they entertained; in a world without TV and CDs, our ancestors told stories that captured the imagination of the people and taught them valuable ethics, how to behave, and how to survive. These eventually became the spirits and deities of the Celtic people that we continue to know today. It can be argued that current Pagan practice has, by the process of apotheosis, deified some of the Celtic archetypes and exalted them to a rank that may not have been acknowledged as such by our ancestors. As society changes, so do the spirits of the Celtic mysteries; this is why they have survived—they are relevant in manners that are beneficial to those who align themselves to them.

A magical ally is a spirit that may express the divine qualities of a god or goddess exalted to a lofty place, ethereal, and sometimes without form. It may be the delicious combination of divinity and the flawed vulnerability of a human being encapsulated in the demigod/goddess. The genius loci may be the spirit of a well or a tree or the echo of a human being who died in a particular place; it may capture a story or recount a fable pertinent to a particular location. The nature of the genius loci is predominantly locality specific.

The Practical Functions of Magical Allies

As is common in Celtic magic, a tripartite structure is as sacred as it is practical. Our allies can be categorized as three distinct groups: gods/goddesses, demigods/goddesses, and genius loci. Magical allies also have three distinct functions, which can be categorized as follows:

- guide
- teacher
- assistant

Guide

Were we to visit a foreign city on vacation, we would no doubt employ a guide. Now this may not necessarily be in the guise of a human being—it may be a smartphone app, a travel guidebook, or a review website. The guide accentuates and brings depth to the experience of visiting somewhere new, of forming a connection to something or someplace. This analogy can be equated to any other function in our lives; more often than not, when faced with a new, challenging, or unknown situation or circumstance, we will reach for a guide. The same is also true for magic.

A magical guide is a sounding board for the formulation of your magic, an ally that acts to give meaning to what you seek to transform or change. It is the subtle power that you converse with in the making of your lists, your pros and cons. It is the ear that listens to you as you plan and plot. Most ordinary decisions are as a consequence of consultation; we may seek the advice of friends or professionals in finding clarity. We turn to the spirits and deities and ask them to lend us their ears, to guide the hand in making the right decision at that time. Approaching the altars of magic usually means that there is something pressing, something needs addressing or transforming; magic is not a knee-jerk reaction; it is not something we turn to at a whim.

We listen, and we respond. Problems at work or in a relationship may be discussed with a friend; this does not imply that the friend makes any decision for you, but he or she acts as a device to clarify the matter in your own mind. Magical guides serve the same function.

Teacher

As teacher, they bring us closer to the mysteries that they represent. Rhiannon is an effective demigoddess in bereavement and grief magic, in humility and steadfastness. Her mythology teaches us the nature of these elements and how we are affected by them. Connecting to Rhiannon to lessen grief would be foolhardy, for that is not her function; a connection to her brings about a deeper understanding of what we are trying to transform and the inherent message within the function of grief. Her legend speaks of assimilating that grief, of making sense of it, and by connecting to her, this quality "rubs off," if you will, and we move to understanding why we grieve.

Rather than reaching for a wand, pointing it directly towards the pain of bereavement, and expecting it to simply lessen by half, Rhiannon teaches the magician the quality of that grief and why it is essential for the human experience. This causes the magician to understand the properties of grief in a manner that transforms it; the magic is enabled and the magician is transformed by the process of connection and understanding. In this case, invoking Rhiannon to understand bereavement is to turn to the teachings of a magical ally that we access by means of our subtle powers and the power of myth and legend. The ally acts as teacher. The teacher's function is to transmit the information and enable us to be fully informed and equipped with knowledge so that when we arrive at the altars of magic, we do so armed.

Assistant

During the act of magic itself, the guide and teacher become an assistant, a hand that is held to enable the magic to be effective. There is power in numbers, so why face a challenging situation alone? However, an assistant in magic may not prevent you from making mistakes. Their purpose is not to scorn or punish—you called them, remember—it is the relationship that matters. The consequence is entirely dependent on your intent, honor, and integrity. For instance, if you needed to perform an act of magic that involved fire or the transforming of something in flames to bring about a result, then it would be wise to align oneself to a spirit or god that is familiar with this art.

In the Celtic tradition, Govannon of the smith would be a natural choice to inspire, guide, and teach you about the nature of fire, its qualities and properties, and, most importantly, its mysteries and function in magic. As you move closer to this energy, your formulation is informed; Govannon offers you teachings that stem from his mythology and the mystery contained therein. So even before you have stepped into your magical space, you are armed with knowledge, and from this knowledge comes understanding. So when you approach the cauldron and raise your wand aloft, you sense that Govannon is beside you, his strength and wisdom swimming in and out of your spirit to enable and activate your magic. But just as a driving instructor will not prevent you from mounting the pavement in your haste to turn a corner, neither will your magical allies prevent you from making mistakes; this, in itself, is an act of teaching. We must listen carefully, evaluate, and examine the need for the magic and be accepting of the consequences.

EXERCISE
THE QUALITY OF COMPANIONSHIP

For this exercise you will need two sheets of paper and some different colored pens. One sheet will represent your allies in the material world, the other your allies or potential allies in the magical world.

Take your first sheet of paper and draw two lines straight down it, equal distance apart, to create three columns on your page. Pop in these titles:

Col. 1: ***Name*** **Col. 2:** ***Quality*** **Col. 3:** ***Qualification***

This is a contemplative exercise where you examine the support systems in your own life, so create a little ambience—light some candles and some fragrant incense, dim the lights a little. Sit comfortably and contemplate the people in your life who serve as allies for your own needs. Who is it that fulfils some of the following criteria?

- Who listens to you the most without ever judging or criticizing you?
- Who is it that will readily come and help you with practical stuff?
- Who offers you a shoulder to cry on and makes you feel safe and protected?
- Who sustains you the most?
- Who nourishes your spirit, be it through inspiration, laughter, or support?
- Who uplifts you the most?
- Who do you call on for specialist advice and help when things get a little rocky, difficult, or just lie outside your expertise or skill base?

The above represents only a fraction of questions that relate to your allies in life. Think on these and more, and in column 1 pop down the names of the people who fulfil these functions. In the second column add the quality that they bring; for instance, my friend Julie brings to my life the quality of steadfastness. She is always there for me whenever I need her; in her company I can let go and just be myself without recourse or judgement. In column 3 articulate why this person is qualified to perform this task. For my friend Julie, it is her inherent rootedness that brings about her ability to make me feel steadfast and secure. She is a part of her locale, she is always there; that is her qualification. Continue in this manner until the page is full.

Think on these qualities and what they bring to your life.

The next sheet should look like this:

Col. 1: ***Spirit/Deity*** **Col. 2:** ***Quality*** **Col. 3:** ***Qualification***

Perform the task in the same manner as the previous list, bearing in mind that these qualities are subtle and magical.

- Who do you turn to for clarity?
- Who do you turn to for access to mystery?
- Who do you look to for magical advice?
- Who do you turn to for spiritual support?
- Who inspires you the most?
- Who do you feel the greatest affinity towards?

Ask yourself these and other questions pertinent to the supernatural beings that you ally yourself to in your magical practice. Now fill in the columns just as you did with your physical allies. An example of this may be:

> Branwen: she brings the quality of communication with the animal kingdom, in particular birds and other winged creatures; she helps you interact with the animal kingdom in a subtle manner. She is qualified by proxy of a legend that recounts her relationship with a starling, which she trains to fly from Ireland to Britain to help rescue her from a cruel husband.

Continue the exercise until you have exhausted your knowledge base of magical allies.

◆ 7 ◆

Celtic Gods and Goddesses

It could be surmised that a god or goddess is a nonhuman entity who forms the foundation of traditions; they are generally attributed a myth or legendary saga that defines their function and quality, and it is this quality and by means of their mythology that we connect to and develop relationships with them. They may represent a force of nature or an aspect of the human condition.

It is not my intention to define what a god or goddess is, for I believe that their magic lies in the fact that we may never truly understand their nature. Our exploration of them only offers glimpses at the world of these enigmatic supernatural beings.

In the following chapters I will examine the gods and goddesses with whom I work most closely and offer rituals and meditations that will help you to connect with them. Not only will this color your own magical practice, it will also facilitate relationship with myriad different deities. In turn, these deities and the relationships you forge with them will function to serve your magical needs. As the exercise in the previous chapter demonstrated, we turn to different friends, family, and community members depending on our needs; the same applies for the gods and goddesses. By sharing my experience of them, I hope to inspire your journey of connection and relationship.

◆ ◆ ◆

Gods and goddesses may exist as entities in their own right who inhabit a world, dimension, or reality that may run parallel with our own or exist beneath the fabric of our own space / time continuum. They may be entities who have attached themselves to the construct of deity created by humanity. The gods can only be examined and explained subjectively, and this in itself is a limiting factor; we are unable to peer at them through a microscope or dissect them in a laboratory. There is no scientific method to prove that the gods and goddesses exist, but this fact has not stopped or hindered humankind in developing relationships with deity. It seems that we intrinsically *want* to be in touch with deity—we hunger and thirst for connection with something that is not human, that is beyond the senses. How we address the question of deific existence must be based on our relationship with it.

A god or goddess may be specific to a particular location—a river, for example, whose name may be etymologically connected to a deity. The river Severn that cuts through England and Wales is derived from the name of a Celto-Romano goddess called Sabrina, called Hafren in ancient British. Now some may argue that Sabrina is simply an anthropomorphic representation of the river and nothing else, but on the other hand it is referring to an actual living, moving entity—a brook that rises from deep within the land, swelling to become a river that snakes through the landscape, irrigating and enriching the earth and the lives of those who dwell nearby. Sabrina's personality and qualities can be seen emulated in the river itself; they are interchangeable. She nourishes, she is fertile, she sustains, and yet there is a hint of danger to her in that she may flood without warning and cause untold damage. She is not representative of rivers in general; she is specific to the river Severn and the dynamic relationship it has with the landscape of England and Wales, and its interaction with the tide and the famous Severn Bore. It is this quality that defines the attributes of the goddess; altars, shrines, and temples sprang up along her banks to honor her, and to this day statues of Sabrina adorn the squares of many towns and villages along her course.

How do we define whether Sabrina is a goddess, a demigoddess, or a genius loci? Perhaps she embodies the qualities of all three. There is a certain truth in this, and it is more than likely that Sabrina began her existence as a genius loci, a spirit of place; over countless centuries of devotion, her quality changed as a consequence of the dynamic relationship between her and the people. She became a goddess, one who is revered to this day.

This demonstrates the fickle, complex nature of the gods, for Sabrina is not transferable to another location: she is locality-specific to a ribbon of a few hundred miles from the west of Wales, through the English border, and to the Bristol Channel—to attempt to transfer her to another location would denigrate and belittle the power and influence of the river itself, as it is indicative of the people's relationship with a place and, by proxy, with a goddess whose power arises from that place. It is inherently dynamic and immensely magical.

It is apparent from Celtic mythology that many of the gods transcend locality and appear entirely nonhuman; in fact, their attributes can appear to be indicative of a more generalized otherworldly component. These gods are transferable to other locations because they are not tied to a particular location; they may have interacted with humanity or been revered in several locations and are not necessarily representative of natural phenomena. They feel entirely "other." These can include but are not restricted to the gods and goddesses of natural weather phenomena—rain, thunder, storms, and the wind.

These deities may have a totemic attribution in that they are stationed as clan or tribe members who move with the people from one location to another in the same manner that the Christian God moved with the founding fathers to the United States of America. Their ethereal quality, which has transcended locality and adapted to the diversity of tribe, allows them to relocate with the migration of the people. This is exemplified in the thousands of Pagans who revere certain Celtic gods beyond the shores of the

Celtic nations. There is connection, and this may be by proxy of heritage and ancestry or something at the far end of subjectivity that we may identify as simply a calling.

The gods act as skeletons that form the bare bones of traditions and mythology; they may have arisen from the landscape or they may represent universal powers. We attire these skeletons with flesh and blood, skin and clothing; it is humanity that gives them a name and carves images in their likeness; we are the ones who perceive them and see them in vision and meditation. And beneath all that swims the energy of the deity—that initial spark that caused an explosion of expression in the imagination and minds of humankind. Our relationship with the gods should be one of symbiosis.

The gods do not nurture ignorance, and neither do they expect us to believe in them without personal evidence of their existence. The beauty of the Pagan traditions is that belief is not a requirement for practice—knowledge and experience are.

I Experience; Therefore, I Know

Belief is generally based on faith, and faith, in return, is mostly blind. Blind faith—the term alone is somewhat chilling, I find; the majority have faith because they are told they must, it is the right thing, do not question anything or anyone, just have faith; *really?* The majority of us who have been raised and nurtured in a Christian society have certain set, almost immovable patterns of belief when it comes to the subject of deity. We are programmed from an early age that there is one superior being, a creator god who rules the universe and is somewhat jealous and will punish his offspring if they do not do exactly as they are told. He is human male in form, and no other gods exist except for him. "I am the Lord, and there is no other; there is no God besides me" (Isaiah 45:5). This standard model influences our lives and can sometimes create teething problems when we transition from one tradition to another. The animistic traditions bear no similarity to the structure of the revealed monotheistic traditions, and in order to transition smoothly between one and the other we must adjust our perception filters.

The revealed traditions cause us to look upwards to the lofty heavens with arms outstretched; we are below and God is above. In animistic traditions, with hands placed gently over the heart we reach inward and back—back through flesh and back through bone, back through the elements that compose us and to the gleaming fire of Awen that underpins the universe. And as we reach back with our senses, we feel the powers of nature as integral aspects of our nature; we are as one. It is here that our gods exist, not separate, not "out there" somewhere. Our gods are a part of us. Just as you are a part of your mother's body, just as the genes of your father and forefathers sing from within you, so too do those beings and energies that we may choose to call gods and goddesses. We experience; therefore, we know.

MEDITATION
REACHING DEITY

Stop for a minute or two—take a breath with the land beneath you, breathe in the sky above you, and deeply breathe with the rhythm of the seas that surround the shores of your land. Pop some cotton wool or ear plugs into both ears so that the sound of your own breathing is heightened. Breathe deeply and reach back—beyond your mind, beyond the rivers and forests, the hills and seas; back, reach back—through your breath, sense the streams of existence that reach backwards from your place in this time and this place. Breathe deeper; listen to the sound of your breath, for within it are the sounds of the universe and your origin at the beginning of time.

Reach back through your heartbeat to the beating spirit of the gods and goddesses; you are one. Back through the rivers, back through the seas, back through the oceans. Reach back through your blood and back through your veins; back through your heartbeat; you are one and the same. Reach back through the forests and then back through the fields; back through the mountains, their mysteries revealed. Reach back to your bones and back through your skin; back beyond your spirit and the Awen within. Sense the gods within the fabric of your being and the very warp and weft of the universe.

Part 2

A Question of Worship

To worship implies subservience and that we are beneath our deities—that they are superior to us when, in fact, they are not. Ultimately it is a choice of words, semantics, but I think that the implications of the word *worship* are associated with the gods of the revealed religions and suggest that they demand our worship without question. Times have changed and so, too, have the people; we no longer needed to appease the gods of nature with sacrifices. Instead, I believe it's more conducive to move away from the sense of worship and walk with reverence and honor.

To honor the gods as aspects of nature or as representations of the human condition is to honor the world we live in and of being human within it. The gods do not demand anything from us; in fact, those who don't align themselves with the gods get on perfectly well in life. I think it foolhardy to fall into the assumption that because we have sets of deities in the Pagan traditions, we must suddenly fall to our knees before them in subservient worship.

Reverence implies respect; to respect the powers of nature is not only wise but also sensible. To honor the passage of human life and the deities that we associate with that is to be conscious of our lives and the things that affect them. The gods and goddesses are not foes; they are not high and mighty beings that sit on some lofty cloud awaiting our unquestionable worship, nor do I believe that they summon us to serve them. I believe that we are drawn to them for a number of reasons: culture, heritage, tradition, and so forth, or simply because a particular god or goddess is a central component of the group, order, or coven that we may join.

To adopt the commonly shared belief that we are created in the image of deity and that it is human is to miss out on the deeply personal and immanent relationship with the gods that is so unique to the animistic traditions.

Lessons from Divinity: Working with the Gods and Goddesses

There are some deities that we are naturally drawn towards; they sing to an aspect of our lives and inspire us to move into relationship with them. The next chapter offers a description of the deities that I work with most frequently. This will provide you with a window onto my own practice, combined with some background to the deities at hand and rituals that have been devised specifically for them. This also acts as a window in time, for as I develop and grow, so does my repertoire of god and goddess allies change with me. You will note by definition of what follows that I am not devoted to one deity; rather, I have a repertoire of deities that I work with depending on where I am, what I am doing, and what my needs or requirements are. My relationship with them emulates the function of my human circle of friends and allies: to each one a speciality, to each an individual function. One may judge this as a form of spiritual promiscuity, but I hope that what follows will demonstrate the individual deific qualities that enhance my magical practice and connection.

8

Mabon and Modron

The traits of the divine child, consort, and lover of the Goddess are a common theme in modern Pagan traditions, but they are particularly relevant and fitting to the Celtic tradition, where their influence affected both Celtic and Roman society.

Mabon, Son of Modron: The Divine Child

The term *Mabon, son of Modron* is derived from the Celtic deity Maponos, son of Matrona, meaning the youthful son of the Mother Goddess. Epigraphic evidence for a cult to Maponos is evident mostly in the northern regions of England and in Gaul, but of particular note is the evidence of a strong cult to Maponos within the garrisons of troops who guarded Hadrian's Wall, which separates what is now England from the northern tribes of Britain. Altars along this region, particularly at Hexham, bear the inscriptions "Apollini Mapono" and "Maponus"; offerings and votives found at these sites are indicative of devotional activity by military chiefs of the Roman army, perhaps indicating that aspects or attributes of Maponos were considered useful to those who served in the armed forces. However, this is evidently not the only attribute afforded to Maponos, the divine son who, within the context of mythology and devotional acts, seems to embody several qualities that adapt to various circumstances, conditions, and seasons.

Devotion to Maponos was seen far beyond the shores of Britain, and he appears in several inscriptions to bear the name "Apollo Maponos," suggesting his adoption into Roman society and his similarity to Apollo, one of their most favored gods. The term *mabon* is a medieval Welsh designation for Maponos, the divine son, and there is compelling evidence to suggest that the etymology of the word *Mabinogi* originally meant "the collective material pertaining to the god Maponos."[24] This suggests that the four branches of the Mabinogi are the myths of the mabon made locality and culturally specific in the guise of Rhiannon and her son Pryderi as facets of Modron and her son Mabon. Pryderi as the mabon or divine son seemingly meets his death in the final branch of the Mabinogi, only to be replaced by another facet of the mabon, Lleu Llaw Gyffes, who resumes the journey.

Perhaps one of the most influential accounts of Mabon comes to us from the pages of one of Wales's oldest tales, the saga of Culhwch and Olwen. In this tale the hero, Culhwch, seeks the hand of Olwen in marriage, but her father presents him with a series of impossible tasks before he will permit him to marry his daughter. One of these tasks requires the assistance of Arthur and his band of warriors to find an ancient being called Mabon to help them hunt down a wild boar who was previously a king. With the help of the earth's oldest and wisest animals, Mabon is discovered to be held prisoner in what is today the city of Gloucester. Snatched from the arms of his mother when he was only three days old, he is held captive in a subterranean prison until freed by Arthur and his men.

---

24 Ford, *The Mabinogi and Other Medieval Welsh Tales*, 3.

The Triads of the Island of Britain[25] record this instance, and Mabon is listed as one of the three exalted prisoners of the Island of Britain, together with Llŷr, one of the gods of the Britons, and Gwair or Gweir, who is cognate with Pryderi, the son of Pwyll and Rhiannon, also stolen from his mother at three days of age, and the mythical prisoner Gweir in the Book of Taliesin poem "The Spoils of Annwn,"[26] all of whom are believed to be representations of the god Mabon.

Mabon can be seen as a character who epitomizes the pan-European concept of the infant in exile and return. This theme of imprisonment and release in the Mabinogi—particularly in the third branch and the Culhwch and Olwen saga—is suggestive of a magical fertility myth. This myth is indicative of the separation of the youthful god from his mother, the great goddess, and the resulting desolation of the land, which is only restored once the youthful god is reunited with his mother.[27] The salmon upon whose back Arthur and his helpers ride a river to breach the prison of Mabon are, as Will Parker suggests in his exploration of the Mabinogi, "potent elements of the mystery of conception."[28]

Parker further elaborates and suggests that

> the mabon would represent the divine child, sacrificial victim or lover of the Goddess, whose perennial imprisonment in the underworld realms follows the seasonal patterns of the plant and animal life of the land, withdrawing as it does into the earth during the winter months.[29]

There is literary evidence to suggest that he was not limited to a single quality. In the Book of Taliesin he takes on a definite psychopompic attribute—a helper to the dead or a deity who initiates the transition from one

---

25 The Triads of the Island of Britain, also called *Trioedd Ynys Prydein*, is a collection of 97 triads from various manuscripts that express an ancient body of lore and mythology. They have been extensively studied by the late Celtic scholar Rachel Bromwich.

26 Bromwich, *Trioedd Ynys Prydein*, 147.

27 Parker, *The Four Branches of the Mabinogi*, 386.

28 Ibid., 215.

29 Ibid.

state of being to another. In poem number 38 of the aforementioned Book of Taliesin we find the following lines:

> Whoever saw Mabon on his white and lovely horse, who mingled before the cattle of Rheged. Unless it were with wings that they flew, only as corpses would they escape from Mabon.[30]

This psychopompic aspect can be seen emulated on a lead tablet that was discovered in Chamalieres (in former Gaul) and written in Gaulish. The tablet—a spell to communicate with the mabon, beseeching action—says:

> *Andedion uediiu mi diiiuion risu Maponon Aruernatin, loites sni eooic sos brixtia Anderon* (I beseech the divine Maponos Avernatis by means of this magic tablet, quicken us named by the magic of the underworld spirits).[31]

Here Maponos is perceived as a god who traverses the fickle line between the under and upper world, the realm of light and darkness; having access to both worlds, he is useful to those who require the qualities of either state. Fertility, birth, and death, in the case of Mabon, are simply opposite sides of the same coin; all are necessary.

In the Book of Taliesin his name is applied to Christ, the newborn child of hope and light, and this theme continues through the Book of Taliesin and into the Mabinogi saga, where the entire four branches can be seen as the birth, imprisonment, life, and death of the hero Pryderi and, later, Lleu Llaw Gyffes, who can be seen to be representative of the mabon. *Mabon* simply means "son"; *modron*, "mother." This implies that all the gods and goddesses of the Celts carry qualities of the divine son and mother, and may, in fact, be representatives of those faceless, nameless deities within the context of the seasons or the human condition. Perhaps most significantly for this discourse is that the magicians' initiatory journey is indicative of and emulated within the mythology of the mabon and the great mother, or modron. In many ways, the mabon is you, a child of the great mother. We may externalize

30 *Kychwedyl am Dodyv* ("A Rumor Has Come to Me," from the Book of Taliesin); my translation.

31 Koch, *The Celtic Heroic Age*, 2–3.

the teachings of the mabon and may perceive him as something other than us, whereas by working with the energy of the mabon we realize that we are essentially him. As adventurers on the great wheel of life, not just passive observers, the key to knowing the mystery lies in the experience of this immanency, of becoming the mabon.

EXERCISE
BECOMING THE MABON

The mabon is immanent; he is the spark of divinity that resides within all of us. We are all children of the great mother. Become the mabon, the sacred child.

Take some time to memorize the *englyn* below until you know it by heart. Then take to a room lit only by candlelight and burn sweet incense to fill the air with fragrance. Sit comfortably and allow your eyes to close gently.

Imagine that you float serenely from a pristine blue sky high above a tidal estuary. The tidal waves, in and out, mimic your own breath. In the center of the estuary is an island, upon which stands a tower of sand-colored stone. A lament rises from within by breath of briny wind to reach your spiritual ears. It is the mabon who sings from within the tower, the top of which is open to the elements.

You descend; as you do, you see a young lad sitting cross-legged in the center of the tower. He sings a song in an ancient tongue; the words are haunting, alien, and yet familiar. Your body sinks into his—your eyes become his eyes, and as they do so, his words become your words as the *englyn* sings from your spirit combined with the mabon.

I am the mabon, I am the child,
I am the mabon, I am the wild.
I am the mabon, I am the tame,
I am the mabon, I am the flame.
I am the son, I am the foal,
I am the hidden secret of soul.

I am you, and you are me,
Child of the mother, let me see.
Secrets and magic of Modron wise,
I call to the mabon in me to rise.
Mabon of Modron, Mabon the child,
Awaken in me the spirit beguiled!

Sense the spirit of the divine child within you: you are the mabon, child of the great mother. When it is time, rise up from the body of the mabon and take to the skies above. Become aware of your breath in tune with the waves of the estuary calling you back to your body, to the here and now.

Give thanks to the mabon. Eat, drink, rest, and, on the morrow, record your impressions in your journal.

Mabon

Spiritual Function: Teaches us the significance of the great wheel and the mysteries of life, death, and rebirth. Teaches the student the importance of assimilation, reflection, and taking time out to reflect and absorb the function of liminality.

Magical Ally Function: Teaches us the function and magic of immanency, discovering the deity within.

Modron, the Great Mother

The medieval designation *modron* has its roots in the earlier Celtic term *matrona*, meaning "great mother"; her name is given to the river Marne in France and to the parish of Madron in Cornwall, along with numerous other place names that are linked to the great goddess. Modron is the deity that links the past to the present. She can be seen within every facet of European spiritual traditions, she gives rise to all things, she represents the earth and the powers of conception and birthing, death and rebirth. Simultaneously she gives rise to myriad archetypes who are representative of her powers and attributes, and they do so by giving her a name and attaching her to facets of the human condition. It could be argued that all the goddesses of the Celts are aspects of the great mother. They are sparks that fly from the central fire—they contain a fundamental component of the source and yet are individuals in their own rights.

In her guise as the great mother, Modron and her son are amorphous; they are devoid of individuation and yet contain the potential to be made manifest and fitting for any season, situation, circumstance, or condition. Within the four branches of the Mabinogi, Modron and Mabon can be seen represented as Rhiannon and her son Pryderi, who form the basis for the entire sequence of events. The great mother becomes the great queen and is representative of a host of human qualities that humans can equate to. So rather than the goddess being something up there, out of touch, out of sight, too amorphous and ethereal for true and meaningful connection, a spark from that source is sent flying into the tales of the Celts, and suddenly we are able to connect to her, to see her in human guise.

Modron's survival through the ages and her continuous influence on modern traditions is a testament to the fact that she transcends diversity and time and remains relevant. She is able to adapt to change and new religions, becoming relevant to all who seek her. Her status as sovereign or that which represents the sovereignty of the land itself is attested in the tale "Washer at the Ford" from northwest Wales. Generally seen as a death portent, this aspect of the great mother has long been feared by the Celtic peasantry, and yet the tale demonstrates her ability to become relevant to new ways and new people, lest she fell into obscurity.

The tale recounts how Urien Rheged, a king of Britain, arrived at the Ford of Barking in Denbighshire to find a young woman washing and surrounded by incessantly barking dogs. The dogs ceased their barking as he arrived, and he was so taken by the young woman that he had intercourse with her, there and then. It transpires that she is cursed to wash at the ford until she begets a son by a Christian man, which she subsequently does. A year later, Urien is presented with a son named Owain and a daughter named Morfyd. The Triads of the Island of Britain refer to this folk tale as one of the "three fair, holy, and blessed womb-burdens of the Island of Britain, of which the second was

Owain, son of Urien, and Morfyd, daughter of Urien, by Modron, daughter of Afallach, their mother."[32]

You will note that Modron is named as the daughter of Afallach, who in turn was the son of Beli Mawr—another great god of the Celts. Afallach was considered a king of Annwn, the indigenous Celtic underworld, and yet his name is also a noun meaning "a place of apples."[33] It is tempting here to veer into the realms of Arthurian romance concerning the Isle of Avalon, which is directly linked to the name Afallach. However, in this case, it is in all probability a reference to the abundance of apple trees that characterize the landscape of the Celtic otherworld and may have given rise to the later renditions of Arthur and his connections to Avalon. What is important here is the fact that Modron is changing her guise—she is being humanized and, as such, is interacting with the world of men in a direct manner. In this case she is awaiting conception by a Christian man, demonstrating her ability to transcend tradition, and it could be argued that the great mother continues to be present in the Christian religion in the guise of the Virgin Mary. Consequently Urien is also directly linked to the deific dynasties of Britain by his union with Modron, thus affirming his sovereignty by proxy of his connection to the goddess as an aspect of the land.

But what can we do on a practical level with this information? What does it all mean—how do we make sense of this ambivalent, amorphous goddess? The magic of Modron (and her son) is in her universality—she is the source, she is the beginning and the end, she is the one that turns the great wheel of life and keeps it spinning. She is the faceless canvas onto which we superimpose all other goddesses; it is by means of the arbitrary goddesses and their attributes that we sense the spirit of the great mother. She is the great wheel of life, and in her skirts hide the faces of all the goddesses that we connect to. They are aspects of her, and they, in turn, represent aspects of us. When we align ourselves to the energy of our goddess allies, we move into the energetic field of the great mother; it is by connecting to our personal goddesses that we sense the power of Modron.

---

32 Bromwich, *Trioedd Ynys Prydein*, 195.

33 Ibid., 274.

As a magical ally, Modron connects us to the great wheel of the year and the nourishing and sustaining qualities of the mother essential for the brewing of magic for healing, nurturing, and stability.

EXERCISE
MODRON'S DAILY DEVOTIONAL

Position a figurine or other representation of the great mother in a central position at the back of your altar or designated ritual space. Place a pillar or taper candle on either side of the figurine. In the foreground position a cauldron or similar vessel. Place eight small candles or tealights around the cauldron; having these contained within small glass receptacles is even better. Each of these candles represents one face of the great mother as she traverses the great wheel of the year that is beloved of modern Paganism.

Stop; take a breath with the sky above you, and draw it into your body.

Take a breath with the lapping waves of the seas that surround your land.

Take a deep breath and draw the power of land from beneath you.

Light the candles on either side of the image or figurine and repeat the following in Welsh while lighting the left-hand candle and in English for the right.

Modron, Matrona, Mam y ddaear, cod a tyd at a fi.
(Modron, Matrona, MAM uh DDAY-arr, cohd AH tId att ah vee.)[34]
Modron, Matrona, Mam y bydysawd, tyd, clyw fy nghri.
(Modron, Matrona, MAM uh beed-US-awwd, tId, KLEEW vuh NG-hree)
Modron, Matrona, Mother of earth, arise and come unto me,
Modron, Matrona, Mother of all, arise and come unto me.

Light an incense stick within the cauldron or drop some incense onto a hot charcoal block. As the smoke rises, repeat the above twice.

Light each of the eight candles, acknowledging the many facets of the great mother as the wheel of the year turns. Imagine her as the following:

---

34 See the pronunciation guide on page 313 for tips.

Winter Solstice/Alban Arthan: the ancient mother, bearer of new light

Imbolc/Gwyl Ffraid: a young girl, innocent, light, and fair

Spring Equinox/Alban Eilir: the blossoming maiden bursting with potential fertility

Beltane/Calan Mai: ripe, fertile, sexually powerful and independent

Summer Solstice/Alban Hefin: the maturing mother, experienced, powerful

Lughnassadh/Gwyl Awst: letting go, untying the apron strings, last blossoming

Autumn Equinox/Alban Elfed: the coming of the grandmother, wisdom from knowing

Sambain/Calan Gaeaf: the old woman, crone, bone hag, and devourer

Cradle the eight candles with your hands; feel their warmth seeping into your palms and sense the great mother. Either look directly at the image or figurine or close your eyes and sense her presence. I use these words:

Modron, All-Mother, giver of life and bringer of death,
I sing my praises to thee,
Modron, Great Mother, weaver of life and death,
arise now and be within me.

Sit awhile and sense the presence of the great mother. Extinguish the candles and then go about your business as usual. Attempt to perform this ritual every day at a time that is convenient for you.

Modron

Spiritual Function: Teaches us about the nature of the great mother and the effect of the turning year on the planet and ourselves.

Magical Ally Function: For acts of magic focused on nourishment, sustenance, healing, and encouragement. Seasonal magic.

9

Rhiannon: The Mare of Sovereignty

With Modron being the great mother, it is the guise of the goddess as Rhiannon, derived from the ancient British Rigantona, who represents the great queen. In Europe she was worshiped in the guise of Epona, the great mare. The four branches of the Mabinogi present a truly unambiguous and complete account of Rhiannon as one of Celtica's most loved goddesses.

Her role as great queen is varied. We first encounter her as a strong, independent woman who appears on horseback from the mists of the Celtic otherworld to lead Pwyll, the hero of the first branch of the Mabinogi, on a chase to win her affections. Here she is seen to be acting against the wishes of her otherworldly family, and this rebellious nature is a powerful attribution that exemplifies the great queen's independent spirit. Try as Pwyll may, his pursuit of her by horseback is never fast enough to catch her. Eventually, in frustration, he calls out to her to stop—and she does, chastizing him for not having asked earlier and exhausting his horse in the process.

There are two distinct periods in the tale where Rhiannon's ties with the otherworld are thin and she moves fully and consciously into the world of humanity. Initially she is fully representative of the sovereignty of the land; the queen atop the horse, and her groom, Pwyll, by means of his marriage to Rhiannon, is perceived as being wed to the land itself. Rhiannon embodies the spirit of the land—she is powerful, sexually assertive, and fiercely independent; she is the epitome of the eternal goddess of land and sovereignty.

Within a year of their marriage, she gives birth to a son and dons the mother aspect of the Goddess, but—as in the tale of Mabon and Modron—her son is stolen from the crib at three days old. Rhiannon is wrongly accused by her servants of having destroyed and eaten her child, and in return she is punished. Forced to behave as a horse, she must offer to carry guests to the king's court upon her back. Rather than being the queen in control of the horse, Rhiannon becomes the horse. In this guise she represents the calumniated wife, the mother wrongly accused, or the suffering queen; she becomes the workhorse.

Bereft and grieving, she accepts her punishment without complaint. Meanwhile, her son mysteriously appears in a stable on May's Eve in place of a foal, and so begins Rhiannon's association as equine goddess and her son as the divine foal god. Eventually they are reunited, at which she proclaims deliverance from her *pryder,* meaning "care or anxiety," and thus the child is renamed Pryderi. In the third branch she appears again with her son, and together they are trapped in the otherworld and treated as horses.

Rhiannon's attributions are simultaneously deific and painfully human. She is the Goddess made incarnate; she is the manner by which we can see through our own tribulations, our own suffering, and sense the divine within. Aspects of Rhiannon in her guise as horse goddess can still be seen within the traditional practices of Wales and Cornwall. The Welsh practice of the *mari lwyd,* where a horse's skull dressed in ribbons hunts from house to house, mimics Rhiannon's hopeless search for her missing foal, and the Cornish "Obby Oss" evokes a distant memory of the divine horse goddess.

She is the nightmare, the whispers of wisdom that come to us in dreams. She is indicative of many traits of the human condition; she instills wisdom and guides her husband to be of greater care; she is loving, faithful, and accepting of her fate. She is the sorrowful queen, the embodiment of grief and bereavement, compassion and humility. Aligning oneself to Rhiannon is to wander into her halls of teaching, of taking counsel before her; by listening to her wisdom, we learn much about our own inherent humanity and of the source of the Goddess that lives within us.

As a magical ally, Rhiannon connects us to the land beneath our feet and our place in time and tribe. She is an effective ally for magic concerning deep emotional healing and help, grief and heartbreak being her forte.

SPELL

GRIEF AND BEREAVEMENT WITH RHIANNON

We all will experience a loss at one point or another in our lives, and with it the ensuing descent into grief and bereavement. All forms of separation and loss can initiate a grieving process, whether losing a job, a home, the children flying the nest, the end of a relationship, or indeed a death. This spell is a simple little ritual that can be done for yourself or for someone who you know is suffering with grief. It does not serve to vanquish or lessen the grief but instead to bring about an acceptance and understanding of it.

The symbol used is based on the White Horse of Uffington in southern England. There are several white horses carved into the hills of Britain, and although their actual meaning is lost to the mists of time, there is no doubt that they were sacred. Rhiannon, Epona, and Rigantona are all representative of the horse, and many British Pagans perceive these figures to be emblematic of the Mare of Sovereignty.

For this spell you will need a small, smooth pebble and some permanent markers or paint. At the appointed time in the spell's verse, you will draw the following image. The entire spell is in the form of an *englyn*, instructions are given in italic verse, and the lines with quotation marks around them are to be spoken out loud in the form of a chant.

As soon as the sun has set its face over the horizon, take to your altar, extinguish all lights, and place a single unlit candle within your cauldron. If you wish, perform the triskelion ritual from chapter 5 at this point. As the light fades and shadows descend upon your space, be inspired by the following *englyn* and call the image of Rhiannon to mind:

Golden hair sweeps o'er tear-stained cheeks, blood stains soft pink skin
A heart breaks beneath the strain of loss, a silent scream within.
At her side a stone-firm mount and men who gather near
To beat her sides with booted feet, at the horse they laugh and jeer.

An image bright to pierce the night, to stone now take to paint
The image of a great white horse to ease thine heart's complaint.
Within the depths of cauldron deep, a light bursts forth to shine
O'er candlelight, the stone in hand, these words shall now be thine:

"Rhiannon, goddess of the horse,
My suffering calls to thee,
To broken hearts and tears give pause,
Understanding come to me."

The goddess in her suffering smiles a knowing look so fair
And wisdom ancient is summoned forth by form of sacred mare.
To live, to hurt, is all the same, and healing comes with time
Look to the horse, Rhiannon wise, and call this ancient rhyme:

"Rhiannon, goddess of the horse,
My suffering calls to thee,

To broken hearts and tears give pause,
Understanding come to me."

With single light that pierces night, the goddess hears your cry
With loss will always come the plea of never knowing why.
But know Rhiannon, ever wise, will walk and hold thy hand
And embrace thy suffering in the lap of knowing in the land.

"Rhiannon, goddess of the horse,
My suffering calls to thee,
To broken hearts and tears give pause,
Understanding come to me."[35]

Remain in the space, calling and singing, chanting or uttering incantations to Rhiannon. As the ritual loses its energy, let the power of it seep into the painted stone you hold in your hands. If you are the one in sufferance of grief, carry it with you or place it under your pillow. If the spell was performed for another, give them the stone and explain its intention. The spell is done.

Rhiannon

Spiritual Function: Teaches us about the importance of humility, acceptance, finding the sacred within the land, the ability to listen and respond, and being held accountable.

Magical Ally Function: For magic and spells that require the energy of a particular location; for healing, grief, and bereavement spells and magic; useful as an ally to enter the realm of the fair folk and to see between the worlds.

35 *Englyn* written by me.

◆ 10 ◆

Cerridwen: The Witch Goddess

Where Rhiannon represents the sovereignty of the land and the connection between the people and the land in her guise as horse goddess, Cerridwen offers us the route to empowerment, magic, and transformation. She is the one who opens the door of mystery and offers us a glimpse to our point of origination. She is the mother in the guise of magician—the great witch. I extensively explored Cerridwen in my book *From the Cauldron Born: Exploring the Magic of Welsh Legend and Lore,* but for the purpose of this book a little recap is in order.

Various poems within the Book of Taliesin refer to Cerridwen as the keeper of the cauldron; she is the goddess of the brew of inspiration, the initiator; she was the muse to the bards of mediaeval Wales and continues to be regarded as the mother of Awen. She is simultaneously a powerful magician and a humble mother, and yet her human guise acts as a conduit for the magic—she is the feeling, loving mother who is moved to magic in order to save her son from shame owing to his ugliness. But of course there is more to the tale of Cerridwen than meets the eye. Her tale, which may appear human on the surface, is full of allegories that relate to deep mystery and transformation.

In the tale of the birth of Taliesin, also known as *Hanes* or *Ystoria Taliesin*, Cerridwen took to brewing Awen, which she intended to be consumed by her son, but the Awen had other plans—and it was a young innocent employed to stir the cauldron who received the drops. In her fury Cerridwen chased the young innocent, Gwion Bach, through the three realms of land, water, and air, pushing the innocent further and further into mystery. In her anger she consumed the innocent, only to find that she was with child. The child, when born, was of such beauty that her heart broke with compassion. She set the child free in a coracle of skin to sail a river in the laps of the gods. This child became the prophet and bard Taliesin, whose name means "he with the radiant brow." He is the embodiment of Awen—the sum totality of its power coalesced into a single being. Cerridwen acts as the initiatrix.

In a similar manner to Rhiannon, Cerridwen is representative of the mother who suffers on account of her offspring, but the manner by which they respond is quite different. Rhiannon simply accepts that her child is dead and takes to her punishment, whereas Cerridwen shows no sign of surrender; instead, she reverts to the arts of magic. Rhiannon's response is passive; she displays humility and wilfully accepts her situation. Cerridwen, on the other hand, is assertive; she responds in a manner that is indicative of strong-willed determination.

We are informed that she is versed in the acts of sorcery, conjuration, and divination,[36] but we are also told that she seeks out another, older form of magic in the halls of the elusive, enigmatic magicians known as the Pheryllt. Her brew of Awen is created according to their wisdom.

Cerridwen is the transformer; she is the source of magic and the great witch queen. Her symbol is the cauldron, that stereotypical emblem of the witch. Together with the demigod Gwydion, she is perhaps one of the most powerful allies in magic that is available to the Celtic magician. She is a help-

36 Ford, *Ystoria Taliesin*, 65.

ful aid for the gaining of inspiration, for clear sight and vision, and for the wisdom of the plant, tree, and animal kingdom.

EXERCISE
ON THE SHORES OF CERRIDWEN'S LAKE

Read the tale of Cerridwen; versions of it can be found online. Take to sitting comfortably with your journal and contemplate the function of Cerridwen as witch goddess. Consider the many aspects of Cerridwen in the tale and her various roles:

- a caring mother, the concern for her son being the primary motive for her magic
- a learned witch
- a mother's fury in defense of her offspring when her potion is imbibed by another
- an initiator and instigator of transformation, forcing Gwion Bach ever further into mystery
- a vengeful mother who is determined to bring punishment to the thief of the brew
- a blossoming mother who acts on instinct and becomes a goddess, offering the child to the sea rather than killing him

Contemplate these things and then begin your meditation.

You stand in a woodland; the trees thin ahead of you, and you can see the reflection of the full moon on water. Wandering forward, your ears pick up the faint crackling of burning wood, and your nose twitches to the smell of smoke and sweet herbs. With the denseness of the trees behind you, your feet crunch gravel as you step from grass to lakeshore.

Before you is a large black cauldron; it hangs from a tripod of metal, a roaring fire licking its belly. Beside it in a gown of deepest blue is a lady, a basket about her right arm. She utters a spell that you cannot fathom; the words of the incantation seem to hang in the air, heavy with power. Her left hand sweeps into the basket and gathers the herbs that lie within it. Her words grow louder—they are old and heavy with energy. She casts the herbs into the belly of the cauldron. Steam rises, the liquid hisses, and the plumes of steam reach your nostrils; they are thick with scent and magic.

The lady is silent; her spell is cast and she turns, sensing your presence. With a brush of her hand she sweeps the gown's hood from about her face and turns to look at you. Her face is wise beyond words and in her eyes are the watery depths of the lake. Her skin is as white as the moon and her lips curl upwards in a smile. She nods her head in acknowledgment.

Speak to the lady of the cauldron: tell her who you are, be in her presence…

When your spirit senses it, bid the lady farewell and offer your thanks for her company. The woods behind you call you to return to your world. Take to your feet and walk away from the cauldron, hailing farewells as you do. Wood smoke wafts in your wake as you enter the silence of the trees, into darkness, away from the moon and the lady of the cauldron and back to your physical form.

Arise and breathe deeply; partake of a little food and go about your business. Think of your encounter no more. Take to your bed as usual and sleep; on the morrow, recall your meditation and record your impressions in your journal. Continue to perform this exercise to strengthen your bond to Cerridwen.

Cerridwen

Spiritual Function: Lessons in inspiration and transformation, listening to the land and responding to it in a proactive manner. She is assertive, not passive, and this quality is reflected in her teachings.

Magical Ally Function: For acts of magic that require deep transformation, inspiration, and clarity. She is useful for all acts of magic as a teacher, assistant, and guide. She is particularly effective in helping with herb and plant lore.

• 11 •

Llŷr: The Mighty God of the Sea

Llŷr is traditionally associated with the realm of the sea and forms the head of the dynastic House traditionally called the House of Llŷr. The divine children of Llŷr—namely Brân, Branwen, Manawydan, and their step-brothers Efnysien and Nisien—form the central characters of the second and third branches of the Mabinogi. Llŷr is cognate with the Irish *lir*; both the Welsh *llŷr* and Irish *ler* are common nouns that mean "sea."[37] He shares a commonality with Mabon, the divine son, in that he too is recorded in the Triads as having been one of the three exalted prisoners of the islands of Britain.

Llŷr's wife Penarddun (meaning "most beautiful") is the daughter of Beli Mawr (a solar deity[38]); the consort of Dôn forms the bridge that connects the deities of the House of Llŷr to the House of Dôn.The House of Llŷr can

37 Ford, *The Mabinogi*, 57.

38 Green, *The Gods of the Celts*, 153; Parker, *The Four Branches of the Mabinogi*, 273.

be seen to represent the powers of the sea realm; the House of Dôn represents the realm of land; and the House of Beli, the sky. Penarddun's previous marriage to Euroswydd, the perpetrator of Llŷr's imprisonment, resulted in the twins Nisien and Efnysien, half brothers to Brân and Branwen. For the remaining discourse to be clear, it is relevant at this point to demonstrate the family trees of the Houses of Llŷr and Dôn.

The House of Llŷr (Sea)

Llŷr♂ *m*> Penarddun♀ *prev m*>Euroswydd♂

| |

Brân♂—Branwen♀—Manawydan♂ Nisien♂—Efnysien♂

The House of Dôn (Land)

Mathonwy♀ (Ancestor Goddess)

|

Dôn♀ (Mother Goddess) *m*> Beli Mawr♂ (Sky) Math♂ *m*> Goewin♀

|

Gilfaethwy♂ + Gwydion♂ Govannon♂ (Amaethon♂[39]) Aranrhod♀

| |

Bleiddwn♂—Hyddwn♂—Hychdwn♂ Lleu♂—Dylan♂

These complex relationships demonstrate that although the deific Houses may seem on the surface to be independent, they are intricately connected by mythological and iconographic means. Llŷr is sometimes referred to as Llŷr Llediaith, meaning "accented or of indistinct speech," or half speech. He is liminal and akin to the sea, and his metaphysical attributes are those of singularity and oneness. He is what connects us to the soul. His offspring, the demigods/goddesses of the House of Llŷr, display extreme human emo-

39 Amaethon, the son of Dôn, is not listed in the genealogy of the fourth branch of the Mabinogi. In the first instance, his name appears in the saga of Culhwch and Olwen in the guise of an agricultural god. See Bromwich and Evans, *Culhwch ac Olwen*, 126.

tional traits that, at times, are their undoing, and yet they are deeply connected to each other and to the powers of nature by means that are not instantly obvious. They interact with the ocean and represent the sovereignty of the islands of Britain. Llŷr is representative of the abundance of the sea and the influence of ocean on land; he is most prevalent in that exquisite no man's land between wave crash and tide line. All the nourishing factors of the sea can be seen in Llŷr; he sustains and simultaneously represents the singularity of the soul.

Llŷr is a powerful ally for deep magic where one needs to tap into the singularity of the universe; he is able to help us understand the light and shadow aspect of ourselves and the deep currents of emotions, helping us to understand why we may respond in certain manners to the different situations in our lives. The ocean's influence is constant; its subtle corridors of currents bring warmth and nourishment to the land. Our weather patterns are affected by the mood and motion of our planet's salty waters. This is the realm of Llŷr; to connect to him is to be aware of the power and influence of the ocean and to honor it for its gifts.

I live on an island, part of the larger islands of Britain; the sea's influence is apparent here. Llŷr is a constant presence in my life, both ordinarily and magically. And yet when the sea is not in sight or the lips do not sense the briny atmosphere, one needs only look to the horizon—where, at some point in the distance, the sky will greet the sea. Our watercourses eventually lead to open sea; they are like veins and arteries that bring the nourishment of the sea to those who dwell on land. To stop awhile near water is to sense its passage into the lap of Llŷr and to be in touch with the mighty god of the sea. Connecting to Llŷr moves us closer into relationship with the singular nature of the earth—one ocean, one planet; we are at one with the planet, we are at one with the world. This is the message of Llŷr: singularity.

EXERCISE

INVOKING THE GOD OF THE SEA

Ideally this ritual of calling will be performed in sight of the sea or ocean. If this is not possible, you will need a clear view of the horizon.

Stop and still your senses; take a breath with the land beneath you, breathe in the sky above you, and deeply breathe with the rhythm of the seas that surround the shores of your land. If you cannot see the sea, cast your spirit to the part of your land that is nearest the sea; visualize it if you can. If you have a particular memory of being near the sea, bring this to mind.

Now look to the skies—follow it to the horizon and imagine the point where the sky meets the sea. It may be the place of sunset or sunrise, where two realms appear to collide.

Visualize the sea, watch the waves, and call to the god of the sea:

O mighty god of the sea,
Llŷr, arise and come unto me!

What does Llŷr look like? Form his image in your mind; if you are at the seaside, imagine him stirring beneath the waves. His hair is formed from curling kelp, his eyes hold the deepest secrets of the ocean's depths. His skin is scaly—half man, half fish, he sings the song of whale and dolphin. He is clothed by phosphorescence. He is the sea. Call his image; watch as he breaks the waves like a dolphin leaping from the briny sea. Call to him:

O mighty god of oceans wide,
Llŷr, by coral chariot ride!

Visualize a chariot of coral: dripping seaweed hangs about its edges, it is adorned by finest pearls. As it rises into the sky, waves reach up to lap at its underside. Call to the god of the sea:

O mighty god of the ninth wave's crest,
I invoke thee, Llŷr the blessed!

If you are by the sea, visualize him rushing towards you. If you are gazing at the horizon, imagine his chariot flying towards you on clouds of white.

Carrion birds—raven, crow, jackdaw, rook; the children of Llŷr—rise to the sky to meet their father. Sense the corvids of your land as they respond to your invocation. Feel the land in love with the sea and call again to the god of the sea:

O mighty god of the sea,
Llŷr, arise and come unto me!
O mighty god of oceans wide,
Llŷr, by coral chariot ride!
O mighty god of the ninth wave's crest,
I invoke thee, Llŷr the blessed!
Be here now!

Repeat the *englyn* in rounds of three until you sense the power of the sea within you and the hand of Llŷr upon you. If you are by the sea, place your hands in the water and offer blessings to the power of this realm. If you are far from the sea, I suggest a bowl of salted water be placed on your altar, perhaps filled with seashells and beach pebbles as a votive to Llŷr.

As the connection to Llŷr nears its end, turn your back on the sea or horizon and bid him farewell. The chariot dissolves into rain that washes down to bless sea and land alike. His power is never dismissed; he is with you always. Relish in the singularity of sea and its personification in Llŷr.

Llŷr

Spiritual Function: Singularity, being at one with the world and the universe, understanding immanency. Coping and comprehending emotions and emotional reactions.

Magical Ally Function: For acts of magic that are based on emotional issues, for clarity of emotions, and for developing coping mechanisms. For magic that requires a connection to the singular nature of the universe.

12

Braint/Brig/Briganti: The Spring Goddess of Healing

The guise of the Goddess as healer and nurturer, sustenance and warmth can be seen in the many names of Brig or Brighid or she who gave her name to Britain—Brigantia, derived from *briganti*, meaning "exalted one." She is possibly one of the most loved and revered goddesses who was worshipped throughout the British Isles and northern Europe. The coming of the church could not eradicate this goddess; her priestesses became nuns and the Irish church incorporated her as St. Bridget; she lives to this day.

Wells and springs, rivers and trees are dedicated to her, and towns continue to bear her name: Bridport in Dorset and Bridstowe, Bridekirk, to name but a few. She is the patron goddess of poets, doctors, and smiths. She is the rising, burgeoning goddess of the spring, and her festival is held around the first or second of February in the Pagan calendar and popularly called Imbolc.

On my native Anglesey, Briganti survives and lends her name to a river that cuts the island in two called *Afon Braint* (Braint's River)[40] and whose waters are famed for their healing properties. She epitomizes the delicious, sublime quality of a great goddess who assumes a local flavor. The name *braint* is believed to have given rise to the Welsh term *brenin,* meaning "king" or "sovereign."[41] The tale of Braint as a goddess who represents the sovereignty and fertility of the land is retold in a fragment of an ancient poem called "*Gorfara Braint* (The Flooding of the Braint)." The poem refers to the death of Cadwallon ap Cadfan, a sixth century king of Gwynedd and Anglesey, and the subsequent flooding of the Braint, believed to be the tears of the goddess crying for her fallen lord. Although the exact date of Cadwallon's death is lost to us, local lore suggests that it occurred in February—and every February since, the Braint has flooded. This further reiterates the common belief that the feast day of this goddess is Imbolc. On the surface this may seem overtly romantic but possibly alludes to the much earlier belief of the king being wed to the land.

What is significant here is that Briganti, long held to be the goddess of healing, sovereignty, and smithcraft,[42] was superimposed onto a river in Anglesey and, in time, her name evolved from Briganti to Braint. Later she would be adopted by the church and renamed Ffraid. Cadwallon was perhaps the last king to be actively wed to the land itself, and this imbues my own spirituality with a sense that we too can be "married" to the land by means of our relationship with it. While her annual flooding may be seen as representative of tears and grief, her life-giving waters simultaneously heal the winter-bitten land and make it green again. People submerge themselves in her waters in the hope that some of her qualities "rub off."

Braint is a feeling, sensing tactile goddess and one that can be seen made relevant to numerous locations throughout Britain and Ireland. Unlike the goddesses I have already explored, Briganti (or, in my locale, Braint) is the practical aspect of the divine mother. She is the healer of ailments, the enter-

40 Ross, *Pagan Celtic Britain*, 47, and Jones, *The Rivers of Anglesey*, 49–50.

41 Bevan et al., *Geiriadur Prifysgol Cymru*, 307.

42 Enright, *The Sutton Hoo Sceptre and the Roots of Celtic Kingship*, 61–62.

tainer, the hard-working smith who creates tools to enable our agricultural endeavors. She is compassionate and sensitive, and she sings the song of the land. By connecting to her attributes we can sense the sovereignty of the land and learn how to connect on a practical level to that power.

EXERCISE

A SPRING RITE TO BRAINT

The instructions for this rite are composed in *englyn* form. The verse in quotation marks is to be spoken out loud.

As the sacred mother stirs and spring begins its wake
A candle white and coin of bronze to a sacred well do take.
And there in shade and moonlight's glow
Bid farewell to ice and snow.
For winter has served the worst it can bring
And Braint now offers the promise of spring.
With flame aloft in the hand of power
Cast a coin to sing back the flowers.
A ribbon bright and knotted tight
A cloutie[43] *tied to a branch of light.*
Call now forth for spring to climb
And to the virgin sing in rhyme:

"Braint, Brid, Briganti, goddess of flame and light
I sing my spell of swelling bud, light shall conquer night.
Bride, Braint, Brigantia, a candle to you I raise
Blessed maiden of the spring, your awakening I praise."[44]

---

43 A cloutie, clootie, or cloughtie is a piece of cloth, a rag, or a ribbon tied to a tree invariably near a sacred well. The practice, no longer restricted to wells alone, is a common function of pilgrimage.

44 *Englyn* written by me.

Briganti/Brig/Braint

Spiritual Function: Alignment with the energies of spring, the understanding of sovereignty, and the gifts of honorable healing. The value of poetry and the practical crafts.

Magical Ally Function: For all magic that involves or requires healing and the use of fire.

• 13 •

Gwyn ap Nudd: Leader of the Wild Hunt

Gwyn ap Nudd, perhaps the most identifiable psychopomp of the Celtic tradition, reflects the folkloric function of a divine mythological collector or a hunter of discarnate spirits.[45] He is a god of transition, leader of the Wild Hunt, and the gatherer of souls. He also functions as a god of the wildwood and of the untamed and animalistic, instinctive aspect of nature. He initially appears in the mythic tale of Culhwch and Olwen, and we are informed that for the hand of Creiddylad, the fairest maiden in all the world, Gwyn ap Nudd—meaning "white son of Nudd"—battles every May Day with Gwythyr, the son of Greidol, and will continue to do so until the end of time. This contains elements that may have developed into the popular modern Pagan myth of the Holly and Oak King battling for supremacy over the wheel of the year.

He is a god-king in Annwn, and his hounds, white with red ears, are known as the *Cwn Annwn* and demonized by the Christian church as the

45 Bromwich and Evans, *Culhwch ac Olwen*, 140.

"Hounds of Hell." His associations with dogs mirror the qualities of his father Nudd, cognate with the ancient British Nodens, who was identified as a god of healing and hunting and whose totem was the dog.[46] He occupies a semipermanent liminal state, existing between the worlds and only appearing in liminal locations or at liminal times—notably at the point of death.

The Black Book of Carmarthen poem "The Dialogue of Gwyddno Garanhir and Gwyn ap Nudd" describes a conversation where Gwyddno and Gwyn meet in an undisclosed location. Gwyn, in admiration of Gwyddno's battle skills, offers him his protection, perhaps implying that the meeting is taking place after Gwyddno's death and between the worlds. What ensues is a conversation where Gwyn describes various situations where he is present at the deaths of historical and legendary figures.

I have been in the place where Brân was killed.
When the ravens of the battlefield screamed.
I have been where Llachau was slain,
The son of Arthur extolled in songs,
And where the ravens screamed over blood.
I have been where the soldiers of Britain were slain,
From east to the north,
I am alive, they in their graves!
I have been where the soldiers of Britain were slain,
From east to the south,
I am alive, they are in death![47]

Within this perplexing poem Gwyn displays an omnipresent quality and an association with ravens who "scream for blood and flesh" and who are also present at the deaths of warriors. Ravens are themselves identified in Celtic lore as death portents and are perhaps fitting psychopompic associates for the enigmatic Gwyn.[48] Gwyddno states that nothing can be concealed from Gwyn, implying an omniscient quality that befits his role as psycho-

46 Green, *The Gods of the Celts*, 88, and Newman, *Lost Gods of Albion*, 95.
47 Skene, *The Four Ancient Books of Wales*, 295.
48 Owen, *Welsh Folklore*, 304.

pomp. This ubiquitous quality does not suggest judgement, for his role, as in all true psychopomps, is simply to facilitate safe passage from this world to the next.

It is likely that the information preserved in the above sources is a fraction of the lore that existed in relation to Gwyn's role as psychopomp. The commonly held qualities of Gwyn as leader of the Wild Hunt and his association with predatory carrion birds and the Cwn Annwn are common folkloric and poetic qualities. And yet it is plausible that, in themselves, these folkloric idiosyncrasies echo an older body of lore that is lost to us. The famed fourteenth-century poet Dafydd ap Gwilym highlighted Gwyn's most Pagan traits and his associations with mist, darkness, owls, and the hounds of Annwn in his various poems, suggesting that the medieval bards were familiar with Gwyn's Pagan virtues. While there is fragmented evidence to suggest that one of Gwyn's functions was indeed psychopompic, it is hardly conclusive or exhaustive, and one cannot be reliant on literature alone. The folkloric record is equally valid, as is personal vision and connection. What can be deduced from the fragments explored is that Gwyn's current role as psychopomp is firmly established with many modern-day authors who identify him as an actual Celtic god of the dead:

> In the Celtic West the role of the huntsman who fetches to his abode the souls of the deceased was fulfilled by Gwyn ap Nudd, a god of the dead and king of the other world.[49]

Gwyn ap Nudd's transition into the Christian faith did not go well, and he was practically transformed into a dark and sinister creature. A remnant of the Pagan significance and power of Gwyn ap Nudd can be seen reflected in the tale of Saint Collen and his encounter with Gwyn. Collen agreed to meet with Gwyn, identified in this tale as the King of the Fairies, but he declined an invitation to eat, drink, or take pleasure in Gwyn's kingdom. Instead, he took a vial of holy water and scattered it in a circle about him, at which point Gwyn and his kingdom vanished. This later tale may be a retaliatory response to the continuous celebration of remnant Pagan deities, particularly amongst

49 Tolstoy, *The Quest for Merlin*, 80.

the peasant class. In all probability, it serves to demonstrate that Gwyn was representative of an enduring Pagan cultus and one that the church was intent on demonizing.[50]

In the tale of Culhwch and Olwen we are informed that the mysterious boar, the *twrch trwyth*, will not be hunted down until Gwyn ap Nudd is found, but that "God has put the spirit of the demons of Annwn in him, lest the world be destroyed."[51] This relentless demonization of Gwyn smacks of too much protesting; the old world (represented in Gwyn ap Nudd) and the new (in the guise of St. Collen) cannot coexist.

Of all the gods I work with, Gwyn is perhaps the one I am most close to. He is the epitome of extreme masculinity that I lack in my own human existence; he is the reaper of souls and a totem for those who work with the dead in the physical world (as I do professionally). He is representative of the turning season and the relentless battle between winter and summer. He teaches us about the nature of the wild and the meaning of death and rebirth. Gwyn is a powerful ally when we need to connect with the ancestors or the otherworld, or when we need to communicate with the spirits of Annwn. He also acts as a bridge between the human world and the world of nature spirits.

EXERCISE
AN INVOCATION TO THE LORD OF THE FOREST

Gwyn appears throughout Celtic mythology in various guises, from hunter to king of the fairies. He has also long been associated with the wildwood. A guardian of the green, in the tale of the Lady of the Well in the Mabinogi collection we are offered a snapshot of a deity that could be perceived as Gwyn ap Nudd in his guise as Lord of the Wildwood:

> A short distance into the forest and upon your right, you will come across a small road; travel along that until you come to a clearing. A mound will be seen in its middle, and you will see on top of the

50 Parker, *The Four Branches of the Mabinogi*, 166.

51 Davies, *The Mabinogion*, 199.

> mound an enormous black-haired man, no smaller than two men of this world. He has one foot and he has one eye in the middle of his forehead, and he has an iron club that would take two men of this world to lift. He is not a violent man, but he is ugly. He is the keeper of the forest. You will see a thousand animals grazing around him.[52]

To approach the forest is to enter the realm of the wild god, the keeper of the wood, and this may have given rise to the following invocation to Gwyn ap Nudd, which it identifies as Lord of the Forest. Welsh soothsayers would invoke his name before entering the forests. The verse was oddly recorded in the fourteenth century in Latin.

As you approach the edge of a woodland or forest, stop. Still your body and mind and sense the fringe of the forest; walk slowly towards the first trees and be aware of their presence and the different energy between open land and woodland. Imagine the collective spirit of the forest embodied as an antlered man sitting cross-legged on a mound somewhere in the depths of the wood. The animals do not fear him; birds rest upon his shoulders and deer graze at his feet. He is the spirit of this place. Take a deep breath, hold the image, and call to him:

> *To the King of Spirits and his queen: Gwyn Ap Nudd, you who are yonder in the forest, for the love of your mate, permit me to enter your dwelling.*
>
> *Ad regime Eumenidium et reginam eius: Gwynn ap Nudd qui es ultra in silvis pro amore concubine tue permitte nos venire domum.*[53]

Enter the woodland thoughtfully and with awareness, making every footfall matter; become a part of the wood.

52 "The Lady of the Well," Mabinogi collection; my translation.

53 Lindahl et al., *Medieval Folklore*, 190.

EXERCISE
A PRAYER FOR THE DYING

This prayer may be spoken in rounds of three as one nears the doors of death. It also can be utilized as part of a eulogy or funeral service.

Son of darkness, ravens cry,
Part the veil for he/she that dies,
Son of mist, beyond death's reach,
Come ye forth to [name] now teach.
Truths of life and truths of death,
Here at edge of life's last breath,
Gwyn, O god who tends the veil,
Let her/him board, her/his ship to sail,
Beyond the sea and to the west,
Gwyn, I ask: permit him/her rest.

Gwyn Ap Nudd

Spiritual Function: Teaches us the mysteries of the ancestors and how to access the otherworld, forms the bridge of connection between humanity and the wild. Mysteries of death and dying.

Magical Ally Function: For magic that involves the ancestors and deep ancestral wisdom. He is useful in winter rites and those associated with death and dying. Psychopomp to assist the dying in their transition.

◆ ◆ ◆

From bended knee we rise to walk hand in hand with the demigods and demigoddesses of the Celtic tradition.

14

The Celtic Demigods and Demigoddesses

The gods occupy the ethereal planes, sometimes without form or substance; we may look up to them, arms outstretched in gestures of praise, for they are the epitome of high mystery. The spirits of place, the genius loci, root us deeply into the soft earth. And sandwiched between the two are the demigods and demigoddesses, those who walk within the experience of humanity as it interacts with the natural world. By their mythologies and legends, their mysteries and magic, we learn what it means to be utterly human.

The demigods of the Celtic continuum are partly divine or have godly parentage; they may be the products of acts of magic, having been created by magicians from the elements of the earth. These half deities or semi-mythical individuals are most prevalent within the Mabinogi collection. In the following chapters I will guide you to a deeper understanding of the nature and function of the demigods and demigoddesses of Celtica and offer you rituals and meditations to connect with them. Those listed here are close to my own practice, and I have grown into relationship with them over the years. I share with you my journey and understanding of them in the hope that you will be inspired to reach out to them as allies in magic.

◆ ◆ ◆

The terms *demigod* or *demigoddess*—half god or half goddess—may appear on the surface to denigrate their power, and this would be an incorrect conclusion. While they may not have the deific status of their parents or creators, they are nonetheless of immense importance to the Celtic magician, for they are the primary teachers of the tradition—they are the bridge by which we make contact with the gods and all magic. And they do this by being almost human—we can identify with them, and this is the key to understanding their nature.

There are three main differences between the demigods/goddesses of Celtica and the gods and goddesses, the first being that they are present—they walk the earth and may appear on the surface to lead ordinary human lives. The second is their interactive quality—they have relationships and friendships with other humans, and they may mate and have offspring. The third is their inherent ability to feel and express human emotions. The demigods may feel what we feel and are subject to the same restrictions and benefits of a sensitive, feeling species. They are fully representative of the human condition.

Being Human

The act of living is a divine act in itself, and it is easy to forget as we traverse the paths into the forests of magic that we are of the world; we live here, now. The beauty of Celtic magic and Paganism is that it does not strive for enlightenment or a way *out* of this world; it is fully present *in* the world. Life is amazing, and the practice of Celtic magic brings a degree of lucidity to that living, where the colors glow a little brighter for we see what causes those colors to happen in the first place, and the rising and setting of the sun becomes a truly awesome event that we are a part of, not just observers.

Celtic spirituality is a true celebration of living, even when that living is hard, tough, or downright awful! The good times and the bad make the experience of living unique. There are many spiritual traditions that serve to disregard the human nature of living, to separate them from the world, living on its edge in a state of constant preparation for what lies beyond the gates of death. Personally, I don't see the point in that; I find it akin to going to the Caribbean on vacation and spending all one's time in the cabin worrying about home—consequently one does not see anything of the Caribbean while knowing that two weeks later, one is headed home again. Getting out there and being a part of that living—of seeing the world and being immersed in it—is a vital facet of Celtic spirituality and magic. We are nature; we do not strive to be apart from it.

As we walk this human path, "stuff" happens to us; seeing that none of us are invincible, these things affect us to a lesser or greater degree. The gods and goddesses can offer us insight into the greater universal mysteries; to know that there is so much more that lies beyond the restrictions of life is all very well, but what about now—what about the stuff that is happening to us right now at home, at work, in our relationships, and on our spiritual paths? This is where the exquisite connection with the demigods and demigoddesses comes into play. Not only can they assist us in our magic as powerful allies, they can also help us make sense of where we are right now and how to actually experience the stuff that life throws at us from time to time without actually losing the plot entirely and being admitted to a psychiatric institution in the process!

Whatever life throws at you, there is a Celtic demigod or demigoddess who can help you make sense of it. I am not implying that these beings are there to alleviate our problems or that by wafting a wand they can make everything bad or confusing go away—on the contrary, aligning with them may exacerbate the situation further, albeit temporarily, but it does so by causing us to look at what initiated it in the first place. Any form of examination is not easy, and yet if we know that we are not alone, if we can find the teachings of the demigods, we are better prepared to deal and fathom the difficult periods of our lives.

Approaching the Forest and Sensing the Spiritual

My first experience of sensing the power of the demigods/goddesses happened over two decades ago as I transitioned from being a Christian to the unfamiliar road of Paganism. Riddled with the tumultuous hormones of late adolescence, with tears and snot running down my face, I had run as fast as my long legs could carry me into the wilderness of the Snowdonia National Park. This was my home, my back garden—a place of sanctuary, it was nonjudgemental and accepting; I felt safe and comforted by its embracing wildness. I was experiencing such a maelstrom of unrelenting emotion—I think things had just become too much for me to cope with—and so I ran, venturing deeper into the solace of the wild and deeper into a place of clarity and comfort.

I recall having had a horrendous argument with my father. I had not long left the church, my faith crumbling, staggered by its attempt to control and unable to comprehend its inability to be adequately questioned. I had questioned the will of God, and that was unacceptable. Perhaps here in the midst of the mountains God himself would speak to me, allow my human mind to question it, and provide me with the answers that I so desperately sought.

The sunlight was failing quickly, casting long shadows through the deep valleys of Snowdonia, each one caressing rock and hillock, sheep and goat, sending a cold chill through the landscape. My hands felt cold and shaky, the tears and snot uncomfortable as they settled and chilled my skin. I doubted that I would ever feel warm again.

Stumbling over the rails of the Snowdon mountain railway, I crashed heavily to my knees, swearing at the sharp pain as bone and skin impacted with hard iron. I vaguely knew where I was, vaguely aware of some childhood fear stirring within me—this place made many feel uncomfortable. Scrambling to my feet, I cautiously walked onto the bridge that crossed the great Sow's River, cursing at the railway line and consciously stepping to the edges of the bridge to avoid the harsh, rust-colored metal. The sound of the river below rose to meet my ears. The old sessile oaks cast weary shadows over the bridge, creating an eerie darkness that enveloped my spirit and froze my flesh.

I breathed deeply. Under no circumstances was I allowing this place to add to my emotional distress; I was safe here, surely? Approaching the edge of the bridge, I peered down in the darkness below. Twenty feet or so below lay the inky black presence of *Pwll Morwyn*, the Maiden's Pool, allegedly the place of countless deaths, in particular of a maid who drowned while washing her master's shirts. My heart quickened as my brain recalled a hundred tales of foreboding and terror, of ghosts and the threat of death, but something else stirred within that body of water: something else spoke to me. At first I felt only subtle warmth, a stark contrast to the cold that seeped from the iron railings of the bridge; fingers defrosted, skin became warm. A certain calmness descended upon me as I stared into the vast emptiness of the inky black water. The sound of crashing water became a song with lyrics I was unfamiliar with, yet somehow it all felt oddly familiar—a contradiction, perhaps the first of many?

For the first time in my relatively short existence I sensed life—sensed the essence of life within everything that surrounded me. I could almost hear the life that brimmed beneath the black surface of the Maiden's Pool, from small fish to snails that precariously held onto submerged rock, the trees and plants that thrived in shadow, fern and nightshade, all gloriously raised their voices in unison. These voices coalesced with the voices that flooded down from the river's source high up in the mountain valleys, the place of beginning, the initiator of all the magic that I now witnessed. Something within me stirred for the first time; I stood still, an enchanted observer. I was acutely aware of somehow being a part of all of it. Here, at this place of liminality and for the first time in my entire life, I started to learn to listen, intently and with all my senses, not just the limited auditory ones.

Beneath the obvious living beings of tree and shrub and river, I began to sense something else—echoes of a time long since passed, stories of people and creatures, the tale of the mountain as she recited the history of the place, of the first stirring of creation that with fire and molten lava created this wondrous land I called home. The river had her own origin, her own sense of birthing, as did the maiden who inspired the name of the pool I stood over. There was nothing to fear here, nothing to run away from; I felt a sudden liberation as something was torn from my mind and cast into the darkness of the river. It was the desperate need to know *why*.

The cold darkness of the mountains felt different now; the sun had long since bid his farewells and sunk into the western seas. I no longer felt the human cold of desolation and despair, but only the beauty of being here, in this place, right now. My mind felt warm, detaching itself from the normal bodily association with cold and replacing it with a sense of bliss. For the first time I felt whole, felt complete within myself, yet aware that there was more to learn, more to sing about with a rejoicing heart. Looking around me at the river and its lover, the landscape, I became utterly aware that what I had associated with God had indeed spoken to me, but not with a voice I had expected; instead it was something more profound, more natural. It was the voice of nature speaking to my flawed human spirit and confirming that I was indeed a part of it. It was all I needed, and all the answers I sought were there, in rock and mountain and river and the spirits that inhabited this place of magic and wonder.

I had approached and entered the forest of my soul, that still, quiet place within all of us that speaks of truth and mystery. I had finally, truly come home.

15

Pwyll: Hearing the Call of the Land

He came as if from a vision—slowly at first, like a shadowy, undefined figure approaching through heavy fog, becoming clearer as he neared. His name seemed to just arrive in my mind: *Pwyll*. I felt a sense of timeless wisdom that came with his presence, and an old magic—older than the standing stones in the next field held. I sensed him walking beside me as his tale coalesced in my mind—unexpected, without cue or reason it seemed, it all came at that moment: a sense of the land calling through the presence of a man whom I knew belonged to the legends of my people.

Pwyll was the prince of Dyfed, a county in the southern reaches of Wales. He awoke one morning with a compulsion to go hunting. Within a grove he set his dogs upon a stag brought down by another pack belonging to Arawn, a king of Annwn, the underworld. To repay his insult, he agreed to take Arawn's shape and form and live in Annwn for a year and a day. There he was asked to meet Arawn's archenemy Hafgan on a bridge on May eve and kill him by striking him only once; a second blow would restore his life. Pwyll fulfilled his duty and returned a year and a day later. He discovered that Arawn, in Pwyll's shape and form, had ruled his kingdom well, and Arawn, in gratitude, bestowed upon him the title of Pwyll Pen Annwn (Pwyll, the head of Annwn). Pwyll later met Rhiannon under magical circumstances and is the father of Pryderi.[54]

Perhaps the most significant part of that tale from the first branch of the Mabinogi is hidden within the very first sentences: that it had come upon Pwyll's heart and mind to go hunting. The majority of readers see nothing within these words other than a man's desire to go hunting, yet I would argue differently—that it was, indeed, the call of the wild, the song of the world hidden within our own reality, that called to Pwyll that dawn. Having conversed with hundreds of Pagans over the years, it seems apparent that at some point in each individual's life, something stirred within them—as if the mysteries of Nature herself began whispering to them, calling them to sing the songs of the wild places.

Perhaps it was a similar "calling" that summoned me to the wilderness of the mountains that evening two decades ago to be stirred by the call of the wild, to begin to listen to its song and respond to it. It was here that I sensed the presence of Pwyll as a demigod, as an ally. It was a calling that only now I am beginning to fully understand, that something within some of us can sense and hear the subtle realms whispering through the story of the land.

Akin to Pwyll that morning long ago, when something entered his heart and mind to go hunting, we need to act upon that instinctual calling of the wild, of the spirit, to respond in an assertive manner to that whispering that we hear, a familiarity that arises from the depths of our spirits, summoning us, invoking us to venture into the wilderness of exploration and finally into the groves of magic. Pwyll himself experienced a profundity of the spirit, a descent into the underworld; his lessons were many and varied, yet he was still fundamentally flawed, human. The remainder of the first branch of the Mabinogi showed him to be nothing other than human; changed, perhaps, yes, but nonetheless human. Whatever we experience and learn along this

54 Versions of this tale are widely available in books and online; enter "the first branch of the Mabinogi" into any search engine.

path into the forest of nature and the shadows of humanity, we mustn't feel inclined to be something other than what we truly are: an individual locked into the experience of being human.

Pwyll's name translates as "wisdom, reason, and understanding,"[55] traits that he learns by means of his connection to the otherworldly realms and his marriage to Rhiannon. Hearing the call of the wild and approaching the forest of the spirit is all very well, but in order to make sense of this we must learn to make sense of ourselves—to utilize our discretion and wisdom, to learn steadfastness and perseverance, traits that Pwyll as demigod and magical ally adequately demonstrates for our own learning process.

Within the first branch of the Mabinogi, we encounter two kings of Annwn, the indigenous underworld of the Celts: Arawn and Hafgan. One could argue that they are simply opposite aspects of the same being, working antagonistically perhaps. This trait can be identified within ourselves, the rational and irrational or the instinctual and unmoving aspects of our personas. We each have colliding forces within us; sometimes their purpose is to keep us safe, in familiarity. Sometimes we go against these safeguards and take risks, learning and growing as we go along; sometimes we fear our instincts—afraid, perhaps, of our own potential to cause change or to affect the tidal flow of our own lives.

Pwyll responded to the calling of the inner observer, the "I" that is our everpresent permanent identity—what has existed since the dawning of the universe; what sings of creation, of evolution, of being. It is this that calls us to hear the song of wild awakening; for some unknown reason it compels us to reach out with our spirits, with our minds, and with our bodies to see the connection between all things and to sing of it with every ounce of our being. Only you and you alone will ever truly know why you have chosen a spiritual path—why you sense something beyond the ordinary denseness of this world and of the societies we live within.

Pwyll teaches us to watch and observe—to trust our instincts and to see the subtle omens that surround us. He did not question the impulse that

---

55 Bromwich, *Trioedd Ynys Prydein*, 486–487.

came to his heart and mind; he simply went with it, trusting that he was doing the right thing. This is a valuable lesson for any magician, to trust and to act on what he or she senses and feels, and trust that, at that point in time, they are correct.

EXERCISE
THE ENGLYN OF AWAKENING

To invoke the wisdom of Pwyll and his teachings, take yourself to a liminal place; I suggest that it mirrors the places of magic that Pwyll himself experienced: a mound of earth or a grove of trees. Take to sitting on the ground with both hands palms-down on the ground beside you, and sing this *englyn*.

Lord of Dyfed, gowned in grey
Hearken to my words I pray
Wise one, King of Annwn deep
Arise and call my soul from sleep.

On this day and upon this hour
Sing to me of ancient power
Let it come to heart and mind
Let Annwn's wisdom be mine to find.[56]

Recite this *englyn* whenever you need your instincts to do the right thing.

Pwyll

Spiritual Function: Listening, acting on instinct, sensing the subtle, honor, faithfulness, wisdom.

Magical Ally Function: Guide to the otherworld who teaches us of the otherworld's reciprocal nature; sometimes it needs our interaction, our noblest virtues. Call as guide in visualization and meditation to the otherworld.

56 *Englyn* written by me.

• 16 •

Efnysien and Nisien: I Would Know My Light and Shadow

We encounter Efnysien and Nisien in the second branch of the Mabinogi; they are the twins of light and shadow. Within the text we are introduced to them as being the half brothers of Brân, Manawydan, and Branwen, the children of Llŷr; with him they share the same mother (Penarddun), however, their father, Euroswydd—whose name means "Golden Enemy"[57]—was responsible for the imprisonment of Llŷr, which is recorded in the Triads of the Island of Britain. In the second branch of the Mabinogi, we are introduced to the twins of light and dark:

> One of these men was good, and he would make peace between two war bands, even when they were at their most angered. His name was Nisien, meaning "the peaceful." Yet the other, he would provoke conflict between two brothers, even when they were at their most amicable. His name was Efnysien, meaning "hostile enemy."[58]

---

57 Bromwich, *Trioedd Ynys Prydein*, 352.

58 The Mabinogi of Branwen; my translation.

Little more is mentioned of Nisien, while his brother, on the other hand, takes over the rest of the tale; although the second branch is commonly called The Mabinogi of Branwen, the daughter of Llŷr, it could just as well be called The Mabinogi of Efnysien. He pushes our buttons, he retaliates against his stepbrother's audacity to give Branwen away in marriage to the king of Ireland, and as a consequence he mutilates the horses of Matholwch of Ireland, an act which also directly attacks the sovereignty of the land and the goddess. He is unruly, hostile, and uncontrollable—and, like it or not, he is a part of all of us. This demigod is a vital teacher.

Within any spiritual or religious tradition there is a requirement to know ourselves intimately, deeper than the normal, mundane opinions we have of ourselves and of those around us. It is imperative on any spiritual quest that we do not fall into the trap of fooling ourselves, of thinking and behaving in a manner that is untruthful or a poor reflection of who we are.

Dion Fortune, a pioneering occultist of the early twentieth century and a woman deep in wisdom, sight, and intellect, once said, "If you could choose to be a blacksmith's forger or an occultist, choose to enter the forge rather than the lodge!"[59] A strange phrase, perhaps, but on closer examination there is much wisdom in those words, for ultimately the blacksmith's forger requires skill to learn a process and apply it as a craft and an expression of art and creativity; the occultist, though, needs to develop the skills to know themselves inside out, and that is no easy task.

We all hide skeletons in our closets; we all harbor deep pools of the darkest, smelliest shit that bubbles and groans within us—but of course shit will assist the growth of the most amazing array of old English roses that radiate the sweetest aroma, joyfully caressing those who come within feet of them. We can mirror that; we too can utilize our own shit in a manner that is positive and constructive, but of course before we can do that, we must stick our fingers in it and have a good poke about! Efnysien can teach us how. By listening to him and working with him, we can make sense of our own festering pits of allegorical excrement.

---

59 Fortune, *The Secrets of Dr. Taverner*, 74.

We are many things at many times to a plethora of individuals that touch our lives. As human beings, we can be fickle, tough, romantic, fantasists, deeply in love one minute and riddled with anger and frustration the next. We are products of our environments, and the circumstances and situations that swim in and out of our lives that mold us, affect us, and transform us cause us to be who we are—or at least seemingly who we are. We can be good actors and at times transparently poor ones too! Each individual who touches our lives—who comes into contact with us—perceives us according to their own experience of that connection, causing us to be a million and one things to a countless amount of people.

To see an element of the spiritual in nature, and to see human nature reflected within that, is a fundamental aspect of my own spiritual path, but sometimes I don't like myself, I don't like the world, I don't want to be sociable and pleasant, I don't want to be good and sweet. I want to scream out in frustration at times—to throw something across the room, to feel angry towards another individual, to feel envious or jealous of something or someone. But, then again, nature itself isn't all sweetness and light either, it just is, and it doesn't apologize for it.

Sometimes I think we swim against the tides of our being so much that an antagonistic, self-annihilating, destructive energy rises up from the depths that is not at all conducive to our well-being. It is imperative—not only in my spiritual and magical practice, but in every path of my life—that I listen intently to what sings from within me. I believe that this is the key to awakening the song of the spirit, which allows us to sing our songs with honor, without fear of judgement or condemnation, and without pacifying others or ourselves, for that matter.

Efnysien's actions were extreme. They demonstrated the unrestrained power of the shadow unleashed, demanding to be heard regardless of the consequences, and we see examples of this suppression of the shadow in our current society. Acts of violence result from the unleashing of the shadow that has never been listened to, and the consequences can be terrible; even practitioners of magic may sometimes revert to immensely destructive methods to pacify the unacknowledged shadow. But if we listen to it—if we give it the time that it needs to be heard—if we look to Efnysien, we learn that it is an essential aspect of us, and only at its most unruly will it destroy.

Efnysien wanted to be heard, and his teachings are applicable to us today. Giving the shadow the voice it needs in a controlled and honorable manner will serve to pacify it and prevent its uncontrolled escape; attempt to crush it, to ignore it, and it will rise in a tumult of destructive energy, whether through cruel and angry words or acts of violence. Our shadow is essential, and for any magical practitioner it is imperative that we understand the nature of our shadow and the power it can have over us if we ignore it.

But the nature of the twins of light and shadow has another story, captured in Efnysien's twin brother, Nisien, the peaceful. You will note that Efnysien shares the "enemy" quality with his father Euroswydd, and yet Nisien has broken the mold, or so it would seem. In the same manner as good news never makes it onto the evening news program, bad news always takes precedence, always packs a bigger punch, and yet every single day of our species' existence sees enormous acts of kindness, compassion, and love taking place. Nisien is the peaceful spirit who shines within our spirits; he is that part of us who inherently and instinctively knows we are all a part of the same divine origin, we are all connected, and that to cause harm to another is no different than harming ourselves. By understanding the nature of the shadow and giving it the voice it needs to prevent its uncontrolled uprising, we also begin to listen to the voice of Nisien; one begins to affect and influence the other.

Our world can be a cruel and merciless place; acts of violence plague society, so much death and carnage, cruelty and war. It is the unruly shadow suppressing the voice of the peaceful. But Nisien exists within us; we are all capable of bridging divisions and realizing that there is so much more that can unite us than tear us apart. But in a competitive world this is tricky business, and even Paganism and magic are not immune to the force of the hostile enemy. One will often come across the unruly shadow who is determined to be a better Pagan than you are; "bitchcraft" abounds even in this beautiful, soulful tradition. But by working with the twins, by getting to know and understand our light and shadow, we are moved to live honorably.

EXERCISE
BRIGHT LIGHTS CAST DARK SHADOWS

Take a long strip of paper, at least three feet long; one of the best items to use is a roll of wallpaper lining, available from most hardware and home improvement stores (in the UK, wallpaper lining is unbleached paper with no chemicals). Place the paper on the floor before you and have at hand a large felt-tip pen. Starting from the top of the paper and working down, without giving it too much thought, begin to externalize aspects of your own shadow and light.

- What are your most endearing and beloved qualities? How did they arise?
- What qualities do you not like about yourself? How did they arise?
- Can you identify circumstances from your past that gave rise to these qualities?
- Who are you in fact? Not to others, but to you? Who are you when the doors are closed and the world has averted its eyes?
- What are the things that anger you? Have events in your past caused you to react angrily or with unruliness? Identify them.
- What are the things that really, truly, maddeningly grind on your nerves?
- What are your most charitable qualities? Where do they arise from?
- How do you express your most sublime qualities?

Write; write in frenzy, articulating your innermost shadows and light, aspects that you would never dare share with anybody else. Keep going until you reach the end of the paper, and right at the bottom write the words "I would know my light and shadow." Now look back at what you have created.

It will no doubt be a mish-mash of all sorts of ramblings and thoughts. Bear in mind that you are not vanquishing anything here; you are simply acknowledging. Melancholy, mood swings, lethargy, depression—all start when we stop giving voice to the shadow. Efnysien cannot live fully without Nisien, and vice versa; they are dependent on each other for balance.

If you ever feel down, take to this little exercise and externalize what hides within you, give it a voice. Allow the twins of light of shadow to express themselves. Listen to them.

Fold the paper and burn it in your cauldron or on a bonfire with a handful of pine needles. (If burning the paper poses difficulties, it can be buried in the earth instead.) Smell the smoke and the healing quality of giving voice to light and shadow as you recite this *englyn*:

Twins of light and shadow, bring your gifts to me this night
By wounded horse and the gifts of peace, lend to me your might.

Efnysien

Spiritual Function: Shadow aspect, perception, gut instinct, sacrifice.

Magical Ally Function: Shadow work, discernment, protection, courage, dealing with anger and negativity.

Nisien

Spiritual Function: Peacefulness, harmony, reconciliation.

Magical Ally Function: Call when working peace and healing magic, to end arguments and heal rifts.

17

The Children of Llŷr: Brân, Branwen, and Manawydan

The children of Llŷr are featured in the second and third branches of the Mabinogi. The second branch takes place near the coast, at sea, or on magical islands where enchantments abound and mysterious events take place. Manawydan is only a passing feature of the second branch but becomes a central character of the third branch.

When we first meet Brân in the second branch, he is sitting at his court overlooking the sea when a flotilla of ships appears on the horizon. It contains the peaceful party of King Matholwch of Ireland, who has come to Britain to seek the hand of Branwen in marriage. Brân agrees to this, and she is given to the king; it is at this point that things take a turn for the unexpected when Efnysien, in his fury, as we previously saw, mutilates the king's horses. To compensate for this insult, Brân offers Matholwch a magical cauldron that has the ability to bring the dead back to life; this he accepts and returns to Ireland. Branwen gives birth to a son, but she is not treated as queen; instead, she is belittled, abused, and neglected. In desperation she tames a starling to do her bidding, sending a message upon his leg to her brother Brân.

Brân and his army amass, and his form becomes gigantic, so much so that he is able to wade across the Celtic Sea to Ireland with his army upon his shoulders; he forms a bridge to cross the Irish rivers to reach his sister. A truce is almost made in a longhouse of shadows, which Efnysien realizes is a trap; he succeeds in killing the soldiers who hide as bags of flour from the walls. Later, Efnysien calls to Branwen's son to come and embrace him, upon which he casts the boy into the longhouse fire and kills him. The resulting battle is terrible, but the Irish have an advantage: the cauldron of rebirth. Regardless of how many men are killed, when placed into the vessel they arise the following day as mute soldiers. Efnysien, remorseful for having caused such tragedy, places himself in the cauldron and stretches himself out; he breaks the vessel into four pieces, and in the process his heart breaks and he dies. The battle ends. From the British army, only seven survivors return to the Island of the Mighty, identified as Pryderi, Manawydan, Glifieu, Taliesin, Ynawg, Gruddieu, and Heilyn. However, Brân is wounded by a poisoned spear, and he orders the severing of his head, which continues to speak and keep company. On her return to Britain, Branwen's heart is broken; she dies on her beloved Anglesey, where she is buried in a four-walled grave.

For seven years the seven survivors, in the company of Brân's severed head, are mesmerized and healed by the three singing birds of Rhiannon at Harlech, and then for eighty years on the island of Gwales in the Bristol Channel. It is here that the seven survivors remained in paradise in a great hall, within which were three doors. Two stood open, whereas the third, which faced Cornwall, remained closed and, according to Manawydan, should not be opened. Owing to his curiosity, Heilyn opened the door, and suddenly all their loss and the bad things that had happened to them became painfully clear. The otherworld and its pleasures vanished. In sadness they took Brân's head to London and buried it within the White Mount (modern-day Tower Hill).

Brân the Blessed: King of Britain and Keeper of the Cauldron

Brân the Blessed[60] was high king over the Island of the Mighty, Britain, and his sister Branwen was the sweetest and loveliest lady to walk the earth. They take their name from *bran,* meaning crow, raven, rook, or other black member of the Corvidae family. Their brother Manawydan does not share their corvid association.

The tale recounts how no house could contain Brân; his form could enlarge by will, allowing him to wade across open sea, and his head survives its severing from his body. It is apparent from these traits that Brân is far more than a mere mortal. His status as king places him in position as defender of the people and of the land; his lessons abound in a sense of loyalty for tribe and family. He is the guardian of the cauldron of rebirth, and one wonders whether his connection to this magical vessel had far-reaching magical consequences, for his head survives death for around eighty-seven years before being buried, thus immortalizing his status as defender of the Island of the Mighty. In a magical sense, the qualities of leadership and loyalty are valuable traits that any magician should strive to maintain, but perhaps for the purpose of this book it is Brân's position as guardian of the cauldron that is most relevant.

If we look to the chronicles of the Celts, we can surmise that the cauldron has three defined functions:

- a vessel of inspiration
- a transformative device
- a vessel of testing

All of the above attributes are contextually expressed within the Celtic material almost exclusively in relation to the divine feminine. References to the cauldron within the British and Irish Celtic sagas perpetuate the position of the cauldron as a vessel of divine, feminine qualities. The importance,

60 His name appears in the Mabinogi as Bendigeidfran, meaning Brân the Blessed; it is commonly shortened to Brân.

relevance, and magical significance of the cauldron is continuously reinforced throughout native Celtic mythology, where it is perceived as a vessel of spiritual and magical function. The tale of Brân is unique, for it suggests that one of the guardians of the cauldron is male, and he also just happens to be a courageous king, a defender of the land—qualities which are essential for accessing the cauldron, which, as we have seen, will not boil the food of a coward.

The primary cauldron of inspiration is found in the tale of Cerridwen, Gwion Bach, and Taliesin. The primary cauldron of testing is alluded to in the Book of Taliesin poem "The Spoils of Annwn." However, the cauldron in Brân's possession belongs to the category of transformative device, of which several appear in Celtic myth. The purpose and intent of these cauldrons are varied, but overall they exemplify a transformative process whereby the initiate undergoes isolation and separation similar to that of death. Within these cauldrons there is a period of reflection and assimilation wherein the mysteries are incorporated into the spirit and body in a cohesive manner. The mysteries have been transmitted, but the mind, body, and spirit have yet to coalesce them into meaning, thus enabling the initiate to articulate them fully. The magical implications of the cauldron as transformative device suggest that in order for the initiate to be fully immersed in the mysteries, he or she must undergo a secondary period of gestational isolation in a womblike vessel. Upon completion of this period of sustained assimilation and nourishment, the initiate appears different; he or she is changed by the experience and steps forth as an adept of the mysteries.

In the second branch of the Mabinogi, Brân states:

> For I will give you a cauldron, and the property of the cauldron is that if you throw into it one of your men who is killed today, then by tomorrow he will be as good as ever, except that he will not be able to speak.[61]

This cauldron is generally referred to as the cauldron of rebirth, where the dead undergo some form of mysterious transformation within its depths,

61 My translation.

the mystery of which we are not privy to. This is further emphasized by the inability of the warriors to speak, perhaps a function that purposefully disables their ability to articulate their experience within the cauldron. Whatever we experience within these vessels is deeply pertinent and indicative of individual connection; to attempt to ride in the slipstream of another's initiatory experience could potentially cause irreparable collateral damage.

It could be suggested that Brân's former guardianship of the cauldron is what gives him the power to survive death, albeit in a liminal state. And it is at this point that the mystery deepens. Firstly, the birds of Rhiannon seem to initiate a separation or the crossing into a liminal state; their singing heals and soothes the assembly of survivors. Secondly, the survivors are held suspended in a place that transcends the lands of the living and the dead. They exist in a temporary liminal state on the edge of eternity. The severing of Brân's head has caused him to become the embodiment of the cauldron as a portal to the immortal, underlying divinity of the universe that is not restricted by temporality.[62] And yet in this instance this is an illusion, for the survivors are not actually dead; they are suspended in a state of being between the worlds. They carry no memory of their former human lives, and yet they exist nonetheless; perhaps this indicates not only the fleeting apparent nature of this life but attempts to demonstrate the existence of the permanent identity.

The illusionary nature of the island paradise is reiterated in a poem in the Book of Taliesin that further links the sequence to one of the otherworld forts of Annwn—Caer Siddi, the fort of illusion.

Maintained is my chair in Caer Siddi,
Neither sickness nor old age afflict those who dwell there,
As Manawyd and Pryderi know well.
Three instruments around a fire play there,
And around its turrets are the wellspring of the sea,
A fruitful fountain is above it,
Its drink is sweeter than white wine.[63]

62 Parker, *The Four Branches of the Mabinogi*, 356–358.
63 "Golychaf i Gulwyd," my translation.

This may seem a contradiction to the illusionary nature of Caer Siddi; it appears idyllic and wonderful, and yet the clue comes in the naming of Manawyd (Manawydan, Brân's brother) and Pryderi, the son of Pwyll. They are two of the seven survivors who return from Ireland. Seven survivors are mentioned also in "The Spoils of Annwn" poem, where Pryderi is mentioned by name in direct relation to the exalted prisoner Gweir's incarceration at Caer Siddi. This is the fort of illusion; everything may seem perfect—until the forbidden doors are opened, that is. In folklore it is the fairy mound, the mount of the Siddhe, renowned for their illusionary qualities. But this illusion is not denigrated as negative or deemed in any way detrimental; it is a sojourn into the otherworld, which implies rest, contemplation, and recuperation, and yet the illusion is acknowledged: they know that they must return, that the limitations of the physical world cannot be avoided forever. I suggest that intentional sojourns into the otherworld by means of vision and the assistance of our magical allies teach us the mysteries of our assumed state and the nature of death and dying.

EXERCISE
JOURNEY TO THE COURT OF BRÂN

Brân is associated with the ancient castle of Dinas Brân (city of Brân) above the valley of Llangollen in North Wales. Imagine yourself as a raven blissfully riding a warm thermal current. Below you is a green valley; a single rounded hill stands at its center, atop which stands a majestic castle. You descend, your raven claws becoming feet as you assume your normal human form. You utter a greeting to the land and enter the castle.

In the center of the courtyard, beneath a vast pavilion, sits the giant King Brân. His eyes contain waves of the sea and the wisdom of eternity shines from them. The courtyard to his left is shrouded in darkness. To his right there is a glowing golden light of unknown source; sitting by his right foot and dwarfed by his stature is Branwen, his sister, with a cloak of black starling feathers about her shoulders. By his left foot sits his brother, the magician and crafter Manawydan. Approach the king and take to a bended knee.

Repeat the following verses three times:

Sure-hoofed is my steed impelled by the spur;
The high sprigs of alder are on thy shield;
Brân art thou called, of the glittering branches.

Sure-hoofed is my steed in the day of battle:
The high sprigs of alder are on thy hand:
Brân art thou called by the branch thou bearest.[64]

You have named the king. Sit before his throne and take counsel from him, his siblings, and his half siblings of shadow and light. Meditate on the curious verse above; what does it mean to be able to identify someone or something by name? Recall this image whenever you need counsel with Brân.

Brân

Spiritual Function: Loyalty, leadership, courageousness, wisdom, understanding.

Magical Ally Function: Guardian of the cauldron; magic involving courage, strength, and stamina; the bridge between worlds.

Branwen: The Tortured Queen

Branwen shares similarities with Rhiannon in that she becomes the calumniated wife, mistreated and crushed. Her son is destroyed in fire by her stepbrother, a tragic event, the death of a child, that still sparks debate and disgust. But things are not as they seem, for her son Gwern—whose name means "alder," the first tree to be mentioned in "The Battle of the Trees"—represents transformation on an initiatory level. It is likely that Gwern's tale was far more significant within the tales than has been recorded. When subject to fire, alder becomes almost pure carbon and is the preferred choice

64 From the Myvyrian Archaeology, translated by Robert Graves, *The White Goddess*, 52–53.

of wood for the making of charcoal. Alder is a colonizing tree and fixes the nitrogen in soil; it more or less creates soil. Nothing in the Mabinogi can be taken at face value—there is far more bubbling under the surface than initially meets the eye.

Branwen's functions are multifaceted, far too many to be explored in this short section, but suffice to say for the purpose of this exploration that Branwen's function as a bridge to the world of birds and winged animals and insects is a vital source of inspiration for magicians. I live on the island of Anglesey, the ancestral home of Branwen and her family, whose palace scars the landscape only three miles from where I type these words. I sense the presence of Branwen constantly, and her primary totem, the starling, abounds in this region. In Wales, the starling—which in the Welsh language is called the *Drudwen*, meaning "pure or blessed Druid"—is considered a magical bird who acts as a bridge of communication to the kingdom of birds. Branwen is a gentle spirit, humble and of good intention, and if we align to her as a magical ally, she can teach us of connection to the kingdom of birds and other flying creatures.

And yet on many levels Branwen is a tortured individual, self-blaming and filled with unjust remorse. There are times in our lives when things are not easy, when the chips are down and we feel at our lowest ebb. Our actions, however good we may consider ourselves to be, may invariably cause pain to another. None of us are perfect, and the majority of us live with degrees of guilt, regret, and remorsefulness for past actions. But we may also take on too much and feel wretched or blame ourselves for things that we are not responsible for. The realities of life can, at times—as they do to thousands of people every single day—be just too much, and as we see in the tale of Branwen, hearts may be irreparably broken. In many cases, when people live with deep regret, remorse, guilt, or pain, they may take the ultimate action and take their own lives.

Branwen was not to blame for the slaughter of her people or the Irish, but she took that blame, she felt that it happened because of her, and—in the same manner as her half brother Efnysien—her heart broke, and she died on the banks of a sacred river.

Branwen teaches us about choices, and from those choices events happen—the family of Llŷr and particularly Branwen teach us the fundamental law of honorable magic, the law of cause and effect. Whatever we may cast in the sea, however transformed, it will eventually return on the tide.

If we look to Branwen and call to her in spell, song, and ritual and sit in her presence, we learn that the qualities of communication, peace, and beauty, however dim they may appear when we are in pain, exist nonetheless. Branwen's heart broke, she became a spirit, and spirit teaches us that there is always hope. However dark the tunnel may seem, look to the light of your own beauty and peace.

EXERCISE

TO EASE THINE HEART'S COMPLAINT

In times of distress, high emotional turmoil, or when one is plagued by regrets, heartache, remorse, or other debilitating emotions of such nature, reach to the spirit of Branwen to assist you or those affected.

With a pestle and mortar, gently grind the following:

- 1 teaspoon pine needles
- ½ teaspoon meadowsweet
- ½ teaspoon dried hawthorn berries
- 1 teaspoon pine resin or frankincense

As you grind, bring to mind an image of Branwen and the individual whom you wish to benefit from this rite. Imagine that Branwen walks towards the intended individual and places both her hands on his or her shoulders. Sense her attributes and qualities flowing from her to the other.

As the moon moves from her fullness, burn the above incense on hot charcoal and place twenty-one hawthorn berries, fresh or dried, into a small bottle of finest brandy. The berries should be inserted one at a time in groups of seven. Bring the image of the individual you wish to heal to mind and recite the following *englyn* as you place the first seven into the bottle:

Birds that flock in skies of blue
Their songs cry in praise of you.
Sister, raven, maiden fair
By incense smoke and into air
Hear my spell and hear my plea
That [name]'s spirit now may see.
Ease her/his/my troubles; ease her/his/my pain
From heartache, guilt, regret refrain.
Lady of two islands that reach
Across the sea, your wisdom teach
Ease the pain of hearts that tear
And find a place to rest, repair.
Branwen, sister, raven queen
Empathy, wisdom shall she/he/I glean.
Let not this heart be torn in two
Your magic sealed within this brew.

Pause and visualize the individual smiling and showing signs of progress and healing. Recite the verse again and insert the next seven berries. Pause and visualize the individual in good spirits and fully recovered. Recite the verse for a third time and insert the remaining seven berries. Seal the bottle and shake. Place on a windowsill for three days. The brew should be ingested by the individual you have in mind by placing fifteen drops into an average glass and drinking this slowly once a day.

Branwen

Spiritual Function: Empathy, compassion, and the ability to articulate emotions and deepen connection to the bird kingdom. Cause and effect.

Magical Ally Function: Rituals or acts of emotional healing and clarity.

Manawydan: Skill, Humility, and Knowledge

> One of the three humble chieftains of the Island of Britain—Manawydan the son of Llŷr.[65]

Manawydan, the son of Llŷr, occupies a unique position in the Mabinogi by straddling the second and third branches. His involvement in the second branch, which retells the adventures of Brân and Branwen and the battle with Ireland, is fleeting, yet he is the primary character of the third branch. Commonly this branch is titled "The Mabinogi of Manawydan, Son of Llŷr."

The third branch follows the interment of Brân's severed head in London and the betrothal of Manawydan to the widowed Rhiannon of the first branch.[66] Pryderi and his wife, Cigfa, form the other significant couplet of this tale. It begins at the Gorsedd of Arberth, the location where Pwyll first laid eyes on Rhiannon. A mist descends; as it clears, it reveals the desolation of their homeland, the county of Dyfed. Nothing, it seems, has survived the mysterious calamity that has befallen the land. Only Manawydan, Rhiannon, Pryderi, and Cigfa survive.

They leave the desolate lands of Dyfed and cross the border into England, which is untouched by the mysterious wasteland curse. To forge a living, they work as saddlers, shield makers, and shoemakers. However, their skills are such that they become the envy of other traders, become the subjects of imprecation and hostility, and are inevitably hounded from each location. Eventually they have no option but to return to their native land. While out hunting, they happen upon a mysterious fort within which hangs a golden cauldron. Within this fort Pryderi and Rhiannon are held captive by the powers of the cauldron and vanish.

Manawydan and Cigfa remain the sole survivors in Dyfed. Try as they may, they are unable to even plant crops, for as soon as the fields are near readiness, the crops are eaten by a hoard of mice. On the third attack by the rodents,

65 Bromwich, *Trioedd Ynys Prydein*, 15.

66 The Mabinogi does not inform us of the manner of Pwyll's death; the first branch closes by stating that years and years passed until Pwyll's life ended and he died.

Manawydan succeeds in capturing one of the mice and prepares a gallows for its execution, whereupon he is visited by a scholar, a priest, and a bishop, who beseech him not to carry out the heinous deed. Manawydan, however, is no fool; he's aware that the entire sequence of their misfortune is an act of magic. The perpetrator is none other than Llwyd Cil Coed, the main antagonist of the first branch, who seeks to curse Pryderi for the wrongs of his father, Pwyll. The captured mouse is Llwyd's heavily pregnant wife.

Three times Llwyd pleads for her life, and three times Manawydan refuses unless there are no more enchantments on Dyfed, that no revenge will be held against them, and that Rhiannon and Pryderi are released. As the curse lifts, Manawydan strikes the mouse with his wand and returns her to human form. The curse ends, and fertility and fruition return to Dyfed as Rhiannon and Pryderi reappear.

There is a lot going on in the third branch. The character of Manawydan is cognate with the Irish sea god Manannan mac Lir, and according to Rachel Bromwich he is a remnant of an ancient archetype much older than the four branches of the Mabinogi.[67] In a practical magic sense, Manawydan represents skill, humility, and knowledge. As the opening epithet of this section reveals, the Triads of the Island of Britain identify him as one of the three humble chieftains of Britain, for in the face of utter adversity he retained his dignity and humility. Even at the end of the third branch where he seeks to execute a mouse, a seemingly illogical and odd turn of events, he retains his demeanor and calm and does not rise to anger. This calm is indicative of his understanding of what is going on beneath the surface—he is responding in a magical sense to a set of magical events.

His qualities set him apart from his siblings, and his name does not contain any corvid associations. While Brân and Branwen are representative of subjective and yet highly valued attributions such as loyalty, courage, empathy, and compassion, Manawydan is practical, highly skilled; he epitomizes the qualities of his siblings by familial association while demonstrating the practicality of the skilled and knowledgeable magician. Triad number 67

---

67 Bromwich, *Trioedd Ynys Prydein*, 434.

expands on this by identifying him as one the three golden shoemakers of the island of Britain, together with Gwydion and Lleu. There is further mystery to be gleaned from this connection.

Gwydion and Lleu revert to magic in the creation of shoes, and shoemaking in particular has a long lineage of occult associations. Lleu is cognate with the older Celtic god Lugus, to whom the guild of shoemakers in Uxama, Spain, is dedicated. While the significance of shoemaking is somewhat ambiguous, some authors have explored the possible associations of shoes with the god Mercury and his role as patron of roads and traveling, particularly of the road between the world of the living and the dead. This psychopompic quality could be related to the magical significance of shoemaking in the third and fourth branches.[68]

In the text of the third branch, twice Pryderi claims he knows nothing of the crafts that will ensure their prosperity, and twice Manawydan assures him that he will teach the lad. Manawydan continuously demonstrates his learned abilities and his proficient skills on both a mundane and magical level, or perhaps the two are intertwined?

In my personal practice, I deduce that Manawydan exemplifies the steadfastness of the teacher, the elder, and the essential qualities required for effective magical practice—humility, skill, and knowledge. Within the spectrum of the occult arts, it seems logical that a practitioner must be in possession of actual occult talents. Manawydan exemplifies this quality. Thinking about magic is one thing; to actually get down and dirty and do it is quite another. The lessons of Manawydan are those of practical magic, the acts of making and doing, and the dangers of armchair philosophy. He is an adept crafter, effective in the arts of making, and yet he is a powerful magician capable of changing the form and shape of an object at will. However, he does not revert to the act of magic as a knee-jerk reaction; there is thought. He demonstrates an understanding of what is going on beneath the apparent veneer, a quality that is useful for any modern magician. In my own practice, I connect to Manawydan when I am crafting and creating my magic and rituals.

68 Kondratiev, *Lugus*, and MacCulloch, *The Religion of the Ancient Celts*, 90–91.

He helps me assess the components of my magic and sense the undercurrents of the situation, and he prevents me from acting brashly.

Manawydan understood the implications of the imprisonment of Rhiannon and Pryderi and that the fertility of the land was dependant on the release of the goddess and her son. He is a demigod who is immersed in mystery but does not get lost in its forests of complexity; he is able to translate the mysteries onto a practical plane as practical magic.

EXERCISE
CLARITY AND DIRECTION

When clarity is required for a ritual or act of magic, when a situation may feel that it is running away with itself or expectations are too high, stop. Sit quietly and assess the situation. Gather paper and a pen and write the following upon it:

Skilled magician, crafter wise, son of ocean fair
Harken to my needs this hour, rise unto my prayer.
Raven's kin, O humble one, you of second sight
Aid me with your ancient power, lend to me your might.

Memorize the verse; allow your eyes to close, and imagine yourself to be in a forest glade at twilight. A dense mist prevents your clear vision of the trees. Chant the verse and imagine Manawydan emerging from the mists, which swirl and dance to his movement. He appears before you, eyes black with ancient wisdom. His voice is the sound of the ninth wave.

Speak to him; tell him of your issues and dilemmas. Listen intently with your spirit. Take to chanting once more and watch as Manawydan retreats into the silence of the otherworldly mists. Bid him thanks and farewell, then return to the present.

Place the paper in a small bowl and pour sea or salted water upon it. Sleep, and on the morrow reassess the situation armed with the wisdom of Manawydan. Dispose of the water and dissolving paper into a water course, the sea, a river, or directly onto the ground.

Manawydan

Spiritual Function: Humility and honor, integrity and conviction, moral and ethical conduct. Being centered, secured, and patient.

Magical Ally Function: Honing one's skills, balance and integration, reconciliation and problem solving.

• 18 •

Gwydion: The Flawed Magician's Lessons in Magic

Perhaps there is no greater magician in any Celtic myth than Gwydion: he is simultaneously powerful yet pathetically flawed; he comes across as arrogant yet immensely compassionate. He has a big heart, and it is sometimes his undoing. There are several references in the Celtic chronicles to Gwydion, such as the following:

> Gwydion, the son of Dôn, who, with his magic powers, made by enchantment a woman of flowers. And he stole pigs from the south, since he had the best of learning.[69]

The most famous is undoubtedly the fourth branch of the Mabinogi. This branch retells the tale of Math, who is the semi-divine lord of Gwynedd and the son of Mathonwy, and his nephews, Gwydion and Gilfaethwy. Unless Math is at battle, he must have his feet in the lap of a virgin, one named Goewin. Alas, Gwydion's brother Gilfaethwy is besotted by her and together

69 "*Kadeir Kerritwen*," the Book of Taliesin; my translation.

they plot to summon Math to battle. Goewin is taken by force. Math punishes his nephews by transforming them, for a year each, into the form and nature of three wild animals: boar, wolves, and deer. In the guise of these animals they are forced to mate, resulting in the birth of three offspring. Eventually Math returns his nephews to human form.

Aranrhod (sometimes spelled Arianrhod), the daughter of Dôn, is summoned for the position of Math's foot maiden, but alas, the question of her virginity is answered when she steps over Math's wand and gives birth to two boys. One heads instinctively to the sea, and the other is concealed by Gwydion, who raises him as his own. Aranrhod, in her fury at being shamed, curses the boy to never have a name, to never bear arms, and to never marry a mortal woman. Gwydion, by his magic and wit, succeeds in breaking each curse in turn. Eventually the boy is named Lleu Llaw Gyffes ("light of skilful hand"). Math and Gwydion summon a wife for him made entirely of flowers, but she too betrays him and falls in love with another man. The adulterous wife and her lover plot to kill Lleu but only succeed in injuring him; in turn, he takes the form of an eagle and seeks solace in the branches of the Tree of Life. Gwydion, by means of his magic and *englynion,* summons the eagle and restores it to the form of Lleu. For her betrayal, the flower maiden, Blodeuedd, is cursed and transformed into an owl.[70]

Gwydion and his uncle Math are immensely powerful magicians. Although it does seem likely when we are initially introduced to them that Math is the most experienced, Gwydion gets the better of him by coercing him away to battle. We are offered scant information regarding Math other than he has peculiar qualities—for example, for him to survive, his feet must rest in the lap of a maiden, and that whatever words are spoken between two men, if the wind were to catch it, Math would hear of it. He is recorded as being the son of Mathonwy, who many assume to be male, but, according to the Celtic expert Rachel Bromwich, this is, in all likelihood, an incorrect assumption. Our Celtic ancestors, as demonstrated in the Mabinogi, were a matrilineal society—the children took their last names from their mother.

70 Versions of this tale can be located online by searching for "fourth branch of the Mabinogi."

In all probability, Math inherited the kingdom of Gwynedd through his mother, who in turn, I would suggest, is a deity that has succumbed to the blurry mists of time.[71]

Initially the relationship between Gwydion and his uncle appears antagonistic; however, they later work in collaboration, and it seems likely that Math was Gwydion's mentor in magic, for it is to Math that he turns for help in creating a wife for Lleu. However powerful Gwydion appears, there are some things that he seemingly cannot accomplish alone. If we compare the manner by which the members of the Houses of Dôn and Llŷr react to various situations, we can gain further insight into their nature. The House of Llŷr reacts to deep emotional traumas and questions of identity, loyalty, and perception; sometimes their reactions are brash and foolhardy—they may descend, as Branwen did, into developing inappropriate coping mechanisms that invariably lead to more pain. However, members of the House of Dôn react in a rather more proactive manner: the magic that Gwydion demonstrates straddles a plethora of human responses from intentional deceit to calculated retaliation and revenge. Ultimately it is a deep sense of love for Lleu as his adopted child and family loyalty that drives his magic; he feels earthy and is almost sticky with the rising sap of trees, and however dishonest his initial magical acts were, they were thought out, considered with care, and meticulously executed. There is an important magical message here.

Gwydion is deliciously flawed, and although his intentions may not be entirely honorable at times, he admits to them nonetheless; there is a vulnerable honesty to him. He is more than ready to hold his hands up and say out loud, "Yes, I did it, I'm sorry, I shouldn't have done; I'm just a bastard at times. I apologize!" Gwydion's initial responses are spontaneous or retaliatory—a flaw that can often plague the most experienced magician. Magical ability may invoke a sense of unrealistic invincibility, a power that may well be abused; one can imagine thinking in this vein: "How dare they piss me off or speak to me like that? How dare they do that to me! Where's my wand—I'll show them! I want that, and if I don't get it, I will make it happen!"

71 Bromwich, *Trioedd Ynys Prydein*, 438–439.

These are particularly "Gwydionic" traits, and we immediately don the negative virtues that the nine maidens of the cauldron embody: the cauldron will not boil, the magic will fail, backfire, or smack us in face—consequences that Gwydion is more than familiar with.

Gwydion's magic had far-reaching consequences, and he had to accept responsibility for them; this is essential for the working of magic—it comes with responsibility, and with that we must develop the ability to respond. This is just one example of the teachings of Gwydion and how he functions as a magical ally. His lessons mirror the virtues of the nine maidens, helping us:

- search for wisdom and avoid the knee-jerk reactions that would highlight our foolishness
- be in awe of magic, have a lightness of spirit, and maintain the innocent disposition of our childhood without consciously working to corrupt others or coerce them to do our bidding against their will or better judgement
- have humility and work for the betterment of others, not just for our own ulterior motives, and be humble enough to admit that we may, at times, be wrong, without arrogantly assuming that we are right and everyone else is incorrect
- have the courage to stand up to injustice and to speak out when need be; to defend others and yourself without avoidance or cowardly hiding in the shadows, hoping that a problem will go away
- be generous of heart, to work magically for the benefit of others out of love or compassion, to be giving of your knowledge and experience, not mean or stingy
- trust in others and in the spirits that act as your allies in magic to see the best in people and situations before judging too harshly; give others the benefit of the doubt

- have a deep knowledge of yourself and why you may react in a particular manner; know yourself well enough to function as an honorable magician and avoid being ignorant
- strive to form good relationships and friendships based on communication and compassion, empathy and connection, and to avoid enmity and hostility towards people or situations that you may not have any experience of; get to know the world and those who inhabit it
- have integrity in your magic: to understand that there may well be consequences and whatever they are, you will take them on the chin; to have the integrity to stand up and admit that you did something wrong rather than project waves of dishonesty that others may see through anyway

---

EXERCISE
MEETING THE INVOKER OF TREES

Before you attempt to call or invoke Gwydion, it is wise to encounter him in the subtle realms. To do this, begin by reading the entire fourth branch of the Mabinogi. Read it once straight through, pause a day, and read it again; let another day pass and read it a third time, but this time attempt to get a sense of what is going on between the lines. What mystery can you sense beneath the words?

Ideally you will perform this exercise in the dark in a woodland setting. If this is not possible, a private space or garden is sufficient. But try if you can to make a concerted effort to get out there into Gwydion's domain and be amongst the trees.

Settle yourself and take note of your surroundings; sense the trees present there and the presence of other animals and creatures in the vicinity. Pick a tree that is preferably directly in front of you; depending on moonlight, your ability to see it clearly will be diminished, but this is helpful. Close your eyes and recall the gloomy shape of the tree; just imagine it, don't force it—let it happen.

What does Gwydion look like? Play with it—what color is his hair, his skin and eyes, what clothes does he wear, how tall is he? Imagine these things; form his shape in your mind's eye.

Now utter these words three times:

Gwydion ap Dôn, of magical powers
Who conjured a woman of flowers[72]
Gwydion ap Dôn, by magician's might
Arise now, come to my sight.

Imagine that the tree before you is changing its shape, and superimpose the image you have of Gwydion onto it: imagine that the tree is becoming Gwydion. Raise some emotional energy from the center of your being and project a greeting towards him.

Now speak to him—tell him who you are, why you are here, and why you would like to get to know him. Keep the image in your mind, but also be fluid in the vision to allow other information to filter into your mind from the subtle realms.

Remain in this space within the trees, in the company of Gwydion. As the energy diminishes and your physical body calls you to return to your material form, sing the above *englyn* again three times.

Allow Gwydion to return to the tree, go home, eat, sleep, and on the morrow contemplate your encounter with Gwydion. I suggest that you practice this exercise at least once a week to further develop your relationship with Gwydion.

---

72 "*Kadeir Kerritwen*," the Book of Taliesin; my translation.

Gwydion

Spiritual Function: The nature of truth and power, magical knowledge and its practical application, humility, and the ability to know one's limitations.

Magical Ally Function: For all acts of natural magic involving trees and plants.

◆ ◆ ◆

And so we move from the realm of the demigods and look closer to the fabric of the earth and to the spirits of place.

19

Genius Loci (Spirits of Place) and the Ancestors

Every single event that happens on the face of the planet or in the realm of sky or deep in the dark depths of the oceans is recorded; it is felt; nothing is entirely lost but becomes a part of the fabric of the space the event occurred within. This is the spirit of place, otherwise known as genius loci. In the following pages I examine the function of the genius loci and the role of the ancestors in magical practice. By reiterating the need for meaningful relationship and developing a connection with the spirits of place and the ancestors, I hope to demonstrate the importance and the quality of connecting to the spirits of your locale and to the shades of the dead. Here I shall explore how and why it is necessary and polite to work with the genius loci in the hope that this will inspire you to seek out the subtle spirits of your own locality.

◆ ◆ ◆

The genius loci are the echoes of things past and the things that are affecting the present; they are the energy left behind from observation and devotion, from humankind's interaction with their locale. They have been named, and some may have developed into powerful gods and goddesses. Through acts of devotion and offerings, through the practice of storytelling and legend and myth, the spirits of place became a part of the personality of a specific location—they are the song of place. It is we who provide the lyrics to the music that they hum, and it is deeply indicative of our relationship with place, which is what the genius loci primarily and fundamentally embody—a reflection of the feeling, sensing relationship between the tribe and the nonhuman characteristics of locale.

The spirits of place can appear as guardians of a particular location; they can be interpreted as the feeling that we get when we enter a place and sense it. The presence of the spirit of place may be a sudden stillness that we feel deep within our own spirits or a cold shiver that runs down the spine, alerting us that we may not be entirely alone. They may be the spirit of a river, a well, a spring, a brook, a cave, or an impression in on a hillside; they may be represented as a chalk figure or an ancient hawthorn hung about with clouties.[73]

Spirits of place occupy a defined location and may have arisen from myth, from an ancient story that is reputed to have occurred at that spot; they may be born from a historic event or they may be something so mysterious that we are unable to give it a reason for being: it is simply there, something that we feel. The spirits of place are everywhere, and to the magician they are vitally important to the practice of magic, for our magic must take into account the spirits of an individual location, whether this is a seaside shore or the back garden of the home that we have lived in for decades.

Often the spirits of place have more presence in one location over the other, and it is true that they may be concentrated at sacred sites, or places that were the focus of ritual activity and devotion. The ancient sacred monuments of northern Europe—from Stonehenge to the lesser-known Crom-

---

73 See footnote 43 on page 99 for a definition of clouties.

lechs of the Highlands of Scotland and the lone standing stones of Wales—all have immense presence.

The spirits of place are not only apparent at sacred sites, they are also apparent at liminal sites, places that by their very nature are betwixt and between—for example, a stile that crosses an old wall or dyke, or a bridge that stretches from one mossy path to the deep, dark green of a forest floor and the river which it spans. Mounds, hills, and the entrances to caves have traditionally been associated with spirits and with those that occupy the world that lies on the edge of reason, just out of sight—we may catch glimpses of it, but just like the elusive fairy tales of childhood, as soon as we attempt to focus on them, they vanish.

By learning about the nature of the spirits of our locale, we move into relationship with them, and they can become powerful allies in our magical workings. By learning the stories that surround the natural places of our locality, we begin to forge connections with our land that we otherwise may not have had. The spirits of place have a multifaceted aspect; they teach us to sense, they teach us the moods and the stories of our land, and they teach us the nature of place. We may pass a lonesome, plain tree on our way to work daily, but how often do we stop and think of it—how often do we stop to breathe the same air as that tree, to watch the dance of the season on its leaves? By stopping and observing, we become aware and begin to develop the subtle senses in a manner that moves us closer to an understanding of the natural world and our function within it.

The Fickleness of Fairy

Spirits of place can be oversimplified and bunched into one category: "the fairies" or "the Fair Folk," and sometimes this happens because we just don't know what else to call them. The Celtic nations are abundant with tales of the Fair Folk. In Celtic Wales the fairies are categorized into three distinct groups that are worthy of mention:

Y Tylwyth Teg ("the Fair Folk"), which are not the small, gossamer-winged creatures so popular in Victorian Britain. They are reputed to be fair and beautiful and taller than the human race. Legend tells us that they have an aversion to iron, but one wonders if this is indicative of an actual magical repulsion or if it is metaphoric of the human Industrial Revolution, a period that greatly advanced our technologies but closed our eyes to wonder and magic. They seem to reside in another realm or dimension and are the least likely contestants for being actual spirits of place.

Bendith y Mamau ("the Mother's Blessing") are the second category, a strange term and one that perhaps poses more questions than it answers. In South Wales the term *Plant Annwn* ("the Children of Annwn") is used for the same category; however, this is not a term in common use today. It has been suggested that the term *Bendith y Mamau* is in reference to a genetic fairy association through the mother's side of some families, and that certain families have fairy blood in their veins. A romantic notion perhaps, but not one without merit, for certain families in the Celtic nations have long been associated as having qualities that are otherwise nonhuman and bestowed with the gifts of healing or second sight. The *Bendith y Mamau* are not human and, like the first category, seem to reside in another world or dimension; they differ from the first category in that they are reputedly capable of mating with humanity.

The *Ellyll* or *Ellyllon* occupy the third category and are perhaps those who assume the standard role of popular fairy, and although the word loses much in translation, the nearest approximate word in the English language would be an elf or goblin. *A Dictionary of the Welsh Language* interprets the term *Ellyll* to mean "goblin, elf, fairy, and sprite, genius of a place, apparition, phantom, or spectre."[74] These are energetic creatures whose forms, unlike the *Tylwyth Teg*, can change at will; they appear as spiritual entities who are directly located in the energetic spectrum of this planet. They do not, it seems, occupy another world; they are indigenous to the earth and to its subtle energies. In current and ancient Celtic cultures, these spirits are indicative of a place; they seemingly do not move from one location to another. Within this category are bundled all the other nature spirits that

74 Bevan and Donovan, *Geiriadur Prifysgol Cymru*, 1209.

abound in Celtic myth and lore such as the *Pwca* or the *Coblynau* (known in Cornwall as the Knockers).

If we observe the three categories above and apply them to the spirit of a place, we will note that perhaps the third category, the *Ellyllon*, is most indicative of genius loci.

Working with the Spirits of Place

It is important is that we learn to identify the energies of a place and in a sense get to know it. The effects of this are threefold: firstly, it causes us to move into a deeper, more observant relationship with our own backyards, with our immediate locality. We may practice our Paganism and magic in a garden, in a wood, or in an inner city park, but wherever we are it is polite and good practice to get to know that area. This relationship causes us to see the wood for the trees—to know what grows in a particular spot and when, which animals and insects call this place home. A garden or a forest is not just a collection of plants and trees, it is someone's home. Secondly, it causes us to utilize and exercise our subtle senses, to develop our awareness of the world around us on an energetic level, to be able to see with eyes closed and hear with ears deafened. Thirdly, we learn about the passage of the seasons and its effect not only on the world around us but on our own physiology.

We cannot assume that the spirits of place will conform to our human understanding of communication; to do so would be to set ourselves up for disappointment. They are not human, so the manner by which we communicate and work them must by definition be different. The energy of a standing stone is quite different to our own: it is slow, dense, and yet sensitive to its surroundings. The standing stone may at some point a hundred years from now suddenly acknowledge that someone walked up to it and poured some mead over its cool surface as an offering with a series of pretty words. Human activity and gesticulation is all well and good, but for the spirits of place to sense us we must meet them halfway. We can chant and recite verses until we are blue in the face, but unless the subtle senses are engaged, we are wasting our time.

To begin with, it is necessary to adjust our frame of reference. It would be silly to march into a natural area that we may use or have earmarked for our magical practice and to expect it to fall into conversation with us; it just won't. In exactly the same manner as getting to know a new friend, we must learn about each other.

MEDITATION
KNOWING ONE'S PLACE

Stop for a minute or two—take a breath with the land beneath you, breathe in the sky above you, and deeply breathe with the rhythm of the seas that surround the shores of your land. Contemplate your own immediate environment; how does it define your daily life? How does it affect the way you live in that place? Why do you choose to walk to work in one direction and not another? How do your neighbors affect the way you behave or engage in your business and relationships? Do you avoid certain areas of your neighborhood? Think of the manner in which you live and why.

Consider the nature of a natural environment you are most familiar with; visit it if you can and contemplate its nature. Why are the roots of that tree visible? Is the soil shallow; if so, why—does it stand on bedrock or is there an old building beneath it? Ask yourself why the branches of that tree grow in that particular shape; is it because the prevalent winds blow from the opposite direction? Why has a bird chosen that tree to nest in? Whose burrow is that? Who lives here, and why have they chosen this place?

Consider the nature of a location and compare it to the nature of your own life. You may find that you are not that different from the creatures who inhabit the wild places.

◆ ◆ ◆

If you analyze the above exercise, you will discover that the experience of your own living conditions and environment have an emotional component. You may avoid one street because it makes you feel vulnerable or you may want to avoid a group of people or an individual. You may choose to place your garden furniture in a spot that brings much joy and pleasure to your heart. The wreath that you hang on the front door and that changes with the season warms your spirit and catches the attention of those who pass by. We do things because they make us feel good or have some meaning to us; our behavior may reflect the restrictions of our environments or the liberties they provide us. Whether we are conscious of it or not, our homes reflect the emotional balance of our minds, which in turn are holistically influenced by our ambient conditions. The same rule applies to nature.

Rather than being reliant on the only form of communication we are most accustomed to (speech), rely instead on your ability to communicate voicelessly and by means of your emotional energy. For example, a pet will avoid you if you are angry or in a bad mood, or they may attempt to move close to you to soothe you; for those who have animals, it is indisputable that they respond to our emotional states. A tree or shrub may not have legs, eyes, and a mouth, but in a Pagan sense it, too, is capable of sensing the emotional energetic field of another being, and it is this that we utilize to communicate with them. We draw emotional energy from the center of our being and project it outwards—towards the object that we wish to communicate with. And we do so consciously and with awareness that the method of communication is subtle. We feel the responses; we do not necessarily hear them through our auditory senses.

EXERCISE
INTO THE DARKNESS

Plan to take yourself away alone in the dead of night to this location. However, it is important that you are familiar with this place and that you have seen it recently in broad daylight. Take a torch so you can find your way safely.

Take with you a small amount of butter, milk, and honey, foods traditionally associated as being good offerings for the spirits of place; this can be dabbed onto a leaf, a tree trunk, stone, or rock. The chant that follows is an old Welsh chant that is perfect for focusing the mind on the task at hand, so if you can, do your best to memorize it fully—and if you are feeling really brave, learn the Welsh version and use that instead.[75]

Take something with you to sit upon lest a damp bottom be the torment of you. Place your offerings on the ground and take to sitting. Now slow down…slow everything down.

Breathe deeply with the land beneath you; breathe in roots from the dark earth. Tilt your chin towards the night sky and breathe in the clouds and starlight. Expand your awareness to the edges of your country or continent and breathe with the seas that surround you.

Become aware of where you are and what surrounds you; you can't see it, so you must rely on your memory and other senses. Imagine the landscape glowing with spectral light, highlighting the trees and shrubs, flowers and grasses. Now address the spirits of this place by chanting this verse three times in either language or both:

O'r glaswellt glan a'r rhedyn man
Gyfeillion dyddan, dewch
Er ddarfu'r nawn—mae'r lloer yn llawn
Y nos yn gyflawn gewch;
O'r chwarau sydd ar dwyn y dydd
I'r dolydd awn ar daith
Nyni sydd lon, ni chaiff gerbron
Farwolion ran o'n gwaith.[76]

From grasses bright and bracken light
Come, sweet companions, come
The full moon shines, the sun declines
We'll spend the night in fun;
With playful mirth we'll trip the earth
To meadows green let's go
With heartfelt joy, without alloy
Which mortals may not know.[77]

75 Sound bites for this and other Welsh terms, *englynion*, and invocations can be found at www.angleseydruidorder.co.uk.

76 Issac, *Coelion Cymru*, 17–18.

77 Owen, *Welsh Folklore*, 87–88.

Contrary to some meditative techniques where one focuses on nothing—on emptying the mind—you will be required to become acutely aware of everything around you. Listen to the natural sounds of the night. Sense the presence of nature around you. Utilize your memory to see through the darkness and identify the plants and trees that inhabit this place. What species are they? What do they look like? Combine your memory of this place with the sense of being here right now.

Now imagine that you are the most gregarious and magnetic person in the world; raise your emotional energy, pull it from your solar plexus, and breathe it out, touching the nonhuman entities that surround you. No need to be all mystical here; just be yourself, just you and the space that you have chosen to be in. Listen: to the wind, to the scurrying of animals in the undergrowth, to the creaking of wood against wood. Become acutely aware of everything around you; become a part of the place.

Recite the verse again, over and over, as a whisper just under your breath; allow it to flow and meld with your emotional energy, and send it all into the night. Touch the world around you. Use your imagination, use your memory, use all your senses—subtle and apparent—to be a part of this place.

Remain in this place for as long as is comfortable. Leave your offerings, return home, and sleep, and as the sun rises on the morrow, think back and allow impressions of that place to flood your mind. Record them in your journal.

Ancestors: Echoes of the Dead

There is another form of spirit that may also imbue a location with energy and memory: the ancestors. The spirits of nature express the mood and qualities of the environment; the ancestors teach us about human interaction with the land. It is through the ancestors that we access the history of the heart. Wherever we live, we can be sure that others have also lived there; their life stories are not forgotten, nature doesn't waste anything, and I firmly believe that this rule applies also to the experience of life. It is not forgotten, it becomes a part of the memory of nature, of a place. The songs of our ancestors are essentially our songs—we are a continuation of the rhythms of their lives and their interaction with the land whether we are directly linked to them by blood or not.

Our human ancestors are connected to us by a common experience of being human—of having struggled and loved, cried and laughed, toiled and reaped the benefits of their lives on the land—and the same applies today. The only thing that really differs between us and the ancestors is that our technologies may make our lives somewhat easier, but that too is a double-edged sword, for perhaps that same technology has also distanced us from the fabric of the soil and our relationship with the planet. But the Pagan traditions serve to narrow the chasm we have created by believing we are more powerful than nature or that we can somehow control it. By listening to the songs of our ancestors, we are listening to the songs of the land and our relationship with it; there is much wisdom to be learned from listening to the ancestors.

The term *ancestor* is not restricted to the distant past, for the recent dead are as much our ancestors as those of two thousand years ago. People's lives and the energy they release on a daily basis affects the world, and the environment records the data. Ghosts, apparitions—all these things arise from the experience of life. Certain buildings and areas are renowned for having a presence, for being haunted, but what does that mean? Far too often they are throwaway words that are used to describe something we may not truly understand. It is suggestive of a human event having a direct energetic influence on an area. The memory of the dead becomes a part of the memory of place; they too can become an aspect of the spirits of place. Nothing is wasted; our memories and emotions are recorded, absorbed into the fabric of the earth, and the practitioners of the magical arts can access these.

The ancestors can teach us about our species' relationship with the land and allow us access to their storehouse of wisdom. The things they learned through toil and sweat are not forgotten; their wisdom has not died, it is remembered—and we can access it. We are the sum totality of all that has gone before us; we are the pinnacle of the human experience, and we stand at its leading edge. Behind us are the memories of our ancestors locked into our genes, into our myths and legends; we find them in tales and lore, in tradition and landscape. In a visionary sense we carry the wisdom of our ancestors within us; all that experience of living, all the learning and knowledge is within us as a product of sum totality. Nothing is forgotten.

A spring or river's bank may be alive with the spirits of place that reach from the fabric of nature; trees, plants and shrub, water and fish, bee and hawk—all contribute to the spirit of a place. The memories of people, of picnics, or making love color it further. At a grave or ancient burial chamber, it is predominantly the songs of the ancestors that we sense, combined with the slow, dense energy of stone and earth.

We live in a closed circuit, an energetic sphere that contains the combined memories of the organism we live upon: the earth. Echoes of our ancestors imbue the earth with memory and song, tale and legend, the tribulations and joys of life. By honoring the dead, we honor the living.

EXERCISE
ANCESTOR ALTARS

Honor your dead by having a special altar, shelf, or space dedicated to their memory within your home. This need not be a glum place but rather a space that celebrates the influence and inspiration of your ancestors. The people you choose to place here do not necessarily need to be family members; the ancient dead may be represented here, or a historical figure that you feel an affinity for.

Place photographs of your deceased loved ones in frames and scatter glass candle jars (the type that will accommodate a tealight) amongst them. Position other items that represent distant ancestors—for example, I have a small clay red dragon to represent the ancestors whom I cannot name on my altar. A chalice embellished with an Awen symbol represents my Druid ancestors of the deep past. Position small bowls or plates on the altar to accommodate offerings for the dead; personally I frequently offer petals of red roses in memory of my little sister Rachel and Everton mints, a British traditional boiled candy, in honor of my grandmother Beryl, who adored them. These little offerings cause me to pause a while and recall the relationship with those who have died—a time to stop and remember.

In central position place a small cauldron or other suitable vessel, and secrete somewhere amidst the photographs and accoutrements a small pad of paper. I find the square stacks of sticky notes to be ideally suitable. Periodically write messages to your ancestors, and encourage your friends and family to do the same—to share their memories of your loved ones if they have any. Fold the paper messages and deposit them in the central cauldron. Leave them there until All Hallows Eve. Whenever you think of your dead, stop a moment, write down your thoughts, invoke their memory, or imagine what they may have looked like if you didn't know them. Be thankful to them and honor their influence on your life.

On the night of the thirty-first of October, as the clock strikes midnight, gather the notes; read each one in turn, and then release the message by means of fire in any way that is suitable and safe for your personal environment. As you do, repeat the following verse as the paper vanishes into smoke:

Shadows of the dead arise, echoes of the past awake
Spirits, hear my words this night, the veil I cause to break.
Sing your songs of land and sea and skies of midnight blue
My spell I chant, these words I sing, in memory of you.

PART 3

By Oak, Ash, and Thorn

Celtic Tree Magic

20

The Magic of Trees

Trees connect us to the natural world; they act as primary symbols of the sheer power and presence of nature. They are steadfast, ever-present, strong, long-lived, and they sing of the earth and their place within it. They are the storytellers of location, and they mold and form the landscape that we are familiar with. They bring personality and attitude to our locales, and they offer respite, shelter, and protection to those who live within them or near them. They are important not only in the spiritual spectrum but also on a purely physical level: they provide us with the clean air necessary for life; they absorb the toxic gasses that would poison and eventually destroy oxygen-breathing life forms.

In the following chapters I shall explore the symbolism of trees in the Celtic tradition and how they were perceived as transmitters of wisdom. I shall examine their role as teachers and allies in magic and conclude with rituals and exercises rooted in Celtica that will enrich your relationship with the tree kingdom. I will also explore the nature and power of the wand as the primary tool of the Celtic magician, how to summon an army of trees for your magical work, and share secrets of the ogam, where trees aid our divination skills.

The Love of Trees

Trees teach us about the nature of where we live or the places that we love to visit and spend time amongst. Even the solitary tree in a courtyard of a hospital or the office block where you may spend most of your day has a story; they have something to tell us about the nature of being and the mysteries of life. They are individuals, each one with its own unique personality and sense of place. To spend time amongst the trees—to observe the turning of the great wheel and the drama of sun and moon on the fabric of their being—alters the way in which we perceive them. We may pass these creatures every day and rarely pay attention to them, and yet they are there, ever-present, silent sentinels of the passing seasons.

They inhabit two worlds. Their roots are hidden in the dark, damp underworld, unseen and yet filled with potential. Their trunks reach up from the soil, strong, resilient, lifting its spirit towards branches that become twigs and buds and leaves; with arms outstretched they reach for the skies, where their cells open to the air. They are simultaneously hidden, apparent, and present. If we watch and if we listen with our subtle senses, they become teachers of mystery; in the Celtic continuum they are transmitters of secrets who whisper of a deep connection our ancestors had with the land beneath their feet. And just as we are the sum total of all that has been before us, so are the trees, for each oak contains the memory of all oaks since the dawning of that species; in a magical sense they are as much our ancestors as the humans that have long since died.

To watch is to learn, to learn is to feel, and that feeling causes us to move closer to the trees and to the mysteries that they are privy to. They absorb the world and process it slightly differently than we do, but they are a part of us and we are a part of them; the particles of our breath are absorbed through their leaves. They sense our stories just as much as we sense theirs.

The only difference is there is no expectation—we don't have to connect to them, to commune with them, to move closer to them in order to learn the mysteries of being—but if we were to, by the gods we would be transformed by it.

The Roots of Tradition

The classical writers inform us that the priests of the Celts, the Druids, worshipped and practiced their religion in groves, which is significant when one considers that the entire landscape of Britain and Northern Europe was literally littered with ancient monuments. And yet the Druids chose instead to practice within groves of trees; why? This must be indicative of something that was pertinent to their tradition, and we find meaning to that in the mysteries of trees and the wisdom that they transmit to us. In fact, the word *Druid* itself is formed from two components: *dru* meaning "oak" and *id* meaning "to know." In the current Welsh language, the word for Druid is *Derwydd*, which contains the *derw* prefix, which also means "oak."

The suffix *wydd* is a mutation of *gwydd*, which deserves further exploration, for within this one word can be gleaned a deeper understanding of the development of words associated with trees and magic. Trees teach us something about the nature of magic and being and the manner by which humankind perceives themselves and their relationship with the natural world, and this can be seen demonstrated in the evolution of words within the Celtic languages. Some words, particularly the aforementioned *gwydd*, would hold different meanings to different people; to some it simply implied a tree or shrub, while to others the implications were far more mysterious.

It has long been accepted in Wales that the ancient Druids may have referred to themselves collectively as the *Gwyddon* or the *Gwyddoniaid*, which, according to the University of Wales's *Dictionary of the Welsh Language*, means "men of learning, wise men, druids, scientists."[78] It also states that the terms *gwyddon* and *gwiddon* could also be used in reference to a

78 Bevan and Donovan, *Geiriadur Prifysgol Cymru*, 1757.

witch, a giant, a wizard or sorcerer, a woodland deity or satyr.[79] These words share the root word *gwydd* and can be broken down to mean one or all of the following: presence, sight, wild, untamed, woody, tree, forest, branches. Figuratively it refers to lineage and genealogy, and may give rise to the Anglicized term "family tree."[80] All in all, the term is in direct reference to the trees, but not necessarily to their physical attributes; it is perhaps more indicative of their energetic value and sublime qualities.

We can take this word even further, for it forms the root of the Welsh word *gwybodaeth*, which translates as "knowledge"—implying that knowledge in itself, in a Celtic sense, is gained from the language of trees, which is attributed the term *gwyddoniaeth*, used today to mean "science." One could hypothesize that the above categories of *gwyddon* and *gwyddoniaid* were practitioners of *gwyddoniaeth*, the language of trees. *Gwydd* has another facet, *gwyddor*, which refers to the rudiments of learning, of first principles and the assimilation of knowledge.[81] And all of this connected to the most steadfast symbol of the Celtic traditions, the tree. By means of ancestry and articulation, words and semantics, we can learn to appreciate the wonder that the trees held for our Celtic ancestors, a wonder that is continuously embraced in modern Celtic magic.

The branches of the tree of tradition reach out from these ancient words that refer to tree, a concept that the genius poet Iolo Morganwg adored and perpetuated in his seminal work on the Druid mysteries called *Barddas*—a piece of work so important to the development of several branches of modern Paganism that without it, these words would not appear, and books of this nature would not exist in the form they do today. Iolo initiated the love for indigenous philosophical and theological exploration, and by his inspiration the modern Pagan traditions of Druidry and Wicca have been colored by a deep love and appreciation of Celtica. We have a family tree, we are connected, it is a lineage that unites us—just like the word *gwydd* itself—to ancestry and heritage.

---

79 Ibid., 1658.

80 Ibid., 1752–1754.

81 Williams, *Gomer*, 95–102.

Trees formed the platforms of initiation and held within them the mysteries of the world. The Celtic Druids surrounded themselves in trees and in symbols of trees, and within the art of the Middle Ages and the Romantic Movement, the oak and its leaves and acorns became synonymous with the Celts and their priests. This tradition continues to this day, and although its actual origin may be lost to us and it may well have evolved and changed over the centuries, its persistence to exist is indicative of the fact that trees were central to the Celtic way of life.

A Trunk to Lean Against: Trees as Teachers

A tree can define a location: they may be the genius loci of your garden or their corner of the woodland or of a lonely and exposed hillside. They can cause us to swim in deep mystery, to be lost in the wonder of profound wisdom; on a simple level, they can teach us so much. If we simply observe a tree, to become still in its presence, it will teach us the mystery of being and the unique relevance of our own personal existence. A tree can impart immense wisdom and knowledge if we are willing and able to receive it.

Think of a tree—in fact, it's even better if you can go outside and sit near one or nestle into its trunk. Stop, still your mind, watch, listen, and be. Smell the tree; allow your senses to blend with it, to become a part of it. As you do, consider this: a rowan tree seeks not to be anything other than rowan; it has its unique nature and personality depending on its location; it has its own function and purpose. Its leaves and fruits are the same as every other rowan within its family tree; it just wants to be rowan. It does not choose to sing the song of birch or oak or yew, it sings its own unique song, unapologetically, without recourse or recompense. It is rowan.

Consider those as human attributes; how often do we strive to sing our own unique song, or do we mostly succumb to peer pressure and attempt to conform to the standards that others have of us or expect of us? I think if we were truly honest with ourselves we would all be guilty of this, of dampening our own unique song for the sake of another, of continuously compromising to our own detriment. This is not the nature of tree; it does not express itself selfishly, it does not sing its own song just to be rebellious or for the want to not conform. It does so for that is its nature, and maybe, just maybe, if we acted in accordance to our own unique songs, our lives would be a little richer, with a dash more color.

MEDITATION
WHOSE SONG DO YOU SING?

Stop for a minute or two—take a breath with the land beneath you, breathe in the sky above you, and deeply breathe with the rhythm of the seas that surround the shores of your land. Whose song do you sing? To what degree do you suppress your own color and the lyrics of your own life for the sake of others? Magic is the act of transformation, and perhaps there is no other act of magic more powerful than self-transformation. Magic causes us to stand in our power and to be aware and fully present with ourselves. Society places restrictions and obligations on us that may crush our own ability to express ourselves fully. Do you compromise your own song for the sake of others? Do you adjust or turn down the volume of your own uniqueness for someone else's benefit? If so, why?

What could you do to change this—to sing your own unique song without emulation, without imitation? On the other hand, do you go out of your way to be so uniquely expressive that you inadvertently offend or annoy? Our songs are special, individual, and yet it is a narrow blade that we traverse between expression for the sake of expression and integrity. Look to the trees.

The Celtic Tree of Life

Consider the physical function of trees—the manner by which they enrich the soil and transform the landscape but also clean and process our planet's air. The Celtic concepts of the three worlds of land, sea, and sky can be seen emulated in the nature of the tree, whose roots reach into the underworld of connectivity and oneness akin to the properties of sea. Its trunk is apparent in the world and on the land, and its branches reach into the potential of sky.

But further mystery can be gleaned when we consider the tree that exists within us, for hidden within the darkness of our chest cavities is a perfect tree; albeit represented upside down, it exists nonetheless, and its qualities replicate its external woody counterpart. It is the bronchial tree.

The bronchial tree exists within the core of our being; it has a trunk and two primary branches that reach into the left and right lungs. These branches then form further offshoots, becoming smaller and finer as they reach ever further towards the edges of the lungs. Surrounding these branches are the alveoli and the fabric of the lungs, the leaves of our own internal tree. Its primary function is the exchange of gases necessary for life in the precise manner of the tree.

The trees of our world teach us to look inward to the place of mystery that resides within us, and we can access this by focusing on our own internal tree. The mystery of being and the truth of magic lie hidden within us and are controlled by what is perhaps the most peculiar of human glands, the thymus. This endocrine gland, which is large in infancy and slowly atrophies as we grow older, sits directly over the base of the bronchial tree and sets inherited patterns. Its endocrine function sets the scene for the rest of our human lives; it predetermines our susceptibility to disease and the natural manner by which we will die (unless death is caused by external, mechanical means). This is the seat of liminality and the place of fate unknown. However determined our attempts to communicate with it may be, we simply cannot. It is voiceless and will not permit itself to be swayed or influenced. It is the result of thousands of generations of genetic predisposition and inheritance. It can be seen as the void, the temporal space in the body, the physiological point of entry to the realm of the spirit. And from this point arises our own metaphorical Tree of Life.

Its roots are hidden in the unseen world, reaching through the thymus gland and into the between places. It is the point of wisdom that feeds us and represents our undercurrent, the magic of physiology and the miracle of life. Its trunk is the body, the physical being, our human anatomy, the visible aspects of who we are; it is our strength and presence. The branches of our Tree of Life can be seen in expression—it is our consciousness, our psychology, and the wonder of the mind. It is the expression of our life force, our beauty; it demonstrates that we are alive.

Consider the following two diagrams:

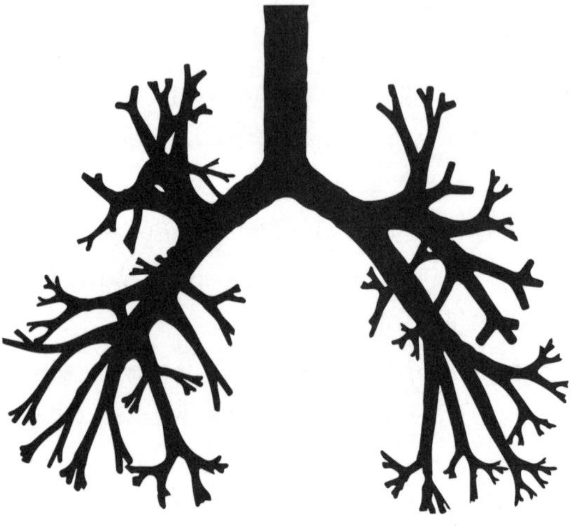

Trees are the lungs of the earth, and this is emulated within our own bodies. Consider the physical role of the previous physiological functions; they are responsible for the exchange of gases and the removal and assimilation of waste, which is unseen yet essentially present. It operates beneath the veneer of consciousness—it happens without us having to see it happening; it is invisible. It is responsible for air quality, communication, breath, vitality, and function. Without the Tree of Life—represented as a physical tree, the bronchial tree, and the mythological or metaphorical Tree of Life—life, as we know it, would not exist. Trees embody the mystery of life, and it's no surprise that they function as important symbols within many spiritual traditions.

Our internal Tree of Life performs the physical function of breathing; the term *spirit* is derived from the Latin *espiritus*, meaning "vital breath." Breath and breathing are synonymous with the mysteries of the spirit. Air is not out there, it is everywhere; when we breathe, our entire being is interacting with the world around it on both a physical and a spiritual level. And this air does not escape the closed circuit of our planet; it remains here as an essential component of the song of the earth. When we breathe with lucidity and perform breathing rituals, we can sense the breath of our ancestors and the spirits of place interacting with our own Tree of Life. It may be silent and unseen, yet it is one of the most profound tools of spiritual development that we have at our disposal.

We are the Tree of Life; it is not something that exists out there or is confined to the dusty corridors of arcane occult sciences: we are it. The Tree of Life is exactly that—*life*—and it lives within you!

MEDITATION
BEING TREE

Stop for a minute or two—take a breath with the land beneath you, breathe in the sky above you, and deeply breathe with the rhythm of the seas that surround the shores of your land. Consider the form of your body. Your feet are rooted to the land; they walk the path of your ancestors. Your body forms the trunk of being and the manner by which you interact with the world. Your expressions and emotions interact with the spirit, with the skies, touching, affecting. You are like a tree. Contemplate this as often as you can, together with your connection to the three worlds: your body as a tree.

Consider the Tree of Life within you; have you ever defiled it by inhaling smoke, narcotics, and solvents? If so, why? By understanding the mystery of our internal tree, why would you defile it knowingly? What does this tell you about your relationship with "you"? Body and spirit are not separate; their functions do not operate apart: all is as one. Sense the teachings of the tree within you.

The Tree of Initiation

Within the Mabinogi collection we find reference to a tree of supernatural quality that is identified as an oak. It seems that the oak was at the center of the Druid religions of ancient Europe, and it acts as conduit between the physical world and the spiritual; it is the bridge between the two. Within the fourth branch of the Mabinogi we learn about the birth and subsequent death and rebirth of the hero Lleu Llaw Gyffes. After his physical death he is transformed into an eagle who sits atop the Tree of Life; its flesh is rotten and maggots fall from it to be devoured by a great sow who forages amongst the roots. Gwydion comes to the bottom of the tree and sings an *englyn* to entice the eagle down through the branches and back to earth, to a life transformed.

In the *englyn* that Gwydion uses to encourage the transformation of Lleu Llaw Gyffes, he specifically addresses the great tree, simultaneously calling to the tree and the eagle as if they exist as facets of each other, both held in the same experience, pivoted between the sky and the earth, in that liminal place between the apparent and invisible worlds. The words he sings are:

Oak that grows between two lakes
Dark is the sky in the valley
Unless I am mistaken
This is because of the flowers of Lleu.

Oak that grows on a high plain
Rain does not wet it and heat cannot melt it
It sustains the one with nine score attributes
In its top is Lleu Llaw Gyffes.

An oak that grows on a slope
A sanctuary for the sweet prince
Unless I am mistaken
Lleu will come to my lap.[82]

It is a sow who leads Gwydion to the Tree of Life, and she is often seen as a direct representation of the Goddess as initiatrix or as a representation of the indigenous underworld. So within this act of apparent initiation into the mysteries we have a magician who is led by a representation of the divine feminine to the base of the tree, in whose branches is held the battered body of the initiate as it awaits transference into its sublime body, into lucidity and knowing. Gwydion sings three *englynion*, and after each one, the eagle descends lower through the branches until finally it is taken up in the magician's arms and transformed.

The above accounts concern the vital transformation of the initiate, the student that becomes the adept, and yet it demonstrates that the journey is far from easy—immensely and profoundly magical, yes, but hardly a walk in the park. This sentiment has been held by groves, covens, and magical lodges and orders since their creation. A magician's life is a learned and practiced one, and the path is fraught with difficulty yet rewarded with wonder and awe.

This particular mystery teaches us the multifaceted aspects of magic and its practice: it is never clear cut; there are always several factors and functions to consider. Gwydion doesn't just take himself off to find Lleu; he employs his intellect and common sense, his association and connection to an animal renowned for its connection to the divine feminine and the underworld, the sow. He employs his prowess as magician by calling to the Tree of Life

82 Fourth branch of the Mabinogi; my translation.

and the initiate; his words have direct influence on both, and each responds accordingly. He employs his compassion, care, and love for the initiate, and the magic, to some degree, travels along this emotional conduit to reach the remnants of human consciousness retained within the body of the rotting eagle. And finally he uses his wand to transform the eagle back into a human being, and at the center of this tale of initiation and transformation is the Tree of Life.

The *englyn* that Gwydion sang above is a translation, and because of that it has lost its nuance and its rhyme. Essentially an *englyn* must rhyme; not only does this aid memorization, but it also acts as a form of mantra that focuses the mind on the task at hand by utilizing the power of sound, the power of words, and the emotional connection one has to the content of the *englyn*. These are not words or pretty little incantations for the sake of it; they are tools in their own rights. Our ability to create effective *englynion* must be a functional process of our magical practice; it requires thought, points of reference, and, above all, connection. With a little poetic license, the previous *englyn* can be rewritten to rhyme as follows:

Oak that grows between two lakes
Shadows cast on sky it makes
Unless a lie I do tell
It is the flowers of Lleu I smell.

Oak that grows in upland soil
Rain nor heat can never spoil
Twenty gifts its branches hold
And Lleu the skilful hand so bold.

Oak that grows beneath the slope
Shelters prince so fair with hope
Unless a lie is spoke of me
Lleu will come unto my knee.

The Teachings of Trees: Singing the Song of Self

When we move towards the energetic fields of trees and begin to listen and work with them as intrinsic aspects of our magical practice, we are transformed by the experience. Practical, energetic, and experiential workings with trees provide an immersive method of exploring the self, and by proxy of this we develop a wondrous reciprocal relationship with the trees. Nothing is separate, we are all connected; by learning and forging relationships with nature, we move into deeper relationship with ourselves.

This exploration is not alien to spiritual traditions, particularly the animistic ones—"know thyself" say the wise words above the temple at Delphi. By listening to the songs of the trees, we begin to listen to the songs of nature and human nature, and the keyword here is *listen*. It is one thing to hear something, to be aware of something on the edges of our spirits, but quite another for it to move the spirit; first we must learn to listen. The trees teach us this. It's all very well contemplating the nature of trees and the messages that they may transfer to our own spirits, but how do we make this real? How do we incorporate this into our own spiritual practice without it just being a whole lot of mumbo-jumbo?

EXERCISE
SINGING THE SONG OF TREE

Find a tree that you are naturally drawn to; greet it, and ask for its company. Study the tree—its color, its texture, the ground that surrounds it. Note its foliage and the patterns they create on its branches. How does the tree interact with other plants in its area? Are there other trees that share this space with it?

Look for a fallen leaf or ask the tree if you can gently take a living leaf from one of its branches. Extend your intent by raising emotional energy from the center of your being. Project this emotion through your body, across the air that separates you, and to the body of the tree. Pluck this leaf of your choosing and proceed to sit beneath the tree and discover its own unique song.

Study the leaf and its pattern. Place upon its undulations (its edge patterns) musical notes that correspond to high or low notes, depending on the distance between the center of the leaf and its outer edge. Start at the stem and offer this the note of D, believed to be the note that the entire universe sings to. Hold the leaf upright between the finger and thumb of your left hand, and beginning on the left-hand side of the leaf, follow its pattern and attribute a note to each section. For example, if the next section extends significantly farther from the middle section, give it a note towards the top of the scale, perhaps an A; if the next indentation is deep, drop down to E. Follow this pattern all the way around the leaf until you have attributed a note to each outward-extending and inward-reaching pattern of the leaf's outer edge.

If the leaf is not toothed to a great degree, simply follow the patterns from its widest point to its topmost tip and around the other edge and back to the stem. You are not trying to be Mozart here, so don't be hard on yourself.

No musical prowess is required; just follow the keys through a single octave: C, D, E, F, G, A, B.

Have a notepad, journal, or piece of paper where you can draw the leaf's shape and chart the notes that you attribute to its patterns.

Now sit still and sense the tree next to you. Begin to hum the music of the leaf. For example, a leaf that I have used for the purpose of this book sounds like this: D, B, E, F, E, F, D, C, D, A, G, B, F, G, D.

Hum the little tune to yourself for as long as it takes to be absorbed in the moment; throw in your voice if you are inclined to do so. Be here, with the tree.

A leaf is unique to a specific tree and akin to our own unique fingerprints; it cannot be replicated exactly by any other tree. It is unique. However, that one single, lonesome leaf is but a single facet that makes up a whole; it offers us a way in, a method to sense the uniqueness of the tree and how that may be represented within ourselves. As we sing and dance the pattern of the plant, we become immersed in that moment, without concern for yesterday or tomorrow, only now. On one level this little exercise develops a reciprocal relationship with another being; it allows the mind and spirit to be precisely focused on the teachings of tree—to be at one, to not know where you end and the tree begins. In itself it only represents a manner of focusing one's mind, body, and spirit on the tree, something that we do not normally do. With the tune in mind and the leaf in hand, sitting under the shadow of the tree, we aim to lose ourselves in the experience. Only you and the tree exist at that moment in time; lose yourself in its song.

21

A Yard of Magic: The Wonder of Wands

The previous account of the life, death, and subsequent rebirth of the initiate Lleu Llaw Gyffes briefly touches on something that may at first elude us: the fact that Gwydion uses a tool to instigate the initiate's transformation. The tool he uses is a wand.

In a Celtic sense wands are the primary tool of the magician, and they appear throughout the myths and legends of the Celts, perhaps more so than any other spiritual tradition on earth. Throughout the mystery tales of the Mabinogi, protected and guarded by the current inhabitants of Wales, we find continuous reference to the use of wands. With each mention, something magical occurs—something is transformed, its shape changed, its function altered by being struck by a wand.

Pointless waving of wands does not occur; each use has a distinct purpose, and each account specifically mentions that the object of the magician's will is struck by his wand. This is telling us something about the functional quality of the wand, which informs of us of the necessity and purpose of the wand in Celtic magic. If a practitioner of Celtic magic has a tool, it should be the wand, the reasons for which I shall explore here.

Symbolically the wand is representative of the living tribe and of the land and the powers of nature; it is present and imbued with an echo of its host's spirit or energy. It represents the natural, symbiotic relationship we have with the world, and it is this collaboration that informs the magician's magic—it is the bridge between the individual and nature. The wand is not simply a tool; nothing in Celtic magic is that clean-cut or straightforward. It is an icon. It is an ally that causes the magician to become one with the powers of nature. A wand is held aloft not in pointless gesticulation but as a symbol of relationship; it has the ability to transform and create, and its creative power or force can be seen emulated in its allegorical association with the penis, a symbol of power, virility, and creativity.

Both Welsh Celtic names for wand, *gwialen* and *hudlath*, are also figuratively used to mean "penis." It is tempting here to veer off into a dualistic approach and assume that this is a male tool, an aspect of the male mysteries, and that there must be a female counterpart. This would be missing the point and the purpose of the wand. Its figurative association with the penis does not limit its function to males alone, it simply represents the creative force that is apparent in both genders regardless of genitalia. *Hudlath* can be seen to have another meaning: a yard of magic, or a measurement of magic, perhaps suggesting that the power of the wand and its efficacy is an indication of the magician's prowess and abilities.

The animistic nature of magic described in the Mabinogi and the use of the wand is informing us of why we use it and for what reason: primarily to cause transformation. Math, Gwydion, and Manawydan are adept at wand use and able to demonstrate the sheer ability of the magician, for not only is he capable of changing the *rith* (shape) of an object or individual, he can also affect its *anyan*. The meaning of the word *rith* demonstrates that something's shape is not necessarily permanent or stable. In turn, the word *anyan* is indicative of something's inherent nature, which the magician has the ability to change.

In the fourth branch of the Mabinogi, Math punishes Gwydion and Gilfaethwy for their transgressions by transforming them into the *anyan* of three forms of animal. It is not their shape alone (*rith*) that is altered but their intrinsic nature; they no longer possess any form of human consciousness. Such is the power of Math's magic. This too suggests that the apparent identity is simply that: apparent, fleeting, and temporary; it also informs us that the magician is not simply a conjurer, a maker of spells—on the contrary, he has the ability to change the shape, form, and nature of anything he so wishes with one strike of his wand.

There is wisdom hidden within the rather dramatic acts of magic that we see in the Mabinogi and other poems of Celtica: relationship. With this in mind, ideally our wands should not be bought from the local trusty occult store, however pretty they look; that would be missing the point of relationship. In Celtic magic the wand is a physical representation of our connection to the spirit of a tree, which sympathetically connects us to the Tree of Life and to the powers of nature. There is symbiosis here: the wand becomes a part of the fabric of the magician, and its ethereal quality is held in the relationship between the magician and the host tree. The stronger the relationship between the two, the more apparent and powerful is the third function: the energetic connection between magician and tree.

For your magic to be effective, it must have its roots in relationship. A pretty wand tipped with crystals, carved with sigils, and bought for $50 in the local occult store is going to be far more reliant on your own abilities than one which has been forged from a deep relationship with nature. The wand is so much more than a nice little tool; it has a multitude of functions that connect us to nature, to natural energies, to the spirit of place, to the spirit of tree, to the Tree of Life, and to deep mystery. One of the central ideas in Celtic myth and poetry is the use of the tree as a metaphor of man as tree; the trees become our teachers, they are the transmitters of mystery, and for centuries the Celts have used trees and plants in personal and tribal names.[83]

83 Haycock, *Legendary Poems from the Book of Taliesin*, 171.

The key message of tree is becoming clearer, and the key state is being—not familiarity or association but being. It is by being tree, plant, animal, and even abstract constructs that the wand gives the magician authority and makes his magic effective. By becoming one with the trees, by not knowing where we end and they begin, by shaping our consciousness into that of a tree so that our *anyan* is temporarily altered, we access old magic and profound wisdom. Therefore, become tree; be the Tree of Life and form a wand that represents this connection.

EXERCISE
CHANGING SHAPE, BECOMING TREE

Take your time with this exercise; although ultimately you will create a wand as a result of it, the aim is to do this with integrity and good intention. Spend time reading the fourth branch of the Mabinogi in preparation; sense the mystery between the words. Identify a tree that has meaning to you and that you are familiar with. If none come to mind, go in search of a tree that draws you; observe and listen to it. Preferably the tree will be mature enough to take the weight of your body leaning against it.

To avoid distractions, place cotton wool or earplugs into each ear canal, greet the tree, and stand with your back firmly against its trunk. Emulate the tree by stretching your arms up over your head so that your entire body is flat against the trunk. Now stop and become the tree.

Yesterday does not exist and neither does tomorrow; only now matters. Be present. If thoughts creep in to distract you, just watch them; don't attempt to fight them off, which will serve only to distract you further. Expect nothing; just let yourself become the tree. You have no mind, no presence, no function; be the tree.

Assimilation and digestion of the exercise can happen later. For now it is essential to allow the tree and yourself to become as one. Do not limit the time spent; just let it happen until it naturally concludes and you become fully aware of you being physically separate. Go home, forget about it, sleep and reflect on the morrow. Jot your experiences and thoughts into your journal.

EXERCISE

A RITUAL OF MAKING: CREATING YOUR WAND

It's the twenty-first century; there is absolutely no reason to hack at a tree with a stone blade or a partially blunt knife. Be considerate to the tree and use good sharp pruning shears or secateurs. The inadvertent gushing of your own blood all over the tree by misuse of a blunt instrument will serve no purpose. Identify a suitable branch for your wand and begin by performing the triskelion ritual.

Then stand facing the tree, arms out to the side, palms facing the tree.

Breathe in with the land beneath your feet and be aware of the creatures and spirits that inhabit this place.

Breathe with the sky above your head and be aware of the creatures and spirits that inhabit that realm.

Breathe with the watercourses of this place and the seas that surround your country and the creatures and spirits that inhabit them.

Sense the spirit of the tree. Greet it and call to the invoker of trees, Gwydion. Begin by imagining him appearing behind you; use all the references you have from your previous encounters with Gwydion—sense him behind you, his hand on your left shoulder; feel his confidence and his magic becoming a part of your energy.

Repeat the following three times, eyes wide open:

Englynion I sing to the son of Dôn
And summon the magic of Gwydion.

Perceive the connections made by the uttering of this single line. You are connecting to Gwydion, who is simultaneously connected to the mother goddess Dôn. Sense the power and potential in this tripartite relationship.

Approach the tree and address it with your emotions, sending waves of emotional energy towards it. Place your hands upon its bark and recite the following three times:

It is not of mother and father that I am made. I am the creation of nine forms, from the fruits of beginning, from the blossoms of trees, from the earth and the water of the ninth wave. The wisdom of sages fashioned me; I had being before this world was made.[84]

Identify the branch for your wand, and sever it from its host with a clean cut.

Sit before the tree, wand in hand, and once more call to the enchanter three times:

I call you, Gwydion, master of tree
Bestow you wisdom on this wand for me
May its nature come shining through
To cast my intent clear and true.

Hold the branch in both hands and recall every encounter you have had with this tree. With as much emotional energy as you can muster, "lock" that feeling into the fabric of the wood. Sense the passing of the seasons upon the tree and all its experience held within this branch. Feel the passage of time, of its interactions with the world around it and your relationship with it glowing from within.

Now sing the final *englyn* to Gwydion. Eyes closed, imagine him in front of you, his right hand hovering over the branch you hold.

Gwydion ap Dôn, I call your name
You of forest magic fame
Sing your englyn, seal the bond
Between me and this forest wand.

Repeat the above *englyn* three times. Sense your connection to both tree and Gwydion.

Now perceive the sum totality of this wand; feel it in your hands. Look to the tree it came from. Sense its roots reaching into the singularity of the soil, connecting it to every other tree that has ever existed. You wand is a part of

84 Adapted by me from "*Kat Godeu*" (The Battle of the Trees), the Book of Taliesin.

this magic. See its branches reaching to the realm of spirit, to the lofty skies, touching the memories of all that has ever been. You wand is a part of this magic.

Sense the spirit of Gwydion next to you, walking beside you, connecting you to deep ancestry and heritage, to the magic of Celtica. You wand is a part of this magic—you are a part of this magic.

Give thanks to the enchanter. Be still, be silent, sit and be in this place. Watch your thoughts but analyze them later. Conclude the ritual as suggested in the triskelion ritual.

Unlike your previous connections to the tree, you will be taking a part of it with you. Remember this as you fashion it, sanding and whittling it to the wand of your making. This is not just a directional tool, a bridge between you and nature; it is a symbol of your relationship with a nonhuman entity. Cherish it.

Create an *englyn* that is specific to the tree. It must be of your making, and yours alone, and it should be representative of your relationship. Sing this *englyn* whenever you reach for your wand.

• 22 •

"*Kat Godeu*" (The Battle of the Trees)

In the Book of Taliesin manuscript there is a mysterious poem enigmatically titled "*Kat Godeu*," which can mean either "the army of trees" or "the battle of the trees." Oddly obscure and frustratingly riddled with nonsensical verses, it seems on the surface to allude to several mysteries. Attempts to classify or seek meaning from this poem by academics and visionaries alike have failed, but what can be deduced is that something remarkable is held within all of its 249 lines.

The eminent and influential Celtic scholar Marged Haycock has identified nine individual components to the poem that can be perceived as chapters, each one with its own story to tell, and the common theme is the supernatural state of knowing that Taliesin has achieved by assimilation of the mysteries.[85] His knowing comes from having been a multitude of shapes and forms, from animate to inanimate, abstract to archetypal. He recounts the abilities of Gwydion to summon an army of trees to do battle with an undisclosed

85 Haycock, *Legendary Poems from the Book of Taliesin*, 167.

enemy, and this spell concludes with a listing of trees, shrubs, and plants and their qualities or attributions. Gwydion summons a magical army of trees "by means of language and materials of the earth to fashion majestic trees,"[86] and his wand plays an essential role in this summoning. It is more than likely that the qualities of the trees recounted in the poem derive from ancient British traditions and beliefs regarding sacred trees and groves and their relevance to the tribe within a magical and spiritual context.[87]

As I have explored, trees can be seen as metaphors for the experience of life and living, and in many ways they resemble humans: they breathe, they excrete waste, they need food and nourishment, they have a hard skeleton that is clothed (with leaves), they bleed when injured, and, just like people, they stand upright and tall. However, their lives are long, and they can seem to be simultaneously alive and dead. To paraphrase the Celtic scholar Miranda Aldhouse-Green, trees have a definite celestial and chthonic dimension to them, and represent a "hyper-metaphor" for the cosmological relationship between humanity and the apparent and spiritual worlds.[88] And this can be seen exemplified in the *"Kat Godeu"* (The Battle of the Trees) poem.

I dislike acts of magic for the sake of magic; I prefer the more disciplined form of thinking magic—knowing why we do something and that there is a true and well-intended reason for the magic to be undertaken. Without a doubt, "The Battle of the Trees" poem involves spellcasting and conjuration, but it is one that is performed with knowing and by means of continuous, honorable relationship with the natural world—a trait that would benefit any would-be magician or witch. The acts of magic described in the old Celtic chronicles are not magic for magic's sake, but they continuously reiterate, strengthen, and affirm the magician's position and relationship with the natural world and the subtle realms.

The poem offers a window onto the special powers attributed to the group of trees that Gwydion summons by magic. We can use this information in current practice, and by absorbing the teachings of the demigods,

---

86 "The Battle of the Trees," the Book of Taliesin, lines 52 and 53.

87 Ford, *The Mabinogi*, 183.

88 Aldhouse-Green, *Seeing the Wood for the Trees*, 22–23.

demigoddesses, and deities of the Celtic continuum and walking with them as allies, we learn the ways of the Celtic magician and the blissful states that Taliesin describes in the opening verses of this poem, where he was myriad shapes before attaining his current human form.

Part four of the poem recounts the following attributions of trees:

Alder was at the head of the line.
Willow and rowan were late to join the army.
Blackthorn was eager for slaughter.
The skilful medlar tree anticipated the battle.
The rose advanced against the host with wrath.
Raspberry took action but did not make an enclosure to save his own life.
The privet and honeysuckle and ivy, despite their beauty, fought fiercely.
The cherry made a commotion.
The birch, despite his good intention, was late to be armored
Not because of his cowardice, but because of his greatness.
Goldenrod maintained his shape, foreigners over foreign waters.
Pine held the place of honor, ruler in battle.
Ash performed greatly for the monarch.
Elm, because of his wealth, did not budge a foot,
He would strike in the middle and the wing and the rear.
Hazel adjudged the weapon for conflict.
The blessed dogwood, bull of battle, is the lord of the world,
Beech flourished.
Holly grew verdant; he was there in battle.
Hawthorn dispensed pain and pestilence.
Vine, the destroyer, attacked.
Bracken was the pillager.
Broom, in the van of the battalion, was wounded in the churned-up ground.
Gorse was not fortunate, but despite that he was marshalled.
Heather, the famous victor, was changed into a host, pursuer of men.
Swift and mighty the oak—heaven and earth trembled before him.
Woad, the brave warrior, his name in a wax tablet.

Pear wrought oppression on the battlefield.
A terrifying army was the surging clover.
Bashful chestnut, an opponent in the ranks of strong trees.[89]

The above section from the Battle of the Trees can be formed into a table of attributions and qualities, although note that some of them are not commonly classified as trees. Clover, for example, is a strange inclusion and deserving of meditation as to why they deemed it suitable for entry in the poem. Others are classified as shrubs, but however we choose to categorize them, they still serve as a method of connecting to and working with the powers of tree while simultaneously linking us to a body of Celtic mythology and mystery. With this in mind, it is good practice to create an apothecary of magically infused potions, tinctures, and infusions that contain the essence and energy of each tree—a magical first-aid cupboard, if you like. Study the above poem in full; online versions can be found easily by entering the term "Battle of the Trees—Book of Taliesin" into any web-based search engine.

I attribute the following qualities to the list of trees and shrubs. Those marked with *** are regarded as toxic or potentially dangerous when ingested; use with caution.

Alder (*Alnus glutionosa*)	foundation of wisdom, knowledge, being, and initiation
Willow (*Salix* spp)	contemplation, love; aids divination, intuition, and deception
Rowan (*Sorbus aucopria*)	patience, thoughtfulness, protection, introspection
Blackthorn (*Prunus spinosa*)	control, coercion, threat, aggression
Medlar (*Mespilus*)	beauty, scarcity, richness, wealth, anticipation

89 *"Kat Godeu,"* the Book of Taliesin; my translation.

Rose (*Rosa* cv)	courage, love, assists development of psychic abilities, healing
Raspberry (*Rubus idaeus*)	action, impetus, affection, emotional stability
***Privet (*Ligustrum ovalifolium*)	protection, steadfastness, humility NOT SUITABLE FOR INGESTION
Honeysuckle (*Lonicera periclymenum*)	inner beauty, prosperity, determination, protection
Ivy (*Hedra helix*)	virility, determination, fertility, protection
***Cherry (*Prunus* spp)	extrovert, confidence, affection, love, attraction USE EDIBLE FRUIT ONLY
Birch (*Betula pendula*)	greatness, vitality, change, eagerness, birth
Goldenrod (*Solidago* spp)	resolution, prosperity, steadfastness, aid to divination
***Pine (*Pinus* spp)	leadership, self-confidence, originality, good health, strength, presence DO NOT USE RESIN FOR TINCTURE
Ash (*Fraxinus excelsior*)	peace, integration, flexibility, perception, nobility, increases psychic ability
Elm (*Ulmus* spp)	perfection, quest for love, vulnerability, delusions, conflict
Hazel (*Corylus* spp)	knowledge, modesty, productive creativity, concentration
Dogwood (*Cornus* spp)	faithfulness, expression, articulation, good fortune
Beech (*Fagus sylvatica*)	prolific, flourish, steadfast, security, justice

***Holly (*Ilex aquifolium*)	intensity, efficiency, tenacity, strength, retribution for wrongs done NOT SUITABLE FOR INGESTION
Hawthorn (*Crataegus* spp)	disarming, determination, destruction, harshness, self-reliance
Vine (*Vitus* spp)	disarming, intoxication, addiction, determination
***Bracken (*Pteridium aquilinium*)	selfishness, self-protection, defensiveness, prophesy NOT SUITABLE FOR INGESTION
***Broom (*Cytisus scoparius*)	harmony, adaptability, vulnerable innocence, unity NOT SUITABLE FOR INGESTION
Gorse (*Ulex europaeus*)	wisdom, synthesis, common sense, courageousness
Heather (*Calluna vulgaris*)	inspiration, magic, turning dreams into reality, activism
***Oak (*Quercus* spp)	strength, endurance, might, overcoming difficulties, truth, empowerment POISONOUS IN LARGE QUANTITIES
***Woad (*Isatis tinctoria*)	beauty, courageousness, self-confidence, assertiveness, warrior spirit NOT SUITABLE FOR INGESTION
Pear (*Pyrus communis*)	lust, single-mindedness, sexual prowess, confidence
Clover (*Trifolium* spp)	success, unassuming, stealth, fidelity, inner strength
***Chestnut (*Castanea sativa*)	nourishment, knowledge, instruction, fertility USE SWEET CHESTNUTS ONLY FOR INGESTION

Summoning the Army of Trees

Use the previous table of attributions and your own connection to the powers of the trees to summon your own personal army of trees. Not only will this deepen your relationship to the natural world, it will also provide you with a cabinet of magical allies always at the ready to assist you in your magic.

Tinctures and essences will keep indefinitely and provide an easy, effective method for activating your rituals and spellwork. The accoutrements and ritual for the preparation of each potion must be mindful of your connection to the tree; this is not simply a task whereby one casts any old item into a pot and stirs, it is simultaneously a ritual of connection. You may identify a tree or shrub and its usefulness to a particular act of magic or you may wish to work through the list, building yourself an army of trees.

Tinctures

Tinctures can be used internally by adding fifteen drops of the tincture to water and ingesting. Externally they can be added to spell ingredients or incense recipes and used to anoint tools, amulets, and other items of magic as necessary. Use a food-grade alcohol—the higher the alcohol content the better—or use 100 proof vodka. This method is only suitable for nontoxic varieties that are safe for human use.

All parts of the tree or shrub are suitable for creating a tincture: leaf, bark, fruit, flower, wood, or root. Place the ingredient in a wide-mouthed jar and completely cover with alcohol, ensuring that no organic material is exposed to the air. Use a 2:1 ratio—for example, 2 ounces of alcohol to 1 ounce of organic material. Shake the jar gently and place on a sunny windowsill for a minimum of two weeks. For best results I would suggest preparing the tincture during the new moon and straining it during the full moon.

Strain the liquid through a fine sieve, discard the organic material responsibly, and decant the infused tincture into a dark glass vial, preferably with a dropper attachment. Label and store.

Essences

Ensure that you have properly studied the properties of each ingredient. If you are unsure or the ingredient is unsafe for consumption by tincture, I suggest preparing an essence. This is not a mechanical process where the volatile properties of the ingredient are extracted; it is an energetic method. During the night of a new moon, pour high-grade alcohol or vodka into a dish and completely cover it with a sheet of clear glass. Place the ingredient on top of the glass and position on a windowsill where it will be exposed to moonlight and sunlight. Leave for two weeks, from new moon to full moon. Discard the ingredients, decant the alcohol into a dark glass vial, label, and store.

Cold Infused Oils

Not to be taken internally, use cold infused oils for anointing and adding to other non-ingestible spell ingredients. Use a 2:1 ratio: for example, place 2 tablespoons of fine-grade oil (avocado, grape seed, olive oil, almond oil, etc.) in a wide-mouthed jar, add 1 tablespoon of organic material, and allow to steep in a sunny position from new moon to full moon. To preserve the oil, squeeze in two or three capsules of vitamin E or add a little benzoin tincture.[90] Strain, decant into a dark glass vial, label, and store.

EXERCISE

INVOKING THE TREES RITUAL

Identify the tree, its location, and its nature. Research its properties in horticultural books or online libraries. Identify any myths and lore associated with the tree or shrub; get to know it. State your intention to the tree. As an example, hawthorn may be used to disarm malicious intent directed towards you or assist in removing unwanted attention and increasing self-reliance. Create an *englyn* for the purpose of gathering the material required; for example:

---

90 Griggs, *The Green Witch*, 246.

Ancient one of the forest's edge
Wisdom forth to shine
Assist me in my cause this day
Make your power mine.

Take the ingredient home. Prepare the materials you need to create your tincture, essence, or oil. Follow these three ritualistic steps:

Step 1: Detachment

Prepare the room, dim the lights, burn appropriate incense, and play some suitable music—anything to make the act different from ordinary activity. You are moving between the worlds; a sense of detachment will send a clear signal to your brain that something extraordinary is about to occur, allowing your subtle senses to come to the fore. This would be the point at which the triskelion ritual from chapter 5 would be performed.

Step 2: Attachment

In this step you will focus your energy, mind, and creativity towards the task at hand; therefore, you consciously attach yourself to the energy of the ingredient. Sense its attributions and properties and recall your connection to it. This is the heart of the ritual, the point where you are between the worlds. Imagine that the fabric of your surroundings loses its cohesion, its edges blur. You can heighten this by completely transforming the light levels in the room or space.

Call to your magical allies here and to the spirit of the trees. Sing *englynion* to them in rounds of three. For Cerridwen you might sing:

Skilful one of the cauldron's brew
Shining one of light.
Be beside me on this day
Help me in this rite.

Step 3: Charging

At this stage you will provide the necessary physical, emotional, and spiritual energy required to seal your intention into the substance. The more energy you raise, the better; the stronger your imagination and visualization, the more effective the extraction will be. I suggest you utilize chants, drumming, singing, voice work, or anything that raises the vibrational quality of your own mind, body, and spirit. Direct this energy towards the ingredients. Continue to maintain this energy for a duration of three, six, or nine minutes. Finally, gather up the ingredients in both hands and hold at arm's length above the receptacle chosen for the extraction. Now charge the item by singing an *englyn* that you have created for this specific purpose, e.g.:

Spirit wise within this tree
Bridge the void that I may see
That which causes me this harm
By your virtue I disarm.

Sing the *englyn* in multitudes of three and then place within the receiving jar or upon the plate of glass. Now stop: be still, silent; nothing matters, nothing is of any consequence, all that exists is you and the tree. Hold your hands above the ingredient and stop. Just be in this place without expectation or desire. Breathe deeply with eyes closed.

Conclusion

Direct your gratitude to the tree, acknowledge the presence of your ally, and return to the here and now. Close the ritual as directed in chapter 5's triskelion ritual. Position your jar or bowl on a windowsill, lighten the mood, put some energetic music on, and go about your business as normal.

Note: The above example was used in the preparation of a wash, which was subsequently used as a home blessing and protection ritual. The individual for whom the wash was created was receiving unwanted attention from a jealous and overly possessive ex-lover. A tincture of gorse was also provided to imbue the client with a sense of courage to face the situation on both a physical and spiritual level and to gain the wisdom required to deal with it effectively. Gorse also helped him to not overact—to think and utilize common sense rather than repetitive knee-jerk reactions, which served only to compound the situation. A wax amulet imbued with oak was created for the client to carry with him.

Magical Amulets

"The Battle of the Trees" poem informs us that woad had his name in a wax tablet. Now, while this reference is obscure and without clear meaning, it can be taken to imply that the attributes of woad were somehow imbued into a wax tablet. I suggest that this can be taken further and applied to the entire list in the creation of magical wax amulets.

Steps 1 to 3 in the previous ritual suggestion should be implemented here with the addition of the following practice in the main body of the ritual. In a double boiler, melt approximately 2 ounces of pure beeswax. Do not use paraffin wax; the properties of such are counterproductive owing to the energetic value of the components used in their construction. The purer the wax, the better the amulet.

A tip here: I use a small single-ring camping stove, the type that takes a cartridge of butane gas. It is wonderfully portable, has adjustable flame control, and enables me to perform the ritual anywhere. I use the same stove for heating my cauldron in all my rituals and magical practice. Place a small quantity of water into a saucepan and place a glass heat-resistant bowl above it, making sure the glass bowl does not touch the base of the saucepan. Bring the water to a gentle boil but do not allow it to boil dry. When steam starts to force its way out between the bowl and the pan, drop the beeswax into the bowl. The wax will melt within minutes; do not stir or disturb it. You will need a mold to pour the melted wax into when ready. I find that an empty tealight case is perfect; when used, keep the empty cases for making amulets. When the wax has completely melted, take a small amount of organic material and hold it in both hands, sense its properties, and imbue it with your intention; for instance:

You are applying for a promotion at work and need a boost of confidence and are able to demonstrate leadership and originality; for this amulet, pine would be suitable. Take a small amount of pine resin and some needles roughly cut into small pieces and sing this *englyn* to them:

> *Spirit wise within this tree*
> *Help me now so they may see*

Virtues of my skills and tasks
By forest power, this I ask.

Drop the resin and needles into the wax and gently shake the bowl to disperse them into the wax equally. Raise a significant amount of emotional energy to charge the liquid; chant, sing, and dance—whatever ensures a good smattering of energy—and direct it towards the melted wax.

Now gently pour the material into the empty tealight case. Allow to cool completely before gently pushing the base of the tealight case, thus releasing your amulet. Carry this about your person. When you sense the amulet has served its purpose, return it to the elements through fire.

Do not assume these amulets must be restricted to pure spellwork for specific reasons; they can be created as gifts for the seasonal festivals or fashioned with specific people in mind and placed onto wreaths or garlands as Yuletide gifts. The same method can be used for plants, flowers, and to enchant items for a multitude of magical purposes.

Amulets of a more permanent nature can be created from slices of wood, the tree of which should be significant to its purpose and creation. Words, images, or symbols pertinent to gods and goddesses can be carved, burnt, painted, or drawn onto the surface; a small hole drilled in it will enable it to be strung, hung, or worn. Various amulets made of wood and other materials have been discovered in Britain and Gaul, several of which depict a sun-wheel symbol, perhaps indicative of a solar deity. Others seem to have been created specifically as offerings and were found in river beds and fords.[91] Remember, these are not spells for the sake of it; this is practice, the formation of items and objects that are sympathetically connected to your life as a magician.

91 MacCulloch, *The Religion of the Ancient Celts*, 328.

23

Tree Divination: The Ogam

When it comes to certain magical practices, I am of the opinion that if it isn't broken, don't fix it. The ogam or ogham (pronounced *oh-wam*) has erroneously been attributed as an ancient Celtic system of divination—when, in fact, it is no such thing. Irish mythology informs us that the ogam was created by the god Ogma and consists of twenty basic letters formed as notches upon a crossbar. A further five letters were added later to account for foreign words borrowed into the Celtic languages.[92] The following exploration will focus only on the original twenty letters of the ogam system.

The ogam as a divinatory tool was invented or created by the twentieth-century writer Robert Graves in his highly influential book *The White Goddess*. Although a greatly admired piece of work and essential reading to the modern Pagan, it is safe to deduce that Mr. Graves came to some rather incorrect conclusions, the ogam being one of them. But something rather

92 Mountfort, *Ogam: The Celtic Oracle of the Trees*, 11–12.

magical happened—however incorrect the belief that this system of divination is ancient, it has become a colorful and appropriate system for modern Pagan practice. The ogam did exist, as the inscribed stones of Britain and Ireland proclaim, and although preserved mostly by the Irish Celts, there is evidence that the ogam was used in the British Isles. The majority of surviving stone inscriptions date from between the fourth and eighth centuries of the Common Era.

There may be little evidence to suggest its use as a divinatory tool, but it was undeniably a system of writing that was culturally specific predominantly to the Irish Celts. Epigraphic examples on stones and wood suggest a commemorative function and a manner by which coded messages could be effectively and covertly disseminated. The fourteenth-century manuscript the Book of Ballymote contains over ninety examples of ogam usage, of which a peculiar mandala-type sigil known as "Fionn's window" is of particular interest to modern Pagans. It places the four *aicme*, or family groups of the ogam, within five concentric circles that radiate out from the central circle to form four distinct paths along a cardinal circuit. While the function of Fionn's window may be lost to us, according to ogam authors Mark Graham and Heather Buchan, it has been adopted into current practice to symbolize the wheel of life and the stages for the evolutionary journey of the human soul.[93] From this aspect a modern divinatory function has evolved.

Symbols are powerful allies in themselves, and the continuous development and usage of the ogam from its misty past through its resurrection in the twentieth century is indicative of its ability to inspire and spark the human imagination. I have a rather straightforward attitude to the ogam in that I like it; I think it's a valuable tool that has had some bad press, mostly due to Mr. Graves and his musings. I have heard many claim that it should not be used as it is not genuinely Celtic. Its divinatory aspect may be recently invented, but that does not negate its value or power. It still has presence, and it does connect us to the lands and the culture of the Celts. We must remember, too, that the Celts were not a group of people that existed only

93 Graham and Buchan, *The Celtic Tree Ogham*, 6–7.

in the distant past, and that for anything to have validity it must come from the past and be of the past. The Celts survive; we are still here, continuously making this spirituality relevant and applicable to a modern world.

Systems of divination are only as effective as the magician's connection to the tool, therefore an understanding, symbiotic relationship with the primary trees of the ogam system will work in a divinatory sense. Using that methodology, one could easily attribute symbols to the trees and shrubs listed in "The Battle of the Trees" and use them as casting tools for divination—there would be absolutely nothing wrong with that, and I would hazard a guess that it would be rather effective. But when it comes to the ogam, the majority feel somewhat put off by its assumed complexity, when in actuality it is not in any form complicated or difficult. As with most things in life, there is a knack to using it effectively, and I aim to share that with you here.

Traditionally the ogam is composed of slivers of wood, preferably taken from each individual tree and fashioned into "staves," little short sticks no longer than around 2 or 3 inches in length and ½ to 1 cm wide. A symbol is then etched onto the stave to represent the individual tree; for example, the ogam stave for alder (fearn) would be represented as:

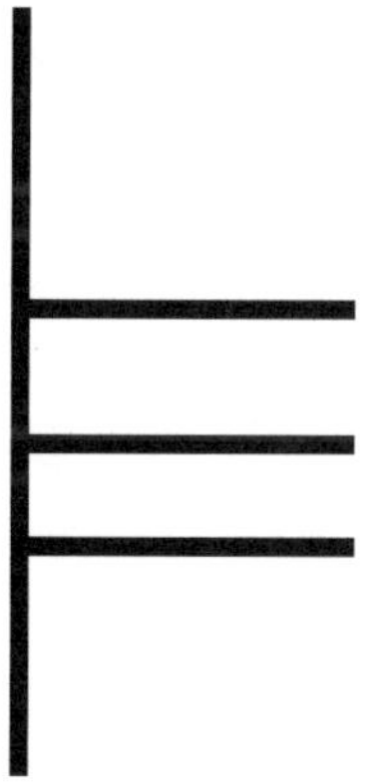

A number of these are then randomly selected from a bag or box and cast onto a reading surface. In the several workshops I have given on ogam divination, the first complaint I hear is the fact that folks do not know what to cast them onto or how to read the staves in a manner that brings meaning to the reading, i.e., the position or pattern they form upon casting. Chapter 29 of this book will provide you with a glyph upon which to cast your ogam staves (and any other form of divinatory tool); this offers a point of reference in conjunction with Celtic myth by which to read the tool against.

Normally books present the ogam as a complete list of twenty trees, with the ogam stave symbol alongside it; these consist of lines etched to the left, right, directly across, or diagonally traversing a central column. Then one is presented with the English name, Celtic name, and their quality. All in all, most people take one look and think, "Well, that's bloody complicated!" and promptly abandon it. Like most things in life, there is an easy way and a difficult way.

First and foremost, it is essential to note that the ogam is split into four *aicme*, which roughly translates as "family, clan or tribe" and is pronounced "AYKH-muh." Each *aicme* is subdivided into a group of five trees, all sharing a commonality within that grouping. To each group I assign a quality that is indicative of the journey upon the Tree of Life and encapsulates the function of each group, which I list thus:

- the branch of beginning
- the branch of gaining wisdom
- the branch of introspection
- the branch of transformation

The separate *aicme* are identified by the Celtic name of the first tree within that grouping; for example, the first tree of the first *aicme* is birch (*beith*), therefore this group is called *aicme beith*.

Faced with twenty bizarre and alien sigils on a stick and a multitude of trees to remember in order is difficult for most people, so the easiest way is to avoid looking at it as a sequence of twenty trees and focus instead on them being four groups. Five trees are far easier to digest than twenty. See the glossary for pronunciation of the Celtic names.

The branch of beginning, *Aicme Beith*, is grouped thus:

ENGLISH NAME	CELTIC NAME	MNEMONIC	QUALITY	SYMBOL
birch	*beith*	birch	vitality, beginning	ᚁ
rowan	*luis*	ran	quickening, insight	ᚂ
alder	*fearn*	away	foundation	ᚃ
willow	*saille*	with	intuition	ᚄ
ash	*nuinn*	ash	rebirth, peace	ᚅ

Look at the tree list. They have something in common: they are mostly colonizing trees—they prepare the ground for new growth and future woodlands. They are the trees of beginning; they pave the way for future generations. On a spiritual or divinatory level, these are the trees that embody our quest, the journey through life and into the spirit. The qualities needed for life are imbued within these trees; to find them in a reading implies innocence, vitality, and the qualities required to create a firm foundation for the future. Focus on the first five trees until you are deeply familiar with them. By proxy of studying this system, you will naturally be drawn to study and observe these particular trees. Relationship will ensue; it is this relationship and the attributions of the trees that you will utilize in divination.

Mnemonics—where the first letter of the English names are replaced with something that will jog the memory into recalling the sequence of trees—will aid memory. A tip: the sillier and more nonsensical the mnemonic, the more it will stick in your mind. The mnemonic provided here is *birch ran away with ash.*

The branch of gaining wisdom, *aicme huath*, is grouped thus:

ENGLISH NAME	CELTIC NAME	MNEMONIC	QUALITY	SYMBOL
hawthorn	*huath*	hawthorn	challenge	
oak	*duir*	or	endurance	
holly	*tinne*	holly	balance	
hazel	*coll*	have	creativity	
apple	*quert*	appeal	beauty, eternity	

The foundation has been set: the land prepared and made ready for new growth, new species, and new experiences. The five trees of this *aicme* are the trees of wisdom. They represent our expressive qualities and the setting of new patterns. On a psychological level they express our coping mechanisms and our ability to deal with the human condition. The patterns laid down by the first *aicme* influence these trees; they are a continuation of the previous qualities. The first steps towards maturity require us to adequately access our own inner strength and creativity, to be functional, well-balanced individuals. This may be hampered or influenced by the functions of the first *aicme*. Focus on the five trees until you are deeply familiar with them. How do you glean meaning from these attributions, and what other qualities would you place on these trees?

The mnemonic of this *aicme* is *hawthorn or holly have appeal.*

The branch of introspection, *aicme muin*, is grouped thus:

ENGLISH NAME	CELTIC NAME	MNEMONIC	QUALITY	SYMBOL
bramble	*muin*	bramble	looking within	ᚋ
ivy	*gort*	is	development	ᚌ
reed (broom)	*ngetal*	ready	harmony	ᚍ
blackthorn	*straif*	but	control, coercion	ᚎ
elder	*ruis*	elderly	change	ᚏ

These are the trees that epitomize our search for meaning, for looking deep within to the place of mystery. They express our desire to fill the void—the deep emptiness that may afflict individuals as they approach the midpoint of life. Our lives may have fallen into repetitive patterns of behavior, secure in our insecurity. The bramble sends out a long, spiky shoot; unaware of where that arching will take her, she leaps, knowing deep down that her arch will touch firm ground and take root. We may long for the sense of being rooted to home, work, lifestyle, spirituality, or tradition. Our attempts to control our own fates and fortunes may lead to inappropriate action—we may long for change while simultaneously fearing it. Reed, or broom, teaches us to live in harmony with our environment, while the danger of blackthorn is its surreptitious attempts to gain control over any given situation, sometimes to its detriment.

What do these five trees tell you? Watch them and the manner in which they interact with their environment. These are trees steeped in lore and legend; seek them out.

The mnemonic for this *aicme* could be something along these lines: *bramble is ready but elderly.*

You will note that this, along with the other mnemonic, contains the actual names of the trees themselves to jog your memory. Play with words, like the above "elderly" that hides the word *elder* within it.

The Branch of Transformation, Aicme Ailm, is grouped thus:

ENGLISH NAME	CELTIC NAME	MNEMONIC	QUALITY	SYMBOL
pine	*ailm*	perfect	objectivity	
gorse	*onn*	groves	wisdom, synthesis	
heather	*ur*	have	gateway, passion	
poplar (aspen)	*eadad*	popular	overcoming, insight	
yew	*idad*	yews	death, immortality	

This is the *aicme* of acceptance, of coming into being, of being comfortable within your own skin—yet it is as challenging and complex as the previous *aicme*. On a psychological and spiritual level these trees teach us about the mysteries of being and transformation. We learn to stop fighting and stand in our own power; it is the power of acceptance, of being who we are and who we want to be in this experience. On the surface of things it seems that this *aicme* leads only to death; however, the nature and message of yew is quite the contrary, for they truly may be immortal. Death is merely a midpoint in existence, and these trees lead us to this understanding. In the journey of life we become elders, experienced; we learn to watch and listen before responding and utilizing our wisdom of the journey to help others on theirs.

Study these trees and learn their mysteries. What other qualities can you add to their attributions?

The mnemonic for the *aicme* could be composed thus: *perfect groves have popular yews.*

◆ ◆ ◆

So there we have it: a snapshot of the window of ogam. Used alone, it can seem cumbersome and messy; used in conjunction with other methods, it bursts into life. Before you attempt to use the trees in a divinatory sense, get to know them—create your own set of staves, try not to jump ahead, focus on one *aicme* at a time; the others will come in due course. The qualities provided are keywords—they serve only to jog your memory; further meaning can be gleaned from research and connection to the trees. Get out there and find the trees, move into relationship with them, and decorate your understanding of the trees' divinatory qualities by proxy of relationship.

I suggest that, when casting, you use no more than nine staves at a time. When creating your staves, fork the bottom end of the symbol with two prongs so that you can immediately identify if the stave is upright or not. If you really can't get your head around the symbols, there is absolutely nothing wrong in writing the name of the tree on the reverse side of the stave.

◆ ◆ ◆

And so we depart from the shades of the forest and cast our eyes closer to the ground, to our companions in the plant kingdom.

PART 4

By Oakflower, Broom, and Meadowsweet

Celtic Plant Magic

24

The Magic of Plants

In the Celtic tradition, if trees are perceived as teachers, the plant world can be seen as our medicine cabinet. The trees nourish and sustain the spirit; the plant world feeds and sustains the body and mind. The creatures of the plant kingdom are our natural resources: they ground us in practice, they cause us to stop awhile and listen with intent and with the ears of the spirit.

We are surrounded by the plant world at every moment of every day. They are our closest allies and yet perhaps are the ones we take most for granted. The following pages will explore the nature of Celtic plant magic and their applicability in modern magical practice. I will introduce you to a body of herbal magical lore in the guise of the Physicians of Myddvai, a medieval collection of plant and herb medicine and magic. I will offer you effective spells and rituals that will connect you to a genuine body of Celtic magical material and a system of divination using the power of plants. The following examples of magical practice will deepen your relationship with the plant kingdom and its spirits while simultaneously connecting you to a storehouse of Celtic wisdom.

◆ ◆ ◆

Plant magic is the nitty gritty, the getting-down-and-dirty-with-nature aspect of Celtic magic, and in no uncertain terms, I absolutely love it. It forms a central aspect of my own spiritual and magical practice that brings color and deep connection to my spiritual workings. I must admit I am no gardener; I would even add that I am a poor gardener. I receive the most peculiar looks from people who cannot understand how I can live with weeds in the garden. However, surely a weed is simply a plant that should not be growing in that particular location? And if that is the case—well, I am perfectly happy for that plant to grow and be alive and thrive where it so chooses. Not, perhaps, the trait of a true landscape gardener, but considering I never aspire to be one, I am quite content with the weeds I have in my garden.

If we were to pause and look closely and sense the plant and its position, we would learn much about its nature—about its preference and the relationship it has with its neighbors. It is this pausing, the simple act of observing its nature, that I classify as communication. There's no need to be airy-fairy here; I am not interested in summoning a tiny little Victorian-inspired creature with gossamer wings from the plant and having some deep and meaningful conversation with it. Being with the plant and listening to its subtle messages is far more effective and useful than being able to see a little fairy. Nothing against fairies, but surely the point of connection is not to have a psychic vision or see a supernatural creature but to form relationship? And the manner by which we do this is just the same as the practice of sensing the spirit of a tree: we stop, listen, and "be."

My own personal perception of the plant kingdom is slightly different to the way I view the trees. The tree kingdom is slow-growing, long-lived, and imbued with a sense of deep wisdom that arises from their longevity; with that in mind, I tend to perceive them as elders, respected teachers, those to whom my ancestors turned for deep, ancient wisdom, a wisdom that arises from the land of now and the land of long ago. The plant kingdom, on the other hand, is predominantly fast—it lives at a bit of a pace. The majority (particularly here in northern Britain) are powerful expressions of the seasons and the drama of moon and sun. They respond to the great wheel, they do their jobs, and those of an annual nature retreat back into the soil to be absorbed into the memory of the earth. Perennial plant allies are quick to respond to their seasonal cues; they arise in a burst of praise to the great wheel, they display their wondrous beauty and individual expressions, and then, with a sigh, they retreat to their core beneath the soil to rest, to sleep until the sun or moon calls them next year. In my mind, that is magic in itself, but gosh—there is so much more!

The Function of Plant Magic

In my own practice, I categorize the plant kingdom as having three distinct functions that are particularly relevant for the magical practitioner:

- the power and inherent ability to heal and facilitate healing
- the spiritual message of locality-specific connection
- the ability to assist in sympathetic magic, spellcasting, etc.

It may well be that you perceive their classification as somewhat different to my own, but let me elaborate. Within the Celtic nations, the predominant alignment the people had to the plant kingdom was that of healing. This makes an awful lot of sense; with no hospitals, no doctors (in the manner we would classify them), and no pharmaceuticals, what do you do? Where do you turn to for help when Death is peeking at you from around the door? The Druids and their priests had the trees as the foundation of tradition, knowledge, and wisdom; they were the facilitators of mystery and formed the bridge to profundity, and it is more than likely that they also perpetuated and disseminated the knowledge of herb magic and healing. But that was the priest caste, the elite of society—what of the common people, those who toiled and turned the land, those who ensured that there was food on the tables of both peasant and elite? They were not doctors or nurses, they had no qualifications to speak of, and yet they had a bank of knowledge about the plant world that would be the envy of the majority today, and the reason for this was necessity.

If we scratch away at the surface of magic and of all spiritual traditions and practices, we will find one simple and overriding component: survival. This is the basic fundamental truth that underlies all traditions, all religions, and the practice of magic: our need to survive and to make sense of that overwhelming mystery at the end of life, death. One could say that all religions are "death traditions" in that they teach us how to live to ensure the best outcome or result when we die. Survival—or, in the case of the revealed religions, learning to live and being present—has been replaced with learning how to die and the preparation for the life beyond this one. But look to the plant kingdom and the messages are quite different. They teach us about being here now, being in the bloom, and singing in praise of living and being; however short, however fleeting, the beauty of life is in its living, and this is the mystery of the plant world.

The effective practice of plant magic is not restricted to qualified herbalists; anyone can practice this ancient art safely and effectively. All that is required is a depth of connection that is based on knowledge, relationship, and study. If we approach the plant kingdom with good intention and honor, and if we utilize their power in a way that benefits ourselves and our communities, if we strive to be in service to nature and the gods, then the plant world will lend us their wisdom and work with us as allies in magic. The message of the plant world is particularly seasonal, and we can learn so much simply by watching, listening, and sensing their response to the great wheel; in doing so, we learn how to harness that power in truly beneficial and inspiring ways.

A snowdrop stirs within its bulb—it senses the pulling of the sun, hears the calling of life, and steadily it breaks through the soil and lifts its head towards the glowing orb in the sky. And for just a few days it simply *is*, with no motive other than to do what snowdrops do: its flowers gently nod their heads in the breeze. Their flowering will ensure the continuation of their kind, but it does so with no concern for its own individual death; it is a reflection of now, of the present, of that window in the great wheel that belongs to it. The snowdrop becomes a part of the song of spring, and its power is the expression of that season and all that it stands for; it is the blooming of life after rest. We emulate this time when we come into the springing of our own life, the fertile time and the period of greatest potential, the attributes and qualities embodied in the snowdrop.

Herb Magic: The Celtic Connection

It was claimed that Gwydion's magic in summoning of the army of trees was fathomed by the "use of language and the materials of the earth,"[94] the power of words, incantations, and charms in conjunction with the kingdoms of plant and tree. Cerridwen, who was skilled in magic, sorcery, and conjuration, took to gathering the herbs and flowers of the land to create her brew of Awen. The creation of Taliesin himself, according to "The Battle of the Trees," was said to have been formed from various items of the natural world, including flowers and plants; all these things claim that the power of plants was not just essential for these acts of magic but part and parcel of the entire process. The magic simply would not have occurred at all had it not been for the plant allies. In one of Wales's most enigmatic manuscripts, *The Myvyrian Archaiology*, we find the following information contained in triadic form:

> The three pillars of knowledge, with which the *Gwyddoniaid* (magicians) were acquainted, and which they bore in memory, in the first a knowledge of divine things, and of such matters, and the homage due to goodness, the second, a knowledge of the course of the stars, their names and their kinds, and the order of times. The third a knowledge of the names and use of the herbs of the field and of their application in practice, in medicine and in religious practice, these were preserved in the memorials of vocal song, and in the memorials of times, before there were bards of degree and chair.[95]

94 "The Battle of the Trees," the Book of Taliesin.

95 Jones et al., *The Myvyrian Archaiology*, 129.

From the above it can be deduced that the Celtic magicians were versed in spiritual matters, the movements of the stars and the divisions of time, and the function and qualities of the plant kingdom. However, what is significant in this triad is the stipulation that the knowledge of the plants was in relation to their medicinal and religious use. This implies that both the physical and energetic functions of the plant were essential knowledge for the practicing Celtic magician. The preservation of such knowledge and wisdom is also stipulated with the suggestion that the power of the voice and song was vital to ensure its perpetuation. What good is knowledge if it is not preserved; what good is information if it is not disseminated? Our task, if we wish to take it, is not only to learn about the power of the plant kingdom but also to ensure the continuation of the knowledge by sharing what we know with others who can continue that work. Our Celtic ancestors recorded their knowledge of the plant kingdom and of their use in healing and magic, and although obscure to many in the twenty-first century, aspects of this storehouse of wisdom are relevant to practitioners of Celtic magic today, and by accessing it we open the doors of ancestral magic.

Plants and the Great Wheel of the Year

Upon the great wheel of the year we see the passing phases of the wheel of life, of our own yearly growth and development through birth, fruition, fertility, vitality and bounty, maturity, reflection, decline, and death. We can capture a glimpse of this in the triad I mentioned earlier, which states that the men of magic knew the order of times. Our aspirations, ambitions, and vocations pass through the seasons of the great wheel, and the more we align to them, the more in tune with the seasons of our being we become.

The entire life cycle of the human can be seen emulated in the above qualities as they traverse the annual great wheel, and our allies in the plant kingdom can teach us so much about the meaning of the cycle of moon and sun and the way in which it affects every single living creature on the face of the earth and down to the depths of our oceans.

All the seasons are miraculous, wondrous, awe inspiring, and filled to the brim with beauty and magic, and if we look to the plants and how they respond to it, we begin to live the year with lucidity, being aware of the cycles of the great wheel in a manner that is conducive to growth and experience. Rather than wishing the winter away—and miss out on the opportunity for reflection and quiet contemplation—we can choose to live it, and our allies in the plant kingdom can show us how. Spring will come; the sun will be reborn; but for the time being, lest we traverse backwards along the Great Wheel in an attempt to halt its incessant momentum, the plant kingdom shows us how to be fully present in time as active participants, not reluctant passengers.

Within the pages of the Physicians of Myddvai, which will be explored a little later, we find reference to only two festivals of the great wheel and the plants that are symbolic of them: the Summer Solstice, to which the powers of the oak and vervain are emblematic, and the mistletoe of the Winter Solstice. This is useful, for it gives us a snapshot of the past and the associations of the plant kingdom that our ancestors considered significant for each festival. These shall be explored at greater depth a little later. These plant associations are indicative of ancestral connection and the relationship our forefathers had with the great wheel.

The agricultural or land-based festivals that punctuate the great wheel are locality specific, and the manner in which we connect to them can only be based on our observation and relationship with the natural world. The four agricultural or fire festivals, as they are commonly referred to in Celtic traditions, are fluid—they are not marked by the stations of the sun, they are the manner by which the land responds to the activation of the sun's power upon it. It is doubtful that our Celtic ancestors would have celebrated all eight festivals that are commonplace in modern Paganism. In British Celtic mythology, only *Calan Mai* (Beltane) and *Calan Gaeaf* (Samhain) are popularly mentioned, and yet the archaeological record informs us that our earlier ancestors certainly marked the passage of the sun against the standing stone monuments of northern Europe. However, in modern Pagan practice, the celebration of all eight festivals is both fitting and a powerful method of connection.

With this in mind, I present the commonly accepted Celtic names of the festivals of the year, together with their common Pagan names and plant associations in northwestern Wales. Contrary to popular Pagan belief, the Celts did not believe that the year ended and thus began at *Calan Gaeaf*/Samhain; it was believed that the year concluded, fell into a period of darkness and gestation, and was reborn anew on the morrow of the shortest day of winter—that is, on the turn of the sun.[96]

CELTIC	COMMON PAGAN	PLANT
Alban Arthan	Winter Solstice	hellebores (Christmas rose)
—the highest point of the winter—		
Gwyl Ffraid	Imbolc/Candlemas	snowdrop, crocus
—the feast of Ffraid, goddess of spring, equivalent to Brid, Brigit, Brigantia—		
Alban Eilir	Vernal Equinox/Eostra/Ostara	daffodil, red campion
—the highest point of spring—		

96 Ab Ithel, *The Barddas*, 417.

Calan Mai	Beltane	hawthorn flower, borage
—the calends of May, the true beginning of summer—		
Alban Hefin	Summer Solstice	St. John's wort, vervain
—the highest point of summer—		
Gwyl Awst	Lammas	marsh samphire
—the feast of August—		
Alban Elfed	Autumn Equinox	sedum, ivy
—the highest point of autumn—		
Calan Gaeaf	Samhain/ Halloween	winter honeysuckle
—the calends of winter—		

Communicating with Plants

We communicate with the plant world in the same manner as we do with trees: we observe, we feel and sense them; channels of communication open by means of this connection, and it is by proxy of this channel that we receive information about the plant. By observing the plants within their habitats, we align ourselves to the passage of the seasons. Our ancestors did not share the same calendar as we currently use; ours is artificial and devised by man, and our ancestors did not rely on the turning of a calendar to inform them that Beltane was near—it would have been the plants that dictated the arrival of summer. This has not changed, and it is by observing plants and the way in which they respond to the seasons that we communicate with them. Remember: they do not have vocal chords, their needs are different to yours, and any communication you have with the plant kingdom will be subtle. For the channel to be effectively opened, you must access your sublime powers in order to perceive them.

As the previous list demonstrates, I tend to identify certain plants with the passing of the season, and their arrival each year is like greeting an old friend. I am familiar with them, I anticipate their coming as they stir beneath the ground or luscious green shoots appear to proclaim their imminent arrival. The daffodils of spring are late in my region, and yet they bring with them the promise of warmth as their golden heads bob in the breeze, mimicking the glowing orb in the sky. I collect a handful of dying heads each year to dry and pound into incense recipes that require freshness, vitality, anticipation, and the promise of a new season.

The red campion is the one I look forward to seeing the most. In my peculiar little mind, there is no plant as gracious or sublime, more beautiful and wondrous as the humble decorator of the hedgerow; it is the plant I love above all others. It is the campion that defines my relationship with the plant world; I sense his coming weeks before his due arrival, and yet I do not long for him during the winter months. I sense his whispers from the warming soil as he sends his body upwards, his pristine pink head bobbing in the noonday sun. To my Celtic ancestors he is known as the *blodyn neidr*, or the snake flower; he is favored and sacred to the snakes and is the plant that they are drawn to the most; he sings of snake goddesses so loved by the ancient Druids. The crushed seeds, according to lore, were used as a salve to treat snakebites. Locally he is also called *blodyn taranau*, thunder flower; it was believed that to pick the flowers would cause thunderstorms, and yet the seedpod is alleged to protect one from lightning strikes. My communication with the red campion has developed into a love affair; his resilience and sheer ability to grow in some of the most hostile and barren grounds belies his strength and determination, qualities that I use magically. A bundle of dried red campion seed heads hangs near the main door to the house to protect us from damage by the frequent thunderstorms we encounter here.

Red Campion Protection Charm

An old charm of unknown source instructs that one make a small red or pink pouch and into it cast nine seed heads of the red campion. Upon its outer surface, with fine ink one should draw an outline of the flower in full bloom with a sharp lightning strike set within it. An *englyn* is then sung thrice while holding the pouch between the palms:

> *Snake flower, thunder flower, fairy flower sing*
> *Make this place a sanctuary and to it may you bring*
> *Protection from thunder and the flashing gods of light*
> *Lend your power to this place, sagacity and might.*

The pouch should then be hung near the main door of the home.

Together with certain charms, his flowers and leaves I imbue into creams and oils, incenses and tinctures to imbue my magic with the properties I perceive him to hold, and this results from the subtle communication between me and the glorious red campion.

Meditation
THE AWARENESS OF PLANTS

Stop for a minute or two—take a breath with the land beneath you, breathe in the sky above you, and deeply breathe with the rhythm of the seas that surround the shores of your land. Read the following paragraph, then put the book down and perform this simple task.

Go outside and approach the nearest plant—do not be selective, simply allow your eyes to fall on a plant regardless of what it looks like or if you are familiar with it. Get as close to the plant as you can. Note its color, its growth, and the patterns of its leaves if it has any. Does it have any flowers? If so, what insects is it attracting? What does the color of the flowers tell you? Who are its neighbors, and what relationship does it seem to have with them—is it growing in competition, is it struggling to get to the light? Notice the plant: touch it, smell it, close your eyes and touch it again. Note how it feels against your skin. What subtle impressions do you receive from the plant, if any? Direct a blast of emotional energy towards it with gratitude and bid it farewell for the time being.

Return to your tasks, go about your business, and think no more of it. Sleep, and on the following day consider the plant and its qualities, look it up online or in books. What properties is the plant purported to have, and do these match anything you perceived? Note these impressions in your journal.

Exercise
BLODEUEDD, THE MAIDEN OF FLOWERS: A RITUAL OF CALLING

> And Math said, "We must endeavour, you and I, to conjure a wife for him out of the flowers, using our magic and enchantment." And so they took the flowers of the oak, the broom, and meadowsweet, and from them they called forth the fairest and most beautiful woman that any living soul had ever seen, and they named her Blodeuedd.[97]

97 From the fourth branch of the Mabinogi.

Blodeuedd was created by the great magicians Math, the son of Mathonwy, and Gwydion in response to the curse that Aranrhod placed upon her illegitimate son, Lleu. Erroneously Blodeuedd is frequently referred to in both human and owl form by the name Blodeuwedd, which is only given to her upon her transformation into an owl by Gwydion's magic. When we are initially introduced to her in the fourth branch of the Mabinogi, she is created and arises from the cauldron, formed from flowers, and she is named Blodeuedd, which literally means "flowers or blossoms." When she is cursed to the night in the guise of an owl, she is renamed Blodeuwedd, meaning "flower face," a typical folk name attributed to the owl; for centuries the owl was commonly referred to as Blodeuwedd.

In her Blodeuedd form she is a force of nature, and not one to be reckoned with. There is an important and vital message to be gleaned from her tale. The magicians create her with every good intention to break the curse laid upon Lleu, but in doing so they also serve to demonstrate ignorance and arrogance—and yet we must not smite their characters for this trait, for that is a necessary function of their personalities; they are flawed. However, they assume that Blodeuedd will do their bidding and conform to the standards they place upon her, but this is doomed from the offset—she is flowers, she wants to be flowers, her ordinary state is held in the color of flowers and the aroma they carry on the breeze. She cannot conform and she cannot be controlled; she is a force of nature.

The two aspects of Blodeuedd offer immensely powerful and profound opportunities of connection and relationship; she can teach us so much about the nature of flowers and their virtues. By developing a relationship with Blodeuedd, we increase our attunement and connection to the plant kingdom.

Begin by reading the fourth branch of the Mabinogi in its entirety.

You will need spring water for your ritual cauldron and an equal quantity of oak flowers (acorns are fine at a push), broom blossom, and the flowering heads of meadowsweet; place these in a bowl next to the cauldron. Suggested magical allies for this rite would be Gwydion or Cerridwen. Perform the triskelion ritual as described in chapter 5. After the vowels of Awen have been chanted, allow your eyes to close gently and recall your impressions of the flower goddess and the mysteries contained within her tale.

With your wand in your power hand, hold both hands over the flowers and repeat the following three times:

Three powers of three flowers, three powers in you combined
Three flowers of plant and tree, your wisdom forth to find.
Oak, broom, and meadowsweet, your powers great to see
Goddess of the blossom, Blodeuedd, I call to thee.

Gather up the oak flowers and chant the following thrice, tossing them into the cauldron on the second repetition and holding your wand aloft over the cauldron throughout:

Blodeuedd, come by blessed oak, stout and strong and fast.
By Druid's shout from ancient times, your magic here I cast.

Next, gather the flowers of broom and chant the following thrice, tossing them into the cauldron on the second repetition and holding your wand aloft throughout:

By sweep of broom its spell is cast
To call you forth by magic's task.
Come, arise, take form and shape
Lift your head, O lady, wake.

Finally, gather the flowers of meadowsweet and chant the following thrice; again, cast the flowers into the cauldron on the second round, holding your wand aloft:

By scent of flowering meadowsweet I sing
Your form and face it doth so bring.
From depth of cauldron, lady, come
Appear to me by day is done.

Now plunge your wand into the cauldron, connecting yourself to the deep, to the hidden world and the abode of the gods. Stir the cauldron anticlockwise with your wand, eyes closed, and recite the following over and over, quicker and quicker, until your mind is concerned with nothing else:

By the power of these flowers, Blodeuedd rise and sing
Form and shape of blossoms, goddess to me bring.
Wisdom from the world of plants and those that humble dwell
On the earth and 'tween the planes, their wisdom forth to tell.

Allow your mind to become lost in the mantralike fashion of the chant; keep it going until you literally lose your mind. When you are utterly and truly exhausted, stop stirring and fall to the ground still, empty, with visions of Blodeuedd your only sight. Sense the power of the goddess and the mysteries she holds and speak to her in that quiet place, in that space between the worlds, held in sacred space.

Conclude the ritual as directed in the triskelion ritual in chapter 5. Think no more of it, return to your daily business, sleep, and on the morrow reflect on the ritual and your connection to Blodeuedd. Record the experience and any insights in your journal.

25

The Physicians of Myddvai

Perhaps the greatest body of herb and plant lore, wisdom, and usage in the entire Celtic world is recorded in a thirteenth-century manuscript that is commonly referred to as the Physicians of Myddvai. This medieval manuscript contains a vast catalogue of plant magic and medicine, with an impressive list of ailments and how to cure them. Some range from the downright bizarre to quite macabre, whereas others are as relevant today as they were in the Middle Ages. Although the manuscript is rather late, it is believed that the information it contains in all probability comes from a much earlier resource and likely dates back to the time of the ancient Druids.[98]

A distinguished Welsh warrior by the name of Rhys Grug had amongst his staff one of the finest physicians in the land, a man by the name of Rhiwallon. Rhiwallon was assisted by his three sons, Cadwgan, Gryffydd, and Einion, who lived in the small village of Myddvai (in current Carmarthenshire) and were collectively known as the Physicians of Myddvai.

98 Hoffman, *Welsh Herbal Medicine*, 4–5.

A vast body of legends and lore, mythology and fables have built up around the physicians, the manuscript containing their medicine and magic, and the mysterious manner by which the information was transmitted to them. This fascinating manuscript informs us that medicine was numbered as one of the nine rural arts known and practiced by the ancient Cymry, or Welsh people. It was believed during that ancient time that the priests and teachers of the people were the *Gwyddoniaid*, or the men of magic—also referred to as the Druids. It was to these men that the art of healing was entrusted, which they seem to have practiced mostly by means of the herbs of the land. If this was indeed true, and I have no reason personally to doubt it, it would seem that after the departure of the Romans and with the Druids now but a distant memory, the magic, wisdom, and usage of plants fell to the peasantry to maintain and perpetuate.

This folk magic can be seen in tales and lore throughout the Celtic nations and within the practice of what modern Paganism would identify as Witchcraft. Suddenly it reappears in the Middle Ages in the form of the Physicians of Myddvai, and if the tale has a morsel of truth to it, it is the powers of nature and perhaps an aspect of the Goddess that presented this knowledge, which had been disparate and fragmented for centuries, and entrusted it to the Physicians of Myddvai.

Rarely retold in modern Paganism, this old tale of love, magic, and devotion should be part of the lore of plants for all Celtic magic practitioners, for it offers a window to the distant past and its wisdom. It combines the beauty of legend and its ability to enchant and inform; it roots the knowledge of the plants and their use in magic and healing as something that has arisen from man's connection to the land and the invisible, subtle yet everpresent powers that inhabit it. Legends and myths are important components of Celtic magic: their retelling aligns us to the cultural continuum of the Celts; we sense the whispers of ancestry rising from their hidden meaning. This is history not of the conqueror, but of the heart—of the people and the unique manner by which they perceived and observed the world around them.

The legend of Llyn y Fan Fach tells of the fate of a young man who happened across a supernatural woman on the shores of a lake in current

Carmarthenshire. Try as he may, he could not win her affections until he baked her the perfect bread. Eventually she agreed to marry him—on one condition: that were he to strike her three times, she would return to her realm beneath the lake. He agreed, and so they married and were blissfully happy. Together they raised three sons until inadvertently he struck her thrice. Upon the third striking, she returned to the lake where they had first met and vanished beneath the waters. Her three sons would wander the hills in the hopes of seeing their mother, and one day she appeared and presented to the eldest son, Rhiwallon, a bag of herbs and instructions as to their usage. From that point on she would frequently meet her sons to give them counsel in the way of herbs and magic. They grew to be the most skilful physicians in the land. In order to preserve their mother's knowledge, they wisely committed the same to writing for the benefit of future generations, and it is this manuscript that has become known as the Physicians of Myddvai.

◆ ◆ ◆

Many believe that it was the Goddess who arose from the lake—from that portal to the otherworld, as all lakes were believed to be in ancient Celtic times. Today, modern writers of Celtic magic and plant lore perpetuate the belief that the spirit of the Goddess and the nurturing and healing powers of the divine feminine can be seen emulated in this old Welsh legend and the manuscript of medicine and magic that sprung from it.[99] The spirit of the goddess of healing can be seen mirrored in the qualities of some of the magical allies that we have previously explored, Cerridwen perhaps being the most obvious choice. Observing, listening, and sensing the power in plants is our primary method of communication, but our allies in magic also serve to bridge the chasm of time and connect us to an ancient storehouse of wisdom that allows us to access the potentiality in plants. Water has long since been attributed healing properties and, as the previous tale recounts, the spirits that sing from that element are intrinsically connected to the powers of healing; we can harness this quality in our rituals and practical magic.

99 Carr-Gomm, *The Druid Plant Oracle*, 5–6.

EXERCISE
INVOKING THE LADY OF THE LAKE

Connecting to the Lady of the Lake (in whatever guise you perceive her) is good practice before and during acts of plant magic. In my own practice, I like to call to her in her Cerridwen aspect just prior to any magical working. All that is required for this little ritual is a vessel of water or, perhaps more fittingly, you may have a pond or other body of water on your property or nearby. If you are using an altar or other designated space in your home for the performing of magic, I would suggest that you have a small cauldron or other vessel of water present. If appropriate and necessary, perform the triskelion ritual from chapter 5.

Take a small piece of lightly baked bread and hold it above the water in your left hand. Close your eyes and allow images of the lady to float into your mind; recall and replay the interaction you have had with the goddess. Then repeat the following or similar:

Perfect baked is my bread
By your wisdom may I be led
To the virtues of these plants
By magic spell and rhyming chants
Let these plants be my aid
And magic here be made.

Now drop the bread into the water and stir the surface with the index finger of your left hand. Imagine as you stir that the ripples are not contained just within the vessel, but by means of the water create a portal to the otherworld, spreading between the worlds, touching the wisdom of ages. Recite the following or similar three times:

Lady of the secret lake, knowledge wise to keep
By the offering of this bread, arise now from the deep.
By flower, leaf, and hidden root, my magic here to make
By the names of your cherished sons, mysteries of your lake.

Lend your wisdom to this rite, my task I here proclaim
Lady of the sacred lake, I call upon your name.

Call the name of the goddess most suitable for this task by name three times, e.g., "Cerridwen, Cerridwen, Cerridwen."

Now acknowledge the power inherent within the plant or plants that you have chosen for your magic by creating an *englyn* that is relevant to them. This means that you will have to spend even more time contemplating the plants and their properties, an excellent opportunity to be fully immersed in the practice.

For example, I recently turned to the powers of borage and hawthorn to make an infusion and tincture for a friend who had been struggling to access and use her own psychic powers; after suffering personal loss and grief, she felt her ability to sense the subtle was failing her. I made a hawthorn tincture by steeping hawthorn berries in brandy for three days; first I pricked the berries and pushed them into a small glass bottle, then I topped the bottle up with brandy. This bottle sat upon my altar along with a fresh infusion of borage leaves and flowers contained in a separate glass jar that had been steeped in boiling water for ten minutes. I placed a photograph of my friend at the back of my altar.

The hawthorn berries would help her with heartache and grief; they also act as a mild cardiac diuretic. The borage would imbue its quality of courageousness and encourage her to know that her abilities were still there, even if a little hidden. The *englyn* I wrote was as follows, and I repeated it in multiples of three until I felt a connection between myself, the energy of the words, and that of the plants:

Yspaddaden,[100] *blessed thorn, flowers of the may*
Steeped herein in brandy bright, your virtue forth to say
Let heartache flee from her this day, her blood run bold and bright
For as your berries tell the truth, day will conquer over night.

100 *Yspaddaden* is the old Welsh term for hawthorn.

Borage, herb of gladness, come; lend your truth to me
Call unto my friend's distress and help her now to see
Courage rises from your leaves, strength and might and power
All these things lie within the magic of the star flower.

By the above example, charge your plant allies by keeping the intent and focus of the rite at hand firmly in mind. Imagine the best outcome for all involved.

When the time feels right, release the energy of the rite and close the space. Imagine a stout, set pair of doors—they are gnarled and battered by the weather; both stand open. Extend your arms out and slowly bring them together so that the palms of your hands meet in a closing gesture; imagine the doors closing as you perform this action and recite the following or similar:

I release this energy from within my core
This rite is done; I close the door.

Go about your normal business, sleep, and on the following day record the ritual and any impressions you have received in your journal.

The Virtues of Plants Recorded by the Physicians of Myddvai

It is evident from the abundance of material recorded in the Physicians of Myddvai that their knowledge of plant wisdom and usage was quite comprehensive. Although attributed to supernatural sources, it demonstrates that study and observation were necessary qualities for the healer—qualities that continue to be necessary today. The following "virtues" are old, quite old, and yet you will find that many modern herbalism books share a commonality with the virtues recorded in Myddvai. This tells us something about the longevity of the wisdom and of its continuous relevance. You may never have come across these virtues before, but they are steeped in the traditions of the Celts; immerse yourself in them, and next time you speak to someone about the properties of plants, tell them about the ancient physicians of an old Celtic land and the magic of the Lady of the Lake—keep it alive.

The virtues in quotation marks that follow are taken directly from John Pughe's 1861 translation of the Red Book of Hergest with some clarifications by me.[101] While the language may seem antiquated, I think they express a certain charm; the charms and *englynion* that follow each virtue were written by me.

The Virtues of Sage

> "This is most useful when boiled and administered as an infusion to strengthen the nerves. If an infusion sweetened with honey is drunk, it is useful for disorders of the lungs. Also pound this herb and apply to a poisoned wound, and it will extract the venom, though the wound be full of corruption it will be cleansed to the very bottom if dressed with this herb. Let some of the sage be taken and pounded small, and the juice mixed with white wine or old mead for a night and a day and strained then drank whilst fasting, it will cure a patient of ills of the nerves. It is a good thing for those in health to drink half a draught in the morning fasting of this potion, in order to preserve health and prolong life."

A Spell for Sagacity

Take a handful of finest sage, preferably grown by your own fair hands. As the moon waxes towards her sixth day, take good bristles of pine and some resin from a generous pine tree; seven stalks of lavender will bestow longevity. With lavender first, sage between, and resin pressed betwixt the gaps, bundle the lot in bristles of pine and wrap around it good firm string; set aside to dry. Place upon both palms and hold aloft and recite this or similar:

Wise one, ye of pungent smoke, by lavender and pine tree
Awaken to my needs this hour, pray, come work with me.
Let all who breathe your scent herein grow in gracious kind
Sagacious sage, eternal herb, wisdom shall be mine.

As the moon nears her fullness, take the bundle and set it alight with naked flame; blow the gift of air upon it until it smoulders forth fine and

101 Pughe, *The Physicians of Myddvai.*

pure smoke. Around the house and garden go, sending plumes of wisdom and sagacity that only the blessed sage can bestow, while lavender offers longevity of wisdom and the pine health and protection.

The Virtues of Nettle

> "Take the juice of this herb and mix it with white wine or mead and strain carefully, and let it cool. Drink some thereof night and morning, it will cure you of the jaundice and renovate the blood and remove any disease existing therein. If the juice is taken mixed half and half with barley wine, it will cure pleurisy of either side and will renovate and invigorate an aged man in body and mind. If the seed of the nettle in powder is taken and mixed with wine, it is very useful for wind colic or a chronic cough and will reduce a swelling, producing a flow of urine without harm to the bladder."

A Nettle Blessing Spell

Take seven whole stems of nettle cut at the ground with a good sharp knife and hang within the home to dry. Strip the leaves from the stem and pound with pine resin with a pestle and mortar. Add to this the needles of larch and six drops of pure lavender oil. Burn upon hot charcoal in home blessing and protection rituals and spells.

Take the stems and cut in half; to each half, bundle-tie the tops with red ribbon and hang the bundles above the back and front doors to ensure protection while uttering the following *englyn*:

> *Blessed nettle, bar the way from all that comes with harm*
> *By your virtue, sting, and kind, all menace will thine disarm.*

The Virtues of Betony

> "He who will habituate himself to drink the juice will escape the strangury (painful urination). If it is boiled in white wine and drank, it will cure the colic and any swelling of the stomach. Pounding it small, expressing the juice, and applying it with a feather to the eye of a man will clear and strengthen his sight and remove specks from

the eye. The juice is a good thing to drop in the ears of those who are deaf. The powder mixed with honey is useful for those who have a persistent cough; it will remove the cough and benefit many diseases of the lungs. If boiled with the leek seed, it will cure the eye and brighten as well as strengthen the sight."

Betony Spell for Second Sight

For those who fail to clearly hear
The shades of spirits that draw near
Let them turn to betony's virtue
And be of hearing clear and true.
For in a pot of good strong clay
Boil the flower and o'er it say—

"Betony, betony, my task is clear
Allow me the fair spirits hid to hear."

Then to a clump of cotton wool
Drop some betony potion and pull
In pieces two and into the ears
Let them rest so you may hear.

The Virtues of Parsley

"The parsley is a good herb of a warm and hot nature. It is useful in all food as a regenerator of the blood. It will remove obstructions of the veins and arteries in a man's body so that the humors (elements) may circulate properly as they should. This it will certainly do. It is also well to employ parsley for the relief of fainting, the ague (fever or shivering), and dropsy, and the juice being taken for three days without any other drink will cure them. It will also greatly stimulate the spirit and strengthen the stomach. It is good for all obstructions of the kidneys and urine, and the juice is useful to destroy unhealthy granulations in a wound."

A Parsley Spell to Increase Lustfulness

To put a spark into your love life and increase lustfulness between yourself and your lover, take a bottle of good white wine, three quarters full, and push within it as much fresh parsley as will fit therein. Shake the bottle well and place in a darkened cupboard. Within the bed chamber place bundles of parsley in vases and a little beneath each pillow. Drink a glass each of this strange-tasting liquor and set forth to kissing. Take another glass and retire to the bed chamber and let the fun begin! To ensure continuous lustfulness, drink a little of this potion every day for seven consecutive nights.

The Virtues of Fennel

> "The fennel is also a warm and dry herb and it too is useful for disorders of the eye. It is good for every kind of poison in a man's body, being drunk in the form of a powder mixed with white wine or old mead. It is useful for the fever, and if the seeds thereof are boiled in water till it is strong of the virtues of the herb, and the head when it is subject to the headache washed therewith, it will greatly benefit and cure the same. When the headache is occasioned by cold or fever, it will remove and ease the headache very quickly."

Fennel Charm for Clear Vision

The physical virtues of fennel's associations with eye health can be utilized in a magical sense to aid, restore, and improve the gift of second sight and psychic vision. Place six tablespoons of the fresh herb into two cups of boiling water and let steep for five minutes. Add honey or maple syrup to taste, and drink before any magical work or meditation. Hold the steaming cup in your hands and recite the following or similar three times:

Above the lower plants it towers
The fennel with its yellow flowers
And in an earlier age than ours
Was gifted with the wondrous powers
Of vision to restore.

Drink the tea, which is quite delicious, whenever a boost in psychic vision is required.

The Virtues of Rosemary

"Rosemary is a warm and dry herb and it is termed a shrub because it is of a kind between an herb and a tree. Take the flowers of rosemary and mix with honey and eat them daily fasting. You will not suffer from nausea, or any other noxious condition, as long as you use this remedy. Take also the leaves of rosemary and wood sage, making them into a potion and adding honey in the same way. It is an excellent remedy for the strangury (painful urination), stone and catarrh. It will disintegrate and expel it in the water.

Also put the flowers of rosemary or leaves under your head in bed, and you will not be troubled with disagreeable dreams or oppressed with anxiety of the mind. Also, if you carry a stick or fragment of this shrub, no evil spirit can come near you, or any one do to you any harm. Gather the leaves of the rosemary and pound them small, strain, and drink the juice; it will remove all phlegm from the head and lungs, curing it with all certainty. A decoction thereof is also helpful to an insane person or one threatened with delirium, indeed it is good for every disorder which can exist in the human body.

To retain youthful skin and appearance you would do well to boil the rosemary and wash yourself with the cooling water every morning, omitting to dry yourself with a cloth but leaving it to do so naturally. Rosemary will also cure impotence in both sexes if used with food; when a couple are childless, let the wife, if young, use rosemary. There is also no better cure for the cold than a tea of rosemary with honey."

Rosemary Blessing Wreath

Always have rosemary plants in pots near the doorstep to purge a house of negative influences and to keep thieves and evil from the home. And as the wheel turns to *Calan Gaeaf*/ Samhain, form a wreath and within it twist a good many stems of rosemary and take to the graves of your ancestors. As you position the wreath, recite the following *englyn*:

Fragrant flower, bring thy power
Here and to this place
Silent spirit lost in death
Arise and to me grace
Your virtue by sweet Mary's rose
Come share, be in this space
O silent spirit from the dead
Your footsteps now do softly tread
Come by Mary's rose I ask
Be here now, my magic's task!

The Virtues of Vervain

"The blessed vervain, most loved by the Druids of old. If one is affected by sores, gather the entire plant and roast it well and powder. Keep this carefully in a well-covered vessel, and sprinkle it on any sore. For the cold and complaints of the chest, take the juice of the entire plant and rub it onto the chest daily. In the winter months, mix the powder with honey and anoint in the same way. The whole plant is good for all diseases proceeding from the lungs, liver, kidneys, brain, eyes and any other part, and it is good for the scrophula (tuberculosis). This plant, most sacred, was best for cleansing and purification."

A Cleansing Vervain Wash

Vervain is ideally suited for cleansing rituals and the removal of negative energies; it purifies and encourages joyfulness and positivity. On the night of the dark moon, gather the flowering herb and hold aloft in the left hand raised towards the skies as you recite the following *englyn*:

Herb of grace, blessed of all
Hallowed vervain, hear my call.
Cleanse this space of all its ills
Bring happiness where thine water spills.

Place the vervain into a vessel of pure spring water and allow to steep until dawn. Use this water to wash away all negativity.

The Virtues of Mistletoe

Note that this is for reference only; DO NOT TAKE INTERNALLY.

> "The mistletoe most frequently grows on the apple tree or the hawthorn tree and occasionally on the oak, which should be preferred, though it is the most excellent plant wherever it grows. Its property is to strengthen the body and spirit more than any other plant. Gather it in Christmas time, when the berries are quite ripe, and pick the berries from the branches, pour boiling water thereon, covering the vessel that are contained within and setting it to stand near a fire and let it simmer for a night and a day. Let the leaves of the plant be bruised small and laid upon a hot baking stone where they should be thoroughly roasted, being stirred about meanwhile so they may not be burned. When roasted enough they should be powdered, the half thereof being used for that purpose and the remainder burnt to fine ash. The powder and the ash should be carefully preserved in separate glass vials.
>
> In any case of bodily debility, whether in the nerves, joints, back, head, or brain, the heart, lungs or kidneys add the above to a salve or ointment and apply to the body. Mistletoe is good for any kind of disease, epilepsia, mania or mental infirmity of any kind, paralysis, all weakness of the joints, sight, hearing and senses. Pliny enumerates some of the plants most in repute among the Britons for their medicinal properties. He mentions the mistletoe, and observes that in Druidical language it signified 'All-heal,' *omnia sanantem*, a name that expresses its efficacy which it possesses, to this day 'Oll Iach' is one of the names by which the plant in question is known to the Cymry."

The Mistletoe Rite

To increase strength or for powerful assistance during healing and fertility spells and rituals, on the sixth day of the new moon take a stout bundle of mistletoe ripe with berries, a good strong cauldron, spring water, a glass vial and some shortening. Follow the instructions laid out in the following *englyn*; the verse in quotation marks should be recited out loud:

With water clear now placed within, set the cauldron forth to boil
Cast the all-heal's berries bright, held betwixt the sun and soil
Into water stir them well and set a flame beneath the pot
Stir the cauldron, chant the rhyme, and let thee worry not.

"All-heal, all-heal, I call upon thy power
Aid me in this rite upon this very hour."

Let the cauldron steep and bubble a night and all the day
Then on the morrow ease thy troubles and set it on its way
Held in vial of darkened glass, this potion shall persist
To all your needs, now from this day, shall always lend assist.

"All-heal, all-heal, I call upon thy power
Aid me in this rite upon this very hour."

Sprinkle, splash, and anoint or set the liquid in a lotion
Carry soaked in cotton cloth, magic from all-heal's potion.
Within an oven's depth do bake the leaves and wood till hard
Then ground into the finest powder and set firm within good lard.

"All-heal, all-heal, I call upon thy power
Aid me in this rite upon this very hour."

And on the day when needs arise to the all-heal let thy rhyme beseech
To he that hangs between the worlds, its lofty realms you'll reach
Whether spring or summer's heat, leaf fall or at deepest snow
Help is always near your grasp by means of mistletoe.

• 26 •

Practical Plant Magic

Preparing for using plants in magic follows the same principles as harnessing the magic of trees: it is our intention and integrity that ensure effective results, and this is entirely dependent on the relationships we forge.

Be aware of the plants; know their moods before you utilize them for your magic. Do not throw a handful of marigold flowers into an infusion just because a book has told you that it is useful for inducing prophetic sleep. Communicate with the plant—use the books as reference, but become reliant on your own senses and connection also; that is where the real magic lies. Ritualize the act of empowering or charging the plant items by following the example given earlier and creating *englynion* and chants to connect with them while you harvest, prepare, and use them in your practice.

Part 4

The Creation of Magical Products

Herbs can be used in a range of effective ways; following is a brief outline and instructions on the preparation and usage for magical purposes. If you require the properties of a baneful herb or other potentially toxic plant, I suggest you use them sympathetically in non-ingestible oil or for inclusion into a crane (charm) bag or in an essence.

Infusion

Essentially this is a tea, where boiling water is poured directly over the plant. For a two-cup measurement of infusion, you would require six tablespoons of fresh plant material or three tablespoons of dry material and steep for three to five minutes. This is intended to take internally; therefore, caution and common sense are required. For sympathetic use that does not require ingestion, add to a bath of hot water. Use immediately; infusions do not store well and lose their volatility quickly.

Decoction

This is a stronger version of the infusion, perfect for casting directly onto surfaces or items to be enchanted. This typically invokes the stereotypical witches' cauldron scenario, for the plant materials need to be boiled in water for a good ten to twenty minutes and then allowed to steep in the liquid for anything up to twenty-four hours. Roots, barks, berries, and other woody plant material will require vigorous boiling to release their properties; pound or crush them a little before adding them to the water. I have an old preserving pan that I use for magical purposes with a designated single-ring camping stove for portability. Add a minimum of four cups plant material to every one liter or quart of water. Decoctions for protection, defense, clearing, purification, prosperity, etc., can be added to your mop bucket for cleaning the house. Use whenever large quantities of material are required. A decoction will keep in a dark glass bottle or jar for six months.

Potion

According to the Physicians of Myddvai, a potion is a draught or fluid prepared according to art. Potions are intended for magical purposes only and are not for ingestion. Items are immersed in spring water and ritually charged before placement in a sunlit position. It is not necessary to strain a potion, and it will keep indefinitely.

Ointments

Ointments are not necessarily absorbed well by the skin and contain mostly fats; they also may be used as a barrier against allergens and other irritants. Magically they can be applied to amulets and other enchanted items. They are prepared by immersing plant material in vegetable shortening, lard, lanolin, or coconut oil and heating in a double boiler for at least sixty minutes. As a general guide, use one part plant material to two parts shortening/oil; for example, one tablespoon plant material for two tablespoons shortening. Press the warm liquid through a strainer, then add to a jar and seal when cooled. The addition of some benzoin tincture or oil will preserve the ointment for several years.

Creams

These are readily absorbed by the skin, passing through the dermis to affect underlying tissues and eventually being absorbed by the body. It is essential that the plant materials you use are safe for application, and before general use it is sensible to dab a small amount on a small, innocuous area of the skin and check for allergies for twenty-four hours. Unlike ointments, an emulsifier is added to the recipe (in this case, borax) to cause water and oil to combine, thus creating a creamy, white substance.

To make:

- Place 1 cup fresh plant material or half a cup dried into 1 cup sweet almond oil or other high-grade oil of your choice in a double boiler.
- Heat for twenty minutes, then strain.

- Return the oil to the double boiler and melt two ounces pure beeswax into the infused oil.
- In a separate pan, heat one cup of water; do not boil.
- Dissolve two teaspoons of borax (sodium borate) in the water.
- Turn off the heat under both pans and slowly pour the water/borax into the oil, beating vigorously with a whisk. The combined liquids will emulsify, pale, and thicken.
- Quickly decant into clean, dark jars and seal when cool.
- Keep in a cool, dark place and ideally use within twelve months.

If you wish the cream to have a particular aroma, I suggest the addition of approximately twenty to thirty drops of an appropriate essential oil into the infused oil before combining.

Tincture

Steep one part fresh plant material in three parts of 100 proof grain alcohol; good vodka is perfect. For example, one eggcup plant material in three eggcups alcohol. Steep for at least 30 days but no more than 120 days in a sunlit position, and shake daily. Strain and bottle. These will keep indefinitely and can be used as components in floor washes, for anointing, or for taking internally if safe to do so.

Crane Bag (Medicine Pouch)

A crane bag, traditionally Irish Celtic, is a useful ally in Celtic magic whereby a selection of plant materials, wood, and other natural substances are placed within a specific fabric pouch that has been hand-fashioned and created for a particular need. These are essentially magical charms and can be carried about one's person or hung in the home.

Cold Infused Oil

These are ideal for anointing magical items or the body and can be easily prepared by steeping one part plant material in two parts good quality oil such as grape seed, sweet almond, etc. Allow to infuse in a sunlit position for a minimum of thirty days before straining and bottling. Keep in a cool, dark place.

Warm Infused Oil

These are a particular favorite of mine; they are versatile and will take on the aroma of the material used. I use an old slow cooker specifically designated for the creation of magical products. Slow cookers are perfect for applying controlled heat over a long period of time without fear of burning. Place two parts plant material to three parts oil and allow to heat in the slow cooker for twenty-four to forty-eight hours, depending on the strength of aroma required.

A tip: if you have a favorite incense, you can transform it into an oil with this technique. Your nose will tell you when the oil has taken on the properties of the material. Strain and bottle.

Essences

These do not contain any physical plant material; instead, they are created by imbuing clear spring water with the energy of the plant. This is an act of magic, where active imagination and visualization are required. Place a small amount of plant material onto a glass bowl or plate that sits atop a bowl of clear spring water or grain alcohol. Allow both moonlight and sunlight to pass through the plant material, thus imbuing the water with the energetic quality or essence of the plant without risk to health. After twenty-four hours have passed, bottle the liquid and label.

A Fresh Supply of Emergency Plants

A wonderfully effective way of ensuring you have access to fresh plants that may well be out of season is to gather them in your normal way and preserve their freshness by freezing. Place small quantities of chopped fresh plant material—enough to almost fill the cubes of an ice cube tray—then top up with water and freeze. Whenever you need them, pop out a cube and allow to melt.

Plant Divination

Using plants for divination is wonderfully simple and although it will consume a few hours of your time, they will last years if you look after them. Any plant can be used for this method. All you will require is raw plant material, some beeswax, and a mold. Casting raw material onto your divination surface is all very well but they don't tend to last awfully long, and frankly, it's just too untidy for my liking. Therefore, I invented a system where nine plants of your own choosing (depending on what you connect with the most) are set into wax "coins." A symbol or the name of the plant is carved into one side of the coin to aid identification, and that's it!

For this method, you will need something that will act as a mold—they don't need to be awfully big, perhaps an inch to an inch and a half in diameter. I found an ice cube tray that is round as opposed to cubic, and it works perfectly.

Melt some beeswax in a double boiler; three quarters of a cup is plenty for making nine small coins. Pour a thin layer of the melted wax into the mold and immediately lay a leaf or flower within it; repeat this nine times so that you will eventually have nine individual coins, each one containing a different plant. As soon as you have set the plant atop the wax, cover it with more melted wax. Allow them to cool thoroughly overnight until quite firm. Make sure you remember which is which, and mark them appropriately. The plants that I use for my set of coins all start with a different letter, so I have carved the first letter of each plant into one side of the coin. They are then ready for use.

Casting these together with the ogam staves and the animal bone oracle (in part 5) will give you another level of insight. The coins that I have currently in use and their attributions are as follows:

Sage: wisdom, immortality, longevity, wishes

Nettle: irritation, annoyance, fear, hidden gifts, unexpectedness

Betony: protection, love, sustainability, the ability to listen

Parsley: lust, attraction, cleansing, refreshes

Fennel: cleansing, clear vision, clarity, seeing the woods for the trees

Rosemary: rest, purification, prosperity, removes blockage

Vervain: magic, reconciliation, potential conflict, unknown influences

Mistletoe: healing, fertility, imagination, inspiration

Agrimony: purification, liberation, new beginnings, transformation

Keep the plant coins safely in a box with your other divination tools. See chapter 29 for an accompanying divination system.

◆ ◆ ◆

And so we lift our eyes from the ground and note the creatures that move upon its surface.

PART 5

By Bone, Tooth, and Claw

Celtic Animal Magic

◆ 27 ◆

The Magic of Animals

We are animals—social creatures who live in packs and protect our offspring and communities with fervor and might—and there are times when we act entirely on instinct. But generally we suppress the animalistic side of ourselves for the more civilized human aspect, one that functions well in polite society. But by connecting to the non-logical, instinctual aspect of the animal kingdom and acknowledging the animal instinct that exists as a part of our inherent nature, we move closer to understanding another facet of the natural world. The following chapters will explore the function of animal magic and lore in the Celtic tradition. Here I introduce you to some of the oldest animals of Celtic lore and explore the power of shapeshifting and animal totems. This section concludes with a Celtic bone oracle that will offer you a unique and effective method of divination reminiscent of ancient Celtica.

◆ ◆ ◆

We have looked at trees and their relevance to the Celts, and also to the plant kingdom, but now we cast our eyes towards our kin—our brothers, sisters, and cousins of the animal and insect world. There is a lot to learn here, and out Celtic ancestors had much to say about their interaction with the animal kingdom. Tales abound in the hundreds and mysteries are relayed as human beings are either transformed into animals or take on the shape and form (and, in some cases, the very nature) of animals. This is interesting, for it tells us that our Celtic ancestors believed that there were lessons to be learned from the animal world. And this wisdom continues to this day for us to look at, study, work with, and be transformed by.

The Celtic veneration of natural powers included those of the animal kingdom, and if we look to the artistic and archaeological record it appears that animals were revered, tended, and hunted and that the Celts admired these traits to such an extent that tribes took on the attributions of certain animals as heraldic or totemic symbols. Examples of animal hunting and veneration are evident in the cave art of prehistoric Europe, and although there are examples of trees and perhaps even plants, they primarily depict interaction between man and beast.

Animals, by means of their meat, ensured the survival of our species, which in itself naturally resulted in acts of veneration and spiritual awareness. In addition, members of the animal kingdom were assigned humanlike qualities, which would cause those qualities to "rub off" when we connected with the animal.

I touched on the significance of the horse earlier, particularly in relation to the Mare of Sovereignty and the goddess of the land, and although we can extrapolate a spiritual significance from this, it also has a deeply practical aspect. The horse enabled the people to tend the land with greater efficiency, increasing their ability to plough effective crop fields. The pig, while revered as a creature of the otherworld and a symbol of the initiate's journey from profane to sublime, also fed the people; a single pig would go a long way to ensure the survival of a family group during the winter months. Like many things within the Celtic cultural continuum, they invariably had a double meaning, and it is likely that the spiritual significance and attributions of trees, plants, and animals belonged more to the caste of priests, magicians, and soothsayers. Everything contained a hidden meaning, which the bards and traveling minstrels disseminated through the channel of innocent entertainment—which also targeted an audience of mystery students and practitioners, disseminating the latest teachings in a changing new world.[102]

While there is evidence to suggest that the Celts revered their animals and even perceived the connection between man and the animal kingdom by means of zoomorphic creatures, there are hardly any actual examples of practical magic associated with the animal world. Therefore, in order to work with the animals in a modern sense that is applicable to twenty-first-century Celtic magic, we must extrapolate meaning from the old mysteries. The previous two chapters, while offering a window of thought onto the manner by which we work with trees and plants, also offered practical, getting-down- and-dirty-with-nature techniques of applied magic. This chapter, by its very nature, is different, and the magic herein belongs almost exclusively to the world of visions and contemplation. Casting a sacrificed cat into your cauldron would be rather frowned upon and alert the attention of the authorities no doubt, but aligning ourselves to cat energy by sympathetic connection, either by means of amulets or shapeshifting, is perfectly appropriate. Where there is an absence of practical lore, it is perfectly permissible for the magician to fill the empty spaces by means of Awen. In ancient times this demonstrated and exemplified the magicians' abilities to connect to the archetypal realms and bring forth that inspiration.[103]

Animals in Celtic Myth

Animals feature heavily in Celtic mythology and legends, where they appear as guides, teachers, or indicators that something otherworldly is about to take place. Within the Mabinogi saga we encounter many animals that are white or have something extraordinary about the way they look. Their

102 Hughes, *From the Cauldron Born*, 15.

103 Parker, *The Four Branches of the Mabinogi*, 101.

appearance informs us that something unusual is about to occur, such as the white hounds of Arawn with their red-tipped ears in the first branch of the Mabinogi. Pwyll seems blissfully unaware that they are indicative of something extraordinary, but the reader is given a clue that the tale is about to take a sudden turn for the unexpected. We encounter a similar situation in the third branch of the Mabinogi, set some years into the future, where Pryderi, the beloved son of the horse goddess, is a young man; his father is dead; and his mother, Rhiannon, has married Manawydan, the son of Llŷr, brother to Brân and Branwen.

Another striking similarity occurs whereby Pryderi and Manawydan go hunting and prepare their dogs; later, the dogs rush into a copse of trees nearby, where they encounter a white wild boar who leads the party towards a fort that nobody has seen before. Against Manawydan's better judgement, Pryderi decides to follow the boar into the fort, and there he encounters a cauldron that is suspended from four golden chains. Upon touching the rim of the cauldron, he becomes mute and his feet become stuck to the spot. His mother, Rhiannon, in her worry goes in search of him, and she too touches the cauldron and loses the power of speech, her feet fixed to the ground. And then, with a clap of thunder and a blanket of mist, the fort and both mother and son vanish.

What is significant here is the occurrence of the white boar, which reiterates the common swine motif within the Mabinogi. Arawn gives Pryderi a herd of pigs as a gift, which Gwydion later tricks him to part with. It is a white sow that leads Gwydion to the foot of the Tree of Life in search of Lleu, and in the epic tale of Culhwch and Olwen, where we first meet Arthur and Mabon, the entire tale is centered on the capture of the Twrch Trwyth, who is a boar. We are informed throughout the legends that pigs, as a species, were a gift from Annwn and are not necessarily indigenous to our planet; they were symbols of food, with pork meat being one of the most sought-after foods for feasting. Their strength and speed made even wolves nervous, and as such they were respected and feared; the act of hunting the boar is captured in the tale of Culhwch and Olwen (incidentally, the name of the hero Culhwch means "slender or lean pig"[104]). Consequently the pig was a primary symbol of hunting and battle. Depictions of a boar can be seen on the plates of the Gundestrup cauldron, where one is attending the zoomorphic Cernunnos figure and another is seen on the helmet of a warrior on horseback. Representations of the boar and other sacred animals were frequently worn as amulets in the belief that some of the qualities or attributions of those animals would be passed on to the wearer; this practice is more than applicable for use by modern magicians.[105]

In subsequent centuries, the pig in Celtic mythology has been associated with the divine feminine and as a symbol of the great initiator. Cerridwen, in particular, has come to be symbolized as a pig goddess; however, there are no actual references to her having been in pig form, but her role as initiator and devourer of the profane can certainly be seen emulated in the function of the pig within Celtic mythology. What is significant to the function of magic is that each encounter with the pig leads to initiation:

- Arawn's gifting of swine to Pryderi initiates Pryderi into the mysteries as he assumes the role of his father.
- The stealing of pigs from the south heralds a set of animal-driven initiations in the fourth branch and also results in the death of Pryderi.
- Gwydion follows the sow to the Tree of Life where Lleu is summoned back by magic as the fully fledged initiate.

For the mind, body, and spirit to be fully knowing of mystery, a transformative initiation must take place, and it is the pig that embodies this. For the sublime to rise, the profane must be questioned, challenged, and ultimately transformed.

Human to animal transformations are prevalent throughout the myths, and we have already encountered some of these as we explored aspects of the Mabinogi legends. The mystery lies in understanding the hidden

104 Davies, *The Mabinogion*, 260.
105 Green, *The Gods of the Celts*, 155–171.

meaning of these transformations. In chapter 21 we explored the meaning of magical terminology in the old Celtic languages, such as *rith* (shape and form), *anyan* (nature), and the manner by which these are employed. There are instances where a human is transformed into an animal against his or her will, but there are also episodes that tell of willful transformation.

Read the third branch of the Mabinogi again, after Pryderi and Rhiannon have been abducted within the vanishing fort; Manawydan is faced with a series of disasters that affect his crop. The culprits are a band of mice; he quickly realizes that there is magic afoot and succeeds in capturing one of the slowest rodents. It transpires that the mouse is none other than the heavily pregnant wife of Llwyd, the perpetrator of the curse; strangely, she is also pregnant in her form as mouse, and the implication is that the transformation from woman to mouse was entirely voluntarily.

I have briefly touched upon the forceful or involuntary transformation of Gwydion and Gilfaethwy as punishment for the raping of Goewin, and also that of Lleu, who is transformed into an eagle. Each of these animals is indicative of mystery, and the manner by which it happens tells us something about the nature of what is going on, or what the tale is attempting to tell us on a subtle level. None of the animals are selected without thought, and many are typical of the common animal iconography of the Celts.

Animal Totems

You may be more than acquainted with the term *familiar,* and no doubt the image that it evokes will be of the stereotypical witch's cat; while I do not doubt that this contains an element of earlier mystery, it may also mislead us into assuming that a familiar is a pet that somehow assists our magic. In actuality, a totem or a familiar is so much more—they may well be allies in magic but they are not necessarily physical animals. In many instances a magician's animal ally may be a zoomorphic beast, such as Cernunnos (half animal, half human) or Blodeuwedd in her owl form. And while these may be representative of an aspect of humanity, they also express the wild nature of the animal kingdom, based on instinct and survival. Animals may well connect us to another facet of the natural world, but within the spectrum of magic they also have other zoomorphic aspects that represent further channels of mystery.

A totem can be perceived as a clan or family member where the animal is not deemed as "other" but instead is a valued member of that particular group; these creatures later may have become emblematic or heraldic symbols. This is not something that has fallen from use. We continue to have animals as part of our modern families; although the focus may have changed a little, our pets are members of the clan, and we invariably treat them as family.

On a magical level, a sympathetic connection to the animal kingdom is a valuable practice, and they can aid and give power to our magic. One of the most effective ways of doing this is to create amulets that have been empowered with connection and are subsequently worn about one's person. Small figures of boars, horses, and other animals have been discovered throughout northern Europe and seem to have been pendants that could be suspended to form a necklace.[106] While their actual function remains unclear, such figures—discovered in bogs, rivers, and other natural sites, together with hill carvings and metal art—likely had both spiritual and mundane functions.

By creating animal amulets, we create a sympathetic energetic link; it is by means of this relationship that the amulets cease to be mundane objects and become charged magical items. They can serve a multitude of functions, and the examples given here contain two specific aspects, the traditional attribution of the animal and also its zoomorphic counterpart. I introduced an aspect of this in the instructions for creating an amulet aligned to Rhiannon to be used for the assimilation of grief and bereavement; these amulets need not be restricted to a single attribute but can embody all functions of the animal and its zoomorphic counterpart.

The amulet itself can be formed from any material you choose. What is essential is that you are comfortable using it and it has a hole or loop attached

---

106 MacCulloch, *The Religion of the Ancient Celts*, 328–329.

to it for threading onto a cord. Bear in mind that there is no requirement for you to be a master craftsman. This is an act of magic; perform it as a ritual in ritual space. Practical magic should not be a chore, and there are allies that we can ally ourselves to if we struggle with confidence or just don't consider ourselves to be particularly crafty. The function of the amulets that you create may have several purposes: they may be emblematic of your group, grove, or coven; they may be created as spell-gifts for a friend or family member who could do with a little boost from that particular beast; they may be created to align yourself to the practice of shapeshifting or to introduce the quality of that animal as a component of your clan. You may have struck difficult times, and the comfort of having a supernatural ally that can imbue its qualities onto your situation may be all you need to get through it.

The symbol of the animal should sing to your spirit; the ones given here are mere examples. Ensure that you take to imagination and meditation to glean an understanding of the animal's quality and, if applicable to you, its zoomorphic attribution. Don't overcomplicate the initial connection. There is a simple technique for getting to know the animal—for example, if you chose to work with the energies of the stag…

MEDITATION

A STAG OF SEVEN TINES

Stop for a minute or two—take a breath with the land beneath you, breathe in the sky above you, and deeply breathe with the rhythm of the seas that surround the shores of your land. Sit comfortably, eyes gently closed, and bring to mind the animal that you would like to work with. Picture it in its natural setting; in this instance, it is a grove in the wildwood. Long shadows dance across the grassy floor. You emerge from the shade of the trees; the sunlight above you warms your face. In the opposite side of the grove a stag emerges. Hold this image; paint it with your imagination: what color is he, how tall are his antlers? Be aware of his presence and ask him to show you his nature—no need to be all mystical and spooky, just ask him to reveal himself to you. Tell him who you are—it's only polite—and be there in his company. Ask him to show you his world and how he interacts with it. Does he have a zoomorphic aspect? If so, ask if you can meet it; it may be in the guise of an antlered man or half stag, half human. Swim in blissful imagination in the company of the stag. When the vision starts to fade of its own volition, offer your thanks and return to the here and now. Have a cup of tea, do something mundane, and allow the vision to assimilate into your being before you analyze it.

Explore the animals in this manner. Note them in your journal and form a picture of their physical lives, any myths and folklore that are associated with them, and how their zoomorphic quality interacts with you. Examples of the most powerful and well-used Celtic animal amulets are as follows:

The Boar

As a magical device, a boar amulet will imbue the wearer with the qualities of leadership, the warrior spirit, and direction, strength, ability, sheer force, and speed. It is a useful animal when faced with new situations and initiations. The sacredness of the pig in ancient times was demonized by the new Christian faith as being dirty, slothlike, and lazy. In its zoomorphic sense it represents the qualities of the Twrch Trwyth, a king transformed into a boar, and the qualities of unrestrained wildness and instinct. The boar can also be perceived as an aspect of the Goddess in her guise as initiatrix.

The Stag

The stag epitomizes the wild spirit and the mysteries of the forest. In Celtic myth, it entices heroes into the otherworld and is often seen as a precursor to supernatural events. It symbolizes majesty, pride, independence, and purification. Its shedding of antlers associate it with the turning Wheel of the Year and with fertility and prosperity. Stags are wholly noble and majestic and represent monarchy and sovereignty. In a zoomorphic sense they are representative of man's connection to the animal kingdom in the various antlered gods of the Celts. In the fourth branch of the Mabinogi, Hyddwn, the hind offspring of Gwydion and Gilfaethwy, matures into a stag and is noted as one of the three champions of Britain.

The Wolf

The wolf may appear as a hostile and fierce predator, which belies its instinctive and well-mannered attributes. The wolf values family and community; it is cunning and highly intelligent. As a magical ally it is representative of the tribe and of learning and understanding the nature of the shadow. It is the perfect creature to align oneself to when a boost in study is required. In a zoomorphic sense it is associated with Bleiddwn, the wolf-cub offspring of Gwydion and Gilfaethwy.

The Horse

A primary symbol of the Celtic people and a representative of the Mare of Sovereignty and the goddess of the land, the horse is a powerful magical ally. They were revered as emblems of sexuality and fertility, as messengers, and as signs of economic strength and success. The war horse was a symbol of immense strength and power. The horse goddess in her guise as Rhiannon, Epona, and Rigantona are representative of the Celtic horse deity par excellence.[107] The horse goddess acts as protectress, but she is not immune from sufferance, and she symbolizes the manner by which we communicate with the goddess of the land.

◆ ◆ ◆

When you are ready to create your amulet, perform the triskelion ritual in chapter 5 and take to crafting. Recall the images and visions from your meditative encounter with the animal and project those impulses into the amulet as you create it. Create *englynion* that are appropriate for the quality of the animal you have chosen. Remain within the ritual space until the item is complete.

---

107 Green, *Gods of the Celts*, 162.

The Power of Shapeshifting

I must admit that when I initially found my path into Paganism and discovered the concept of shapeshifting, I was somewhat disappointed to discover that nobody could actually change their physical form into a toad or a badger or any other animal, for that matter. It took a while and some years of study to come to the realization that the shapeshifting accounts within the tales were expressing mysteries of the spirit, and that is when the magic of these encounters started to make sense to me. As it happens, shapeshifting is a reality in the magical world and a practice that any of us can do with a little study, devotion, and practice. We can learn a lot from the animal kingdom, and the shifting of the spirit's form into that of an animal is a common theme in Celtic myth.

In the tale of the birth of Taliesin, we encounter the following verse:

I have fled with vigor; I have fled as a frog,
I have fled in the semblance of a crow, scarcely finding rest,
I have fled as a wolf cub; I have fled as a wolf in the wilderness,
I have fled as a thrush of portending language,
I have fled as a fox, used to concurrent bounds of quirks,
I have fled as a martin, which did not avail,
I have fled as a squirrel that vainly hides,
I have fled as a stag's antler or ruddy course,
I have fled as a fierce bull bitterly fighting,
I have fled as a bristly boar seen in a ravine,
I have fled as white grain of pure wheat.[108]

Taliesin claims to have been all these things as well as numerous other animate and inanimate objects. It is tempting to assume that he is speaking of linear, or sequential, incarnations, but we must consider that the spirit is not bound to the limitations of linearity and temporality. Taliesin experiences these encounters, and by proxy of that he becomes them, albeit temporarily. In *The Life of Merlin: Vita Merlini*, he elaborates on this ability when he says:

108 Guest, *Mabinogion Legends*, 132.

> *I was taken outside of myself and I was as spirit, and I knew the acts of peoples past and was able to foresee the future. I knew the secrets of things and the flight of birds, the wandering motions of the stars and the way by which fish glide.*[109]

He knew the secrets of things, in particular the nature of certain animals, something which he reiterates in other poetry, and the key to this is that he was taken outside of himself and was as spirit. What is happening here is that Taliesin is not changing his form or shape; he is projecting his spirit into the form of targeted animals and other states of being, and as a consequence his spirit swims with the energy of that creature and he is able to experience the life of that animal and its secrets. This is the true nature of shapeshifting. Just as a shaman in some tribal cultures could cause his spirit to join that of an eagle in order to seek counsel, the shifting of shape should really be called the shifting of the spirit from one experience to that of another.

This is all very well, but does this have an actual practical function in modern Celtic magic? Yes, I believe it does, for it creates another bridge by which we become ultra-aware of our environment and the creatures and spirits that inhabit it. The act of shapeshifting causes us to appreciate and understand the nature of where we live and the manner by which other forms of life make up the song of that place. We can be a selfish animal; we tend to go about our business with little thought for what is around us; but the magic of Celtica teaches us to listen and be aware of everything that surrounds us, not as separate aspects but as parts of the whole.

To explore the function of shapeshifting, this exercise will require some study on your part. Read the Celtic myth of Culhwch and Olwen in its entirety (it is readily available online or in book form as part of the Mabinogi collection). You will have already been acquainted with Mabon, the son of Modron, and the fact that Arthur went in search of him, but in order to locate him he had to seek the help of the world's oldest animals. It is to these animals that we look for the mystery of shapeshifting; connecting to them will also facilitate a deeper understanding of the Mabon mystery.

109 Geoffrey of Monmouth, *The Life of Merlin: Vita Merlini*, 33.

The birds within this tale are recalled in the Triads of the Island of Britain as the "three elders of the world," and it seems likely that there existed a substantial body of lore relating to these animals and the wisdom they transmitted. This body of folklore can be seen mirrored in Irish and Scottish mythology, and the antiquity of the oldest animals motif can be seen in Indian and Persian myths.[110] There is much wisdom here; the sheer age and ancestry of these tales suggest that there is something relevant and important—so important, in fact, that they continue to mesmerize and baffle academics and visionaries to this day.

As visionary practitioners, we must look to Awen to fill in the gaps, to cause us to swim with the experience of the oldest animals, and we do this by the process of shapeshifting, of being beside ourselves and being as spirit and projecting that stream of consciousness and energy into the shape and form of the oldest animals. By doing so we are connecting to iconography and a body of lore that is hundreds, if not thousands, of years old. It is here within the hidden realms and by means of our subtle senses that we access the mystery teachings of these tales. Attempting to understand them by studying the words alone is futile; for the mysteries to be discovered, you must be outside of yourself and as spirit.

Within the tale we encounter five ancient animals:

- the blackbird of Cilgwri
- the stag of Rhedynfre
- the owl of Cwm Cawlwyd
- the eagle of Gwernabwy
- the salmon of Llyn Lliw

110 Bromwich, *Trioedd Ynys Prydein*, 235–237.

EXERCISE
MEETING THE OLDEST ANIMALS

The following exercise can be recorded onto an electronic device and played back to facilitate a guided pathworking journey.

Take to a comfortable chair; in a group setting, ensure that everyone is comfortable and capable of being relatively still for at least forty minutes.

Breathe deeply to the beat of the land.

Breathe deeply to the rhythm of the seas.

Breathe deeply with the breath of sky.

Focus entirely on your breathing for several minutes, slowing the body down; focus your mind on each limb and tell to it relax and let go of the day. As your body slows to the rhythm of your breath, begin your meditation.

◆ ◆ ◆

You stand on a peninsula; an ancient forest thins to reach the seashore. There is a clearing in the wood; within it is a small stone platform, and upon it sits a tiny marble of what appears to be iron. The delightful song of a blackbird draws your attention to the nearest tree, whose lowest branch holds the form of a blackbird. It looks deep into your spirit. You offer it a greeting and nod your head to acknowledge it. Now send your spirit towards the blackbird—in a flash, sense what it sees from its vantage point; imagine looking back at yourself from the form of the bird.

Sense the age of the bird and the following mystery. The stone platform held an anvil, black and heavy. See the sun setting in the west, hear the sound of the ocean, and feel the bird alighting from the tree to land on the side of the anvil. The bird bends its head and rubs its beak against the anvil. Sense the longevity of the bird and the wisdom of its spirit as it watches the passage of time and alights onto the anvil and rubs its beak against it each evening. Over millennia it erodes the iron, and the anvil grows smaller and smaller until nothing more remains than a small iron nut. At this point, sense the spirit of the blackbird swimming with yours and ask it questions that are pertinent to your journey; what mystery and wisdom can the blackbird relay to you and your experience? Through the eyes of the blackbird you see a band of men approach. Now leave the body of the blackbird, thanking it as you do.

Take your place amongst the men. You turn to look at the bird, who utters these words:

> *"I know nothing of the man you ask; however, what is right and proper for me to do for Arthur's messengers, I will do. There is a species of animal that was shaped before me. Go there; let him be your guide."*

A mist descends on the peninsula, and as it clears you see a fern-covered hill. Walking gracefully through the tall fern is the form of a stag. It walks steadily towards you; the morning air is cold, and his breath is visible as he exhales. You send him a greeting and extend your spirit towards him, and he accepts you with the wisdom of ages. Suddenly you see yourself through the eyes of the stag—you *are* the stag. What is this world that the stag inhabits? Where is this place, and what wonders has the stag seen? You turn in the guise of the stag and notice a small red stump on the ground; the mists of time rush towards you, and you see in its place a mighty oak. The stag takes to his antlers and rubs them against the tree. And time moves forward, and with each rubbing the oak grows ever smaller until nothing remains but a small stump. At this point, sense the spirit of the stag swimming with yours and ask it questions that are pertinent to your journey; what mystery and wisdom can the stag relay to you and your experience?

The stag turns and sees a band of men approaching through the mist. With a blessing, your spirit leaves the stag and appears beside the men. As you take your place amongst them, the stag opens his mouth and utters these words:

> *"I know nothing of the man you seek; however, since you are Arthur's messengers, I shall be your guide and send you to another who was shaped before me."*

The mists rush towards you, and the stag and the fern-covered hill vanish. You find yourself on a hillock overlooking a large, lush, green valley; you sense the rivers running through the trees and the lives of a million creatures. A hoot from behind you takes your attention; you turn to see the shape of the owl of Cwm Cawlwyd before you on a branch of oak. He nods at your greeting, and your spirit rushes towards him; with a dizzying turn, your view changes and you see yourself and the vast valley behind you through the eyes of the owl. The sun runs backwards and the moon rises, darkness becomes light, and you sense the backward turning of thousands of years.

The forest groans as you watch a band of men destroy it; bark cracks and the smell of burning wood reaches you. The sun rises and the moon sets and the wood is destroyed. But on your branch outside of time you watch as saplings grow and a new forest emerges, but again the men come and destroy it. A third time the forest regrows. At this point, sense the spirit of the owl swimming with yours and ask it questions that are pertinent to your journey; what mystery and wisdom can the owl relay to you and your experience? From the woods to your left, a band of men appear and offer you a greeting; you sense them to be Arthur's messengers and leave the form of the owl. As you take your usual form, you turn just as the owl opens its beak and utters:

> *"I know nothing of the man that you seek, but I shall be your guide to meet the oldest animal in the world and the one who has wondered the most."*

As the mists descend, your form moves from one place to another, and as they lift they reveal an alder tree, in whose branches is held the form of an eagle. You offer it a greeting, and your spirit is taken outside of yourself. See what the eagle sees, hear what the eagle hears, and as it takes to the wing, flying over your human form, you sense the wisdom of ages. In the form of eagle you alight onto a rock, and from here you attempt to pick at the stars, but the sun rises and sets, and the moon shines her face, over and over, and with each setting and rising the rock grows ever smaller. At this point, sense the spirit of the eagle swimming with yours and ask it questions that are pertinent to your journey; what mystery and wisdom can the eagle relay to you and your experience? You take to the wing, and beneath you a movement catches your eye: a salmon sleekly swimming through a narrow creek. You descend, sensing the rush of air and the hunger and instinct of eagle. Your claws pierce the back of the salmon, but lo! He will not come easily. Instead, you are pulled beneath the surface and the mighty salmon takes you deeper, threatening to drown you; your talons retreat, and you make for the surface. As you land breathless near the riverbank, a band of men appear from the trees and summon your spirit from the form of eagle, who says:

> *"I know nothing of the man you seek, but I know of one who may; he is the salmon of Llyn Lliw."*

The salmon appears at the surface and stares at you; you feel your spirit tugging at the edges of your body, and suddenly it rushes towards the form of salmon. You take its shape and rush through the waters; swimming quickly, you sense the floodwaters around you growing stronger, inundating the land, and as your head in salmon form breaks the water's surface you hear the most dreadful cries—stout walls ahead of you conceal the lamenting and moaning of Mabon, the son of Modron. Sense the spirit of the salmon swimming with yours, and ask it questions that are pertinent to your journey; what mystery and wisdom can the salmon relay to you and your experience?

Your form swells, and you sense the approach of Arthur's men. As they leap from the riverbank to alight on your back, your spirit is propelled from the shape of salmon and soars into the piercing blue skies; beneath you the cries of Mabon rise to meet the spirits of sky.

The mists envelop you, and as they do your body becomes denser, limbs relaxed, and you sense the chair against your back. From the center of your being send a greeting to the blackbird, the stag, the owl, the eagle, and the salmon. Return.

◆ ◆ ◆

Stretch, move a little, have a bite to eat, do something mundane, and think no more of it. Take to your bed as usual, and on the next day recall your impressions of your journey into the form of the oldest animals.

Part 5

A Cloak of Feathers

We encountered Blodeuedd in the previous chapter, but now we strive to call her in the form of an owl and the magical attributions of that enigmatic and mysterious bird. At the culmination of the fourth branch of the Mabinogi, Gwydion strikes Blodeuedd with his wand, cursing her to change her form and shape, and thus she is renamed Blodeuwedd. She became the first of her kind, and all subsequent owls would be cursed to the night and be scorned by all other birds. Now while this may appear somewhat harsh on the surface, we cannot take it at face value, for it represents a deeper mystery. Blodeuedd was a maiden made of flowers and turned into the shape of a human being, yet she possessed the inherent uncontrollable powers of nature that just wanted to express its own inherent nature. Finally, she is returned to the wild in the guise of the owl.

In her cloak of feathers she has become synonymous with ancient wisdom, the secrets of the night, and of shadow and potential; she heralds transitions and acts as a conduit for messages relayed from the subtle realms. She is extremely cunning and stealthy and is the epitome of instinctive intelligence. All of these attributes are held within her form; she is the owl goddess, and her cloak of feathers connects us to the wondrous world of the owl.

The cloak of feathers in itself is a typical symbol of Celtic mysticism and magic, and yet there is no evidence to suggest that it existed in ancient times; motion pictures and later legends have immortalized the concept, and it has become a familiar and well-loved notion of Celtic magic. But there is merit and validity here, for to create your own cloak of feathers is to participate in a ritual that has all the signs and feeling of being Celtic while simultaneously causing one to move closer to the bird kingdom, developing relationships with our winged cousins. This ritual will help you construct such an item.

We live in a want-it-now society where even spirituality can be purchased; we want spells that can secure that flashy car, we want it NOW! Why should we have to wait? Cerridwen had to wait—in fact, she had to work hard for just over a year, toiling and tending the cauldron; it was an act of devotion and deep commitment to her craft, and without it the cauldron would not boil the essence of Awen. Sometimes magic and the crafting of magic needs to take time; we need to be fully there and present at every turn, working towards a goal that we have set in mind, worked on, and committed time and effort to achieve. And while a cloak of feathers is not an essential requirement in Celtic magic, it is a rather wonderful manner of connection and the perfect tool for working animal magic.

To create a cloak of feathers, you will need:

- 1 plain cotton cloak of any color
- a range of feathers
- a strong steel needle (a darning needle works well)
- cotton thread

Your cloak may take you six months to create or it may take ten years—the time it takes will reflect the manner by which you connect to the kingdom of birds and develop your own ability to practice augury, divination by studying the movements of birds.

You will need to find as many feathers as possible, and bear in mind that you will need a *lot* of feathers, perhaps over a thousand or more. They can come from any source as long as is responsible; however, do consult your own local laws regarding the possession of feathers. Feathers can invariably be found as a result of death, road kill, accidents, natural causes, or hunting for the purpose of food. What is important is that wherever the feathers come from, take it as a sign of that bird's message and attributions. If you don't know which species it came from, find out: look it up. Learn about the birds and their symbolism.

As you collect the feathers, keep them in a safe place, and then periodically, as the moon turns her face to darkness, take to stitching the feathers onto your cloak. The most effective form of a feathery cloak is to make a cape of feathers that covers the shoulders and extends to the middle of your back, this will still require several hundred feathers, but its effect is striking. Stitch a feather in place securely by pushing a needle and thread through the quill and into the fabric; there is no right or wrong way of doing this, but by piercing the quill a few times it will ensure a good grip. However, be careful that you do not over-pierce the quill and consequently weaken it. If you start from the top of the cloak, you will need to start the second layer of feathers underneath the first layer, which will pull back and out of the way easily. Stitch the second layer of feathers starting from halfway down the first layer; this will eventually result in a rather lovely layered effect.

As you stitch, call to the owl goddess:

Flower-face goddess, to thee I sing
Shame of eagle, Gronw's delight
To my cloak of feathers bring
Wisdom and secrets of the night.

Return your cloak to a safe place until it is complete. Finally, when you are happy with its progress, read the fourth branch of the Mabinogi and acquaint yourself fully with Blodeuwedd, then take to your visions...

With a breath from the land, and one with sky and another with sea, imagine a stout branch beneath your feet. In place of your eyes, two blooming flowers form the shape of an owl's face; your human form loses shape, and as you cast the cloak of feathers about your shoulders, you become the owl and the spirit of Blodeuwedd floods your being. What does it feel to be human-turned-bird; what mystery does she transmit? Imagine being the woman of flowers turned into a bird, and sit in your cloak of feathers imbued with the wisdom and magic of Blodeuwedd.

Bee Magic

It is easy to fall into the assumption that only the grandest animals most replete with Celtic heraldic symbology are the ones worthy of examination, but when we consider that the most revered of birds was the smallest—the wren—perhaps we must also look to the miniature world of the insects for further teachings of mystery and magic. There is an ancient adage that says we should "ask the wild bee what the Druids knew." Where this phrase came from is wrapped in mystery, and yet it points at a greater mystery and connects them to the priests of the ancient Celtic world. Bees were sacred insects in almost all civilizations and societies, famed for their honey, a rich carbohydrate that ensured nourishment during the cold months. Mead—fermented honey, probably the world's first alcoholic beverage—was famed to be fit for the gods, and the old Celtic term for being intoxicated was and continues to be *meddwi*, to have had too much mead!

Bees live complex lives and have powerful methods of communication; they utilize pheromones and intricate vibration dances to relay information that can accurately pinpoint the location of a flower to within feet. They act as individuals but never at the cost of the hive, where upon entry they lose their identity as a single insect and become an aspect of the collective mind. Man's relationship with bees is as long as our need for sweetness and light, and probably stems back to the dawning of our species. They are abundant in metaphysical significance and were considered to be messengers of the gods and were believed to carry the souls of the dead to the borders of the otherworld. On a practical level, bees and their keeping and observation align us with powerful seasonal energies, for the bees react to the seasons in a manner that most of us cannot. We can learn much by watching the bees and attempting to understand the singular nature of the hive's mind.

It is thought that the bees take a particular interest in human affairs, and it is therefore considered expedient to inform them of certain occurrences. It has been a custom in Celtic lands to inform the bees of a death in the family, and not necessarily the domestic hive; to inform the wild bee is equally customary. If this was neglected, it was thought that another death would soon follow the first. In many parts of Wales it was usual for the hive to be turned around so that the entrance did not face the funeral procession. The bee hive would often be placed in mourning after a death by placing a small black ribbon onto a stick and inserting it into the hive's roof.[111]

The month in which the bees swarm is considered of greatest importance, and this makes perfect sense, for the sooner they swarm, the longer their summer and therefore the greater the quantity of honey. A late swarm cannot gather honey and may well suffer. This belief has found its expression in the following verse:

---

111 Owen, *Welsh Folklore*, 337–340.

A swarm of bees in May
Is worth a load of hay
A swarm of bees in June
Is worth a silver spoon
A swarm of bees in July
Is not worth a fly.[112]

It is, however, considered very fortuitous to find a strange swarm of bees in the garden or a tree belonging to your property. However, stolen bees are considered unlikely to produce honey.

EXERCISE
A MEDIEVAL CELTIC BEE SPELL

From finest clay make the form
Of three small bees, stout and strong
Within a bag now should you place
And heed these words of grace
These three bees within this bag
Will bring you all you need
Health, wealth, and sweet happiness
Is where you will succeed
So hang them high within your home
Near window and front door
Place within your brightest room
So you should want no more.[113]

112 Owen, *Welsh Folklore*, 338.
113 *Englyn* written by me.

28

The Celtic Bone Oracle

Within my own personal practice I utilize four different divination tools: the ogam, the plant oracle, the tarot, and the bone oracle. The tarot stands apart as an entirely different system based within a particular cultural frame, that of the Western Mystery Tradition and the Cabala. However, of all the systems I use, the bone oracle is my favorite. The oracle itself is quite simple, for it consists of nine bones from nine different animals and is used in conjunction with the glyph divination sytem in chapter 29, but the beauty of it lies in the fact that as a system it must be worked with quite intensely. The ogam can be purchased or made, the plant oracle is rather easy to make, but the process of finding various bones to construct an oracle is rather time consuming—and then there is the question of whether or not you can find the bones of an animal that you are particularly drawn to working with.

The bone oracle works on two precise and important levels. Firstly, the bones contain an echo of the life of that animal; an energetic residue remains within the fabric of bone. This in itself will contain an echo of the life story of that animal, and if you are well practiced in the art of psychometry—the occult science of sensing impressions and information from objects—you will be more than capable of discerning data from the bones. Secondly, it will require you to get to know the animal and its living kin, and by proxy of this you will develop associations that you will utilize as qualities to represent the human condition in your readings.

You may approach this oracle with particular animals in mind, and herein lies further magic—for the chances of that actually happening is slim unless you have a collection of dead animals nearby! The bones will normally present themselves to you when you least expect it; for instance, one of the bones in my oracle is a porpoise, and although they are not rare in the waters of Anglesey, I had never seen a dead one until a cold winter's day where I came across one fully decomposed on the beach.

I sat with the bones for a while and caught a sense of its life and its death. I took a piece of its vertebrae home with me, and it is now a valued member of my oracle. The other was that of a hare who had met its death on the path to Wayland's Smithy and someone had placed its body in the hedgerow to return to nature. A small plastic bag was caught in the wind ahead of me, and it flew headlong into the hedge; I was annoyed, I hate litter, I went to pick it up and was faced with the skeleton of the hare. She and her attributes joined the growing oracle.

The bone oracle is imbued with attributes from the life of an animal but also with the environment where you found it, for it interacted with the world in its own unique manner, and this will have transferred into the fabric of its physical body, an echo of which will have been retained by its skeleton. As far as is possible, ensure that the animal has died naturally, which also includes predation. I would also encourage you to consult your local laws and any restrictions concerning the possession of bones. Look to the natural world and to natural processes. A rat that has been caught by a hawk, half eaten, and tumbled from a nest to decompose at the foot of a tree is fine, whereas bludgeoning a rat to death to retrieve a bone is neither honorable nor civil.

Nine bones are all that is required to create your oracle. Ensure that the bones are clean and that no organic material remains. With a permanent marker or paint, mark a small, inconspicuous area of the bone with a symbol or letter to denote which animal it belongs to; believe me, to begin with you may not be familiar enough to define which is which. However, this will develop with time and use, and you will become less reliant on having to catch a glimpse of the symbol to determine which is which. When your oracle is complete, spend time with them, experiment with them, cast readings for yourself and your friends, and get to know them as a collective tool. Keep them wrapped in fabric and safely held within a box.

I am a hater of endless correspondence lists, so to give you a flavor of a bone oracle I will share mine with you. I have been using this particular set of bones for around nine years now, but I hasten to add that it took some time for me to decide on the right combination; this one feels good to me and I am comfortable with it. All in all I had thirteen bones; after much contemplation and meditation I whittled them down to nine, eliminating the bones that I did not particularly connect to.

Rabbit

The rabbit is a natural creature of the underworld. It spends the majority of its time underground and consequently takes on that liminality. It is easily unnerved and quite anxious in the upper world, yet it is aware of its necessity; it is a risk taker. It can be prone to promiscuity and flirting and therefore is associated with fertility and sexual expression, although this may well be exaggerated. It is quick to take action and yet can be slow on the uptake; it startles easily. The rabbit is undeniably faithful, with strong nurturing instincts.

To find the bone of rabbit in a reading indicates that the seeker may be conceiving new ideas and must hold them in the heart and mind with calmness. It may indicate a new beginning or the fact that risks are needed to ensure that the required outcome is achieved, and yet it is important to be calculated lest one is startled into acting against instinct.

Porpoise

This cetacean dweller of the sea may appear secretive and shy and come across as aloof or standoffish; the porpoise is a small, subtle creature of immense poise and beauty. It is a family-centered creature whose sense of community is a vital aspect of its nature. It is the epitome of emotional connections and relationships; however, casting the porpoise—particularly into the realm of sky—may indicate that the seeker is prone to extremes of emotion without applying equal amounts of logic. The lesson of porpoise is to inform us of balanced emotions; a little heart and a little head in equal quantities, never too much of one. The porpoise is a creature of balance and walks the knife's edge between emotional opposites, yet its lesson is clear: the opposite of our most revered emotion, love, is not hate but rather indifference.

The casting of the porpoise is indicative of deep emotional issues. It is poised between land and sea, sandwiched, and sometimes the pressure from either can be too much, causing extreme reactions or indifference. The lesson of porpoise is to be in tune with one's emotions.

Deer

The deer is a land-based creature and yet it shares a liminal quality with the rabbit in that it is drawn to liminal places and often heralds interaction with otherworldly events. The lesson of deer is to be kind to others and be aware of your own inner majesty and serenity. The deer is a graceful creature that walks softly into our consciousness, bestowing a quality of gentle reassurance. Deer are reminders of spiritual evolution and the patience required to allow our spiritual unfolding. The deer is patient and mysterious; its teachings tell us to wait, to not rush headlong into situations that may be to our detriment. Although gracefully majestic and seemingly confident, they can be nervous and easily spooked; situations and places that are new may cause them undue distress and spark irrational fears and worry. They are good actors and can be akin to the graceful swan, gliding serenely on the surface yet peddling like fury beneath the water. Deer tend to shy away from crowds and large gatherings, sometimes to their detriment, and they may appear aloof as a consequence or come across as too sure of themselves.

Drawing the bone of deer implies that we need to take note of how we are presenting ourselves to the world and what our inner majestic qualities are; are we sometimes being too hard on ourselves, and do we occasionally judge others harshly? Deer is indicative of being aware of where we are and how we are interacting with the people who inhabit our world.

Hare

The hare is divinely feminine; she is the lover of the moon and is commonly depicted as the moon gazer. She exudes magic and serenity, and to cast the bone of hare is a sure sign that the subtle is being brought into focus. The hare has a delicious gracefulness and yet immense inner strength and determination; she represents our psychic abilities and our spiritual aspect. She is the epitome of mystery and its realization. She is curious, self-driven, and intuitive. The lesson of hare is that we must listen to our gut feelings, to instinct and intuition, and act upon them, trusting that all will be well. To cast the bone of hare is to bring into focus our spiritual path and journey and our abilities to perceive, utilize, and express the subtle.

Raven

In a mythological sense the raven straddles the realms of sky and sea. It takes to the wing as a creature of the sky yet is symbolically connected to the children of Llŷr and the gods of the sea. This imbues the raven with incredible and insightful qualities. It is an immensely sociable creature and will often be seen in large groups; there is an extrovert nature to the folk who cast the raven, particularly if it lands on the realm of land. The raven is indicative of supreme intelligence, and its opportunistic nature ensures that it rarely misses out on anything, but this also implies that it can be easily overwhelmed and exhausted. There is no malice to the raven, but to those folk who are naturally introverted the raven can appear cocky and overconfident. To cast the raven in a reading implies that the qualities of protection, self-realization, self-knowledge, confidence, and stamina are coming to the fore and need particular attention.

Cat

The cat is a purely sensual creature and the epitome of acute perception and intuition. It is cunning and can appear sly and calculated, yet it has no malice. It can be self-centered but only because it knows that there is something inherently special about itself. The cat is quick of wit and mind and has a pouncing intellect; it does not take any prisoners. If the bone of cat is cast in a reading, it indicates that there are situations that require the seeker to have their wits about them and to be able to have new perspectives in order to deal with fresh and possibly challenging situations. It implies that the seeker should be using their kindness and humanitarian qualities in the situation at hand. It may also indicate that regardless of another person's best interests, their actions may not have your best intentions at heart. Cat also calls the seeker to question whether they have someone else's best interest at their hearts. The cat may indicate that the seeker is apt to self-righteous behavior, and no matter how justified it is, first impressions count; be careful not to come across as self-opinionated and arrogant.

Hedgehog

This little prickly creature is representative of the earth and its qualities of security, surety, and stability. Its belly rubs against the ground, against mother earth; it is a creature that embodies sustenance and particularly the home. To draw the hedgehog is to be focused on your domestic situation and issues thereof. The hedgehog also has hidden talents, and although it can be highly skilled it can also appear clumsy, overprotective, and too defensive for its own good. It is prickly and easy to temper, and yet it is not an aggressive creature. If one is injured by the hedgehog it's because we got too close to it. This bone represents your personal space and the manner by which you defend it; it represents all those things that you hold dear in the material world, and issues regarding family and work are all part and parcel of the life of hedgehog.

Rat

This member of the rodent family is perhaps the most reviled creature to walk the earth; the mere sight of a rat can cause most people to shriek, but why? The rat is an extremely devoted creature and makes an excellent parent; it is highly industrious and demonstrates ingenuity when faced with problems. The rat is necessary: it cleans up other people's messes and utilizes those castoffs as resources for its own benefit. It is immune to many of humanity's diseases and afflictions and is highly resilient. It will survive and thrive in any given environment. The rat is an indication that certain situations need to be dealt with efficiently and quickly; the seeker may need to employ their cunning and take advantage of any offers that may be coming their way—they may be highly rewarding. The rat is lovable and yet it naturally repels; this may indicate that the seeker is projecting an image that is repellent or antagonistic and may be exacerbating the problems that they seek clarity for.

Wild Boar

To cast the bone or fossilized tooth of a boar or pig is to connect the seeker with the present and the landscape of their lives and of their ancestors. It implies that the situation being questioned is best dealt with cautiously, and yet the drawing of the boar implies that the seeker's immediate reaction is to rush headlong into the situation, with little thought. Employing the strength and stamina of the boar is fine, but bear in mind that the boar does so with little thought of consequence or recourse. Questions of doubting one's abilities are raised here, as well as issues of being overprotective.

What will *your* bone oracle consist of?

◆ ◆ ◆

Having explored the ogam, plant, and bone oracles, the following part will provide you with a unique system of casting that is rooted in the Celtic tradition.

PART 6

The Islands of Annwn

A Celtic Divination System

• 29 •

The Forts of Truth

Divination is a meta-language—it is a method that we employ in service to our communities whereby we seek the assistance of nature to divine the present and the shades of future events. The systems of divination that were presented to you in the previous chapters—namely, the ogam, plant, and bone oracles—must not be seen as methods of "fortunetelling"; on the contrary, they serve a deeper purpose. Any magician worth his or her own weight is in service to the tribe, and this will naturally include offering counselling and advice, whereby members of the community may seek us out to help them at times when things in their lives are challenging or difficult; others may need clarity, a little encouragement, or a push in the right direction—and sometimes it is difficult to see the woods for the trees. This is when the diviner comes into play. By being impartial we are able to see the wood in the trees. Being outside of a given situation and in tune with the tools of our magic provides us with the ability to help those who seek us out.

There may be times when we ourselves need a little assistance, and by working with oracles and divination tools we employ connection and the use of subtle language to connect to the spirit and to the gods and demigods of Celtica by means of tree, plant, or animal magic.

The unique system of divination I present to you here has been in use for a number of years; it has not been "invented" for the purpose of this book or just for the sake of appearing different. It differs from other divination systems in that its effectiveness is entirely dependent on your connection and experience of the attributions and symbols held within it. The glyph on the facing page arises entirely from the Celtic cultural continuum and offers you a method for casting your tools. Simply throwing a handful of ogam staves onto the ground or onto a tabletop is all well and good, but for it to be effective one needs a point of reference; the following glyph will provide you with this.[114]

The glyph is based on a journey in search of the cauldron through the island forts of Annwn as presented in the Book of Taliesin poem "The Spoils of Annwn." In it we witness the perilous adventures of Arthur, his warriors, and Taliesin as they encounter seven challenging forts in the seas of Annwn. In my book *From the Cauldron Born*, I briefly described this journey and offered an interpretation of the forts and their qualities.[115] The journey through Annwn is indicative of the initiate's quest through regions of the self, and each fort (or *caer* in the original language) is representative of the human condition—our coping mechanisms and how they influence and affect our lives. By connecting to these themes and to the symbols created for the individual forts, we are accessing a known storehouse of ancient wisdom and descending into the fabric of mind, body, and spirit in unison. This is the practical act of bringing forth inspiration from the deep, emulating the words uttered in the primary ritual: "The Awen I sing, from the deep I bring it."

And so to the glyph itself—you will note that it is composed of eight divisions, seven of which correspond directly to one of the seven forts of Annwn. The eighth division represents Caer Pedryfan, of which no actual

114 Glyph by Taryn Shrigley, www.taryn-shrigley.co.uk.

115 Hughes, *From the Cauldron Born*, 74–81.

Forts, clockwise from top one o'clock position, and what they govern: Feddwit (communication, thyroid, intoxication), Pedryfan (vitality, immune system, protection), Goludd (passion, pancreas, emotion), Wydr (predestined, thymus, ancestors), Rigor (impulse, adrenals, rigidity), Ochren (reflection, pineal, perception), Vandwy (power, ovaries/testes, creation), and Siddi (illusion, pituitary, control)

journey is made to; it represents the place of being, your current location. The divisions arise from a central black sphere that represents the potentiality of Annwn; as they radiate outwards, they are subdivided into three sections, each one representing from the center to the outward edge the realms of land, sea, and sky.

The sigils of the forts, which are included in the following *caer* descriptions, can also be utilized as visionary meditative tools and are not restricted to divination alone—they may be drawn on cards, stones, etc. Focusing the mind on the sigils will allow you to access the attributes and wisdom of each fort in a manner that is purely visionary. They may also be painted or traced on the body for healing purposes in oils or by using minerals, with each sigil corresponding to one of the seven endocrine glands.

In a divinatory sense, the tools of divination—i.e., ogam, the plant and bone oracles, or indeed all three—would be cast onto the glyph drawn on paper, cloth, or another smooth surface; I find that wallpaper lining offers a cheap and effectively large area for the glyph to be drawn on. However, taking the time and effort to create a casting cloth or mat by your own creative means is immensely rewarding.

The position in which the divination tools fall provides the reading. If one or more divisions are empty—if a divinatory tool does not fall on it—that division is disregarded in the reading. If a tool falls beyond the edge of the glyph, it too is disregarded. But if a tool lands in, for example, the sky and land realms of Caer Wydr, one would also take note of the empty realm, sea, in that its quality may be required to resolve or bring clarity to the situation at hand.

The realms represent the following attributions:

Land: physicality, the present, here and now, material affairs

Sea: emotions, passion, vocations, fluidity, movement

Sky: aspirations, un-manifest, concepts in motion without form, spirituality

Annwn: potentiality, the seed of movement, concepts and ideas, the unknown

Depending on what divinatory tool falls within each realm, the above interact with the fort divisions, giving further depth and meaning to your readings, based entirely on the Celtic cultural continuum. The fort sigils and their attributes are as follows:

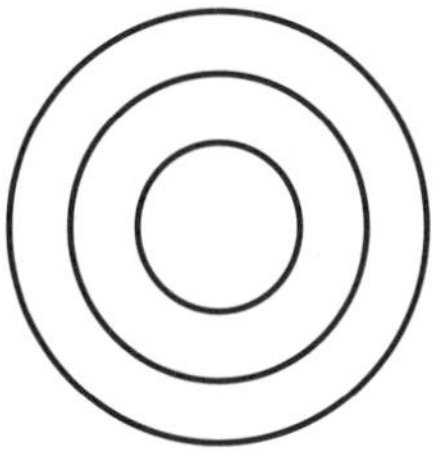

Caer Siddi: The Fort of the Mound

Three flaming circles of illusion surround the fort. It equates to the pituitary gland of the human body.

Attributions

This is our assumed earthly state, the point from where we make our initial assessment of the world around us, even if our view is obscured or clouded by judgement or preconception. It is the place of illusion, for it will do anything within its power to retain the status quo. Its purpose is to remain steadfast and keep us in the illusion that it knows best. It is the seat of influence, and its power has the ability to convince all the forts beneath it that it is the only truth. It is extremely convincing and can lock us into habitual patterns of repetition. Our clarity of mind comes from this place; we may be imprisoned here and held by the heavy chains of illusion, but to acknowledge its illusionary nature is to lessen its power over us, thus allowing it to become the place of the fire in the head. Its dictatorlike quality is not one gained from malice but one that simply strives to keep everything just as they are. It is simultaneously protective and restrictive.

A divinatory tool that falls within this division represents the status quo, what is illusionary or habitual. This is the place that we know the best, and, however illusionary, we may be secure in our insecurities and will do anything to prevent its walls from crumbling. If the bone of rat were to fall onto the sky realm of Caer Siddi in a reading where the question was in relation to clarity within relationships, it would imply that the person concerned, while extremely devoted, may have their own intangible reasons for taking advantage of the situation and perhaps of the querent to maintain the status quo. It would imply that the emotional and physical needs of the person involved may be cloudy, undefined—they may have lost their way and, believing themselves to be doing what is best, their actions may come across as sly or cunning.

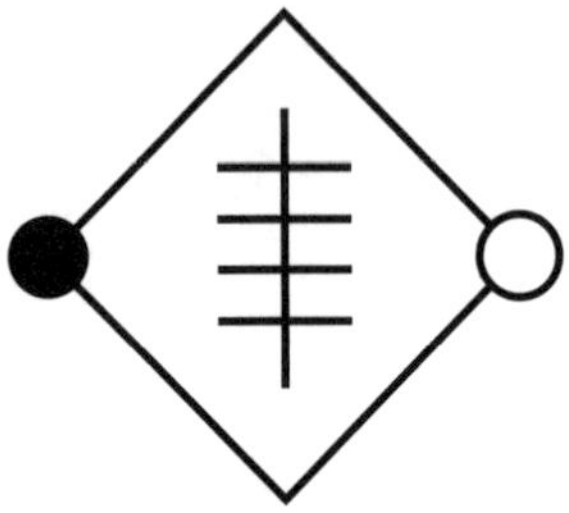

Caer Feddwit: The Fort of Mead Intoxication

The ogam symbol for poplar (aspen), the tree of insight, expression, and communication, is captured within the square of Caer Pedryfan, the place of being. The dark and full moon sit on either side to display the polarity of our own ability to express and communicate. It equates to the thyroid and parathyroid glands of the human endocrine system.

Attributions

This is the place of communication and the manner by which we express ourselves outwardly to the world, and by proxy the way which we interact and engage with it. Our words can soothe and bring pleasure, comfort, and encouragement; they can also cripple and destroy. Caer Feddwit's qualities are those of nourishment and sustenance; it is the place where we express our inner environment. It is how we present ourselves vocally and affect the world around us by the action of words. Speech can nourish, but it can also poison; its effect on the world around us and on our own internal physiological environment can be profoundly affecting. What sustains us can also poison us. Everything that we find pleasurable and intoxicating in life is expressed through this fortification.

A divinatory tool that falls onto this division is indicative of our communicative position and the manner in which we wish to be perceived. This is the place of expression and our ability to nourish ourselves and others. If, for example, nettle fell onto the land realm of Caer Feddwit and the ogam stave for bramble fell in the realm of sea, it would demonstrate that the situation the querent is facing is causing them some annoyance, and this irritation may well be arising from too much emotional connection; distance may be needed. A touch of sky is required in order to allow the querent to objectively look inwards to discover the reason why the situation is annoying them so much.

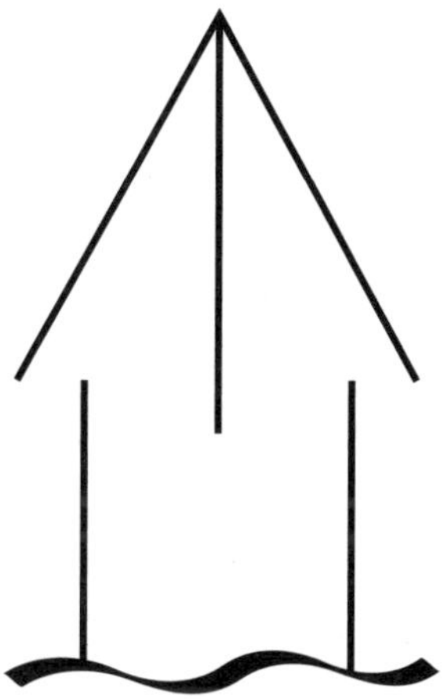

Caer Goludd: The Fort of Impediment

The threshold between the worlds, liminality; an arrow points up from the pillars of land and sky that sit atop the sea. It points to gain, growth, and riches, and it is also representative of Awen shining with passion and inspiration. It equates to the endocrine function of the pancreas.

Attributions

Caer Goludd represents what we feel in the pit of our stomach. The fort of impediment is a fickle place, for we may sense our anger rise from here, shattering the windows of the forts, cracking the walls or its turrets, and yet it is the seat of our creativity. This fort represents the riches we enjoy in life and those things that make us feel good about ourselves. But in a compromised situation, we may feel the claw of envy, jealousy, or anger rise from the center of our being, gathering momentum as it rises to burst forth through the portal of Caer Feddwit above. We are easily frustrated in here and may feel that sometimes we are fighting a losing battle. Caer Goludd is that secret place within us that defines how we learn, what we learn, and what influences us; our vanity comes from here, as does our smugness and snobbery. The first stirrings of lust and carnality rise within the heat of this place; as sugars burn through the blood, so too does this place cause the screaming of our sex hormones to raise their heads and demand attention. This is the seat of our emotions; it is the vice that grips the core when we are in grief, anguish, or despair. The dizzying heights of elation and happiness can be felt here, as can the butterflies in the stomach when faced with the rush of attraction or anticipation.

If a divinatory tool falls onto this division, it is indicative of our passions—our emotional stability or instability, as the case may be. It is the origin of expression. If a querent needed insight into why a certain project feels hindered or is not meeting their expectations and the bone of cat is cast onto the sea realm of Caer Goludd, it would imply that the emotional connection the querent has to the material is one-sided, and this passion may appear superior and self-inflated. Total absorption in the project may have resulted in the querent appearing aloof and unapproachable. The answer to this would be to bring these aspects down to land and ground them in foundation, depending on what tools are falling on other parts of the glyph.

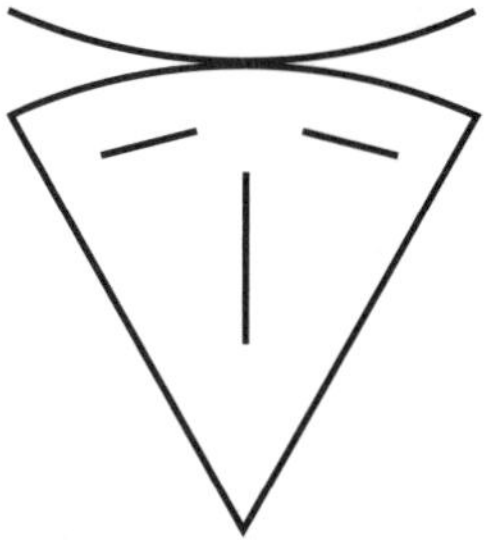

Caer Ochren: The Fort of Edges

The beast with the silver head, with the moon shining between its horns. It equates to the pineal gland.

Attributions

This is the fort of reflections, the great tower of mirrors. It appears as a mirrored enclosure, its walls silvered; it is the place where we see ourselves—or, rather, our reflection. Within its walls we see reflected what we want to see, not necessarily what is actually there. We may be pleased or displeased by our own image, and yet we may not realize that a mirrored reflection is not a true representation. The image is reversed; it is not how the world sees us. Its lunar associations teach us about the nature of perception. Remember that the moon does not shine by its own light, however beautiful it is; it shines by means of reflected light. Its true nature may well be hidden in its dark face that never sees the light of the sun; what we see is simply an illusion of mirrored or reflected light. We may judge ourselves harshly within the confines of Caer Ochren, for it is the seat of perception and effectiveness. We may conform to the standards and expectations of another here. The limitation of intelligence may impede our experiences, and we are in danger of becoming overanalytical within its mirrored courtyards.

If a tool is cast onto this division it is indicative of perception, intelligence, logic, rationality, and the manner by which we physically interact with the world. If the plant symbol for rosemary were to fall on the land aspect of Caer Ochren in a question where the querent felt that they were being misjudged, it would imply that a time-out is urgently needed. If the ogam symbol for oak fell in the sky realm of the same division, it would imply that the querent has endured too much of a situation that was untenable—the strength of oak would need to be grounded in order to bring rationality and logic to what is being perceived as a problem. Rosemary asks for time out to reflect, for temporary separation; oak in sky may have forced the querent into a corner where they feel they must continue to behave or act in a manner that arose out of want rather than necessity.

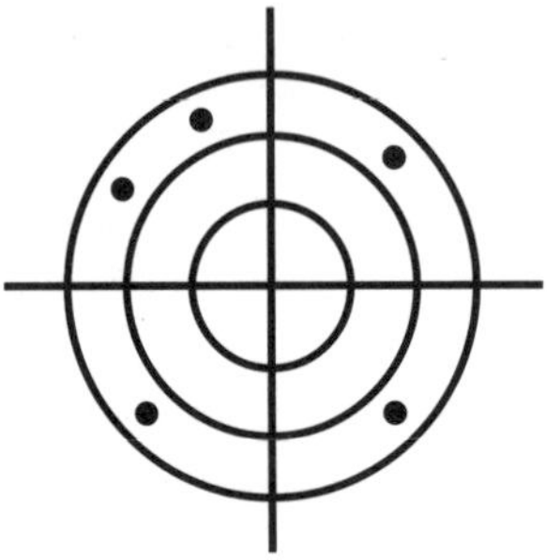

Caer Vandwy: The Fort of High Mystery

The glyph incorporates all other forts within its circles, which it intersects with the equal-armed cross. The point where the cross meets implies the origin and answer to mystery. It equates to the ovaries and testes of the endocrine system.

Attributions

This is the place of high mystery, wisdom, and knowledge. Caer Vandwy is the primal driving force of the human experience; it is the seat of reproduction, carnality, and lust. This fort can cause "lust blindness" and cause us to fall into the consuming flames of irrationality and obsession, and yet it is the place where we maintain the continuation of our species. This is the place of spirituality and the way in which we sense and perceive the subtle forces of the universe. It is a place of comparison, conformity, and competition, where we maintain or become victims of our vanity. Our confidence and self-esteem, so intricately tied to our sexual drive, sing from this place, but so too does inexperience and the inability to conceptualize.

For a tool to fall onto this division implies that the actual foundation of all that you are familiar with is being questioned. Issues of sexuality, love, and relationships come to the fore in this fort. If the ogam stave for yew fell in land and the bone of raven in the realm of sea in relation to the querent's sense of spiritual development, it would imply that a situation must end for transformation to be grounded. Body and spirit must unite; raven in sea would imply that the courage to create this change is being muddied by waves of emotion. The querent needs to ground in spirit and evaluate the need for transformation; raven may imply that too much emotion is pushing out the use of the intellect. Bring heart and mind together in unison.

Caer Rigor: The Fort of Rigidity

Balance and imbalance; the circle represents the self pivoted above the line of balance.

Attributions

This is a difficult fort. In a divinatory sense, any tools that fall within its realms will be challenging and possibly painful. It is the place of stumbling, rigidity, hardness, falling, and the ego. It dictates the manner by which we develop coping mechanisms that deal and make sense of the other forts. These may be appropriate or inappropriate. It is the most dangerous fort; here we can fall into the "I'm not good enough" or the "I'm right and you're wrong" mentality. We can become immovable and stubborn here. Our insecurities and those things that threaten us are realized here; it is the place we are most threatened and we ourselves may threaten. The qualities of Rigor are many, and it can propel us into action with sheer determination. It is a constructive place where personal strengths can be utilized effectively, and yet its opposite side can be immensely destructive.

For the division of Rigor to be selected by a divinatory tool implies that the situation may be inflexible, rigid, petrified, or cold. It points to the manner by which we are dealing or coping with the situation at hand. If the bone of rabbit were to fall on the sky realm of Caer Rigor when the question asked was in relation to a new project and anxiety therewith, it would imply that although a degree of trepidation is healthy and will avoid unnecessary risk taking, the querent may be too easily unnerved and may be overreaching their ambitions into intangibility, then panicking when things do not go according to plan. The quality of rabbit needs to be pulled down to sea and bridge the gap between what is tangible and what is ethereal. The querent may want to appear to be in full control, and yet their anxieties are too overwhelming; they are reaching too far, too quickly. Pull back.

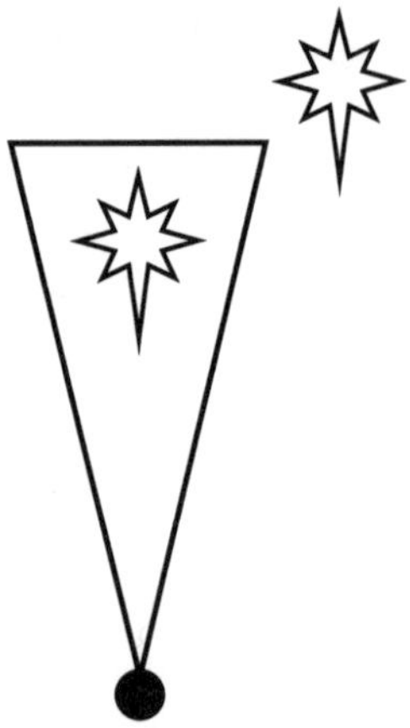

Caer Wydr: The Fort of Glass

The sigil represents a shard of glass reflecting the constellation of the Great Bear, Arthur (*arth* = bear in Welsh), which points to the place of being.

Attributions

This epitomizes inherited patterns that we have no control over and sets the scene for the remainder of our human lives. However determined our attempts to communicate with it are, we simply cannot; it is voiceless and will not permit itself to be swayed or influenced. It is the result of thousands of generations of genetic predisposition and inheritance. Caer Wydr expresses the fact that you are the sum total of all that has been before you. This function may appear mysterious and perhaps unfair, and yet it is a vital aspect of our human experience—we are influenced by the past, by blood and by memory, and this is held within the vast halls of Caer Wydr. Its influence can be seen within every subsequent fort. If Caer Siddi's illusion can be perceived, we must then also see through the walls of Caer Wydr, for its glass surface may obscure what lies beyond its borders. Glass is a peculiar substance; we may believe that we can see right through it, but light, shadow, and reflection can alter the view, preventing us from actually seeing what is there.

For a tool to fall onto this division in a reading would imply patterns of behavior, of ancestry and heritage and what we perceive as the foundations of our life—family, profession, relationships, etc.—are being addressed. If alder was cast onto the land realm of Caer Wydr and the plant oracle for mistletoe in sky in relation to a relationship crisis, it could imply that the foundation of the relationship has changed, and yet the behavior of those involved has not developed or evolved appropriately. Mistletoe in sky suggests that there is the potential for fertility and inspiration, but the absence of anything in sea implies that emotional separation may have ensued from complacency.

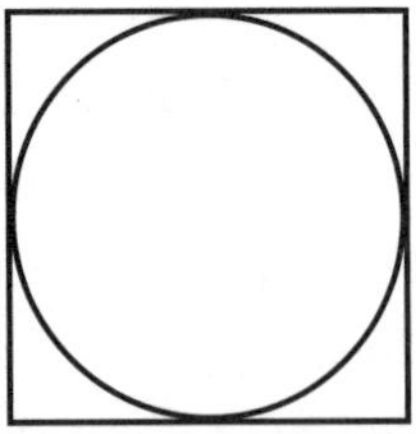

Caer Pedryfan: The Place of Being

A four-walled enclosure surrounds the circle of Annwn.

Attributions

This fort represents all that is physical, which may include but is not exclusive to your home, your body, and to all that you hold familiar and knowable. Anything that may be cast onto this division is indicative of your place in the here and now; therefore, if the question is in relation to the home and the ogam stave that represents rowan falls within its realm of sky, it would imply that the issues at hand are lofty and intangible, and may well be figments of your own imagination. Rowan would imply that insight and the ability to look within to bring the issues from the intangibleness of sky and into the form of land before is necessary before this issue will resolve itself. However, finding blackthorn in the realm of sea may imply that something or someone is attempting to take control of the situation by influence of coercion, instigated by an emotional and possibly irrational reaction.

A Sample Reading

Beth is a mother of three older children and works full-time. She is a talented artist and has recently been asked to offer workshops and talks on sacred art. She asked the oracle if she should risk taking time out from work and her family commitments to go part-time in order to pursue her artistic talents.

From a box containing a mix of bones, plant coins, and ogam staves, she randomly selected nine divinatory tools, held them in her closed hands while pondering the question, and allowed them to fall onto the divination cloth.

The bone of hare fell directly onto the circle of Annwn, demonstrating that the potential for this situation to arise is already forming in the sheer potential of Annwn and bubbling up to affect Beth's life; this is not simply a dream. Hare indicates that the time for causing this to be manifest on the physical plane is imminent. Hare is subtle, powerful, enigmatic, sensitive, and in tune with the subtle; this implies that Beth needs to be reliant on more than her physical senses to judge this.

The ogam for birch fell onto the land aspect of Caer Goludd, which implies that Beth is intensely passionate about this project, and it has imbued within her the sense that this could create a new beginning and colonize a new era of her life with new projects and possibilities. However, the presence of the ogam for blackthorn crossing from the sea realm of Caer Goludd into land indicates that there is some emotional displacement going on here; she needs to control the situation and think logically about the consequences of her action. Blackthorn may indicate that she is reacting with too much emotion, and this may cloud her vision a little. She needs to have the passion of Goludd, but she also needs to prevent it from running away with itself and becoming unruly or resulting in uncalculated risks.

Hawthorn in the land aspect of Caer Siddi indicates that she may well be overanxious about the risks to the material, work, and family aspects of her life. Hawthorn presents challenges, yes, but she may be worrying unnecessarily about what impact this project will have on the physicality of her professional situation. Her children are grown up; although living at home, they are financially independent, and yet Beth is maintaining the apron strings instead of bringing some rational emotions (sea) into the mix, with a clear idea of her aspirations (sky). With her talents being recognized, she is still maintaining the illusion that the money she earns is vital to the wellness of her domestic life, but hawthorn is suggesting that this is not the case.

Agrimony in the realm of sea in Caer Feddwit is reiterating the new beginning of birch in Goludd; this is the vocalization and the outward expression of that passion made manifest. She needs to liberate this impulse and give it voice, combining the feeling aspect of the place of communication with the foundation aspect of her passions in Caer Goludd. The absence of any tool in the realms of land and sky of Feddwit are indicative of the fact that emotional balance is key; do not be overcautious to maintain material security, and do not be flaky in your aspirations and have unrealistic dreams. As an artist, emotion in her work will touch people deeply.

Deer fell in the sky realm of Ochren and fennel in the land realm of the same division. Again, this is reiterating the need for emotional rationalization and stability to enable this situation to progress with positive results. These two aspects are in relation to the way Beth sees herself; naturally she is anxious and nervous to make such a change in her life after years of the status quo. Self-confidence has always been an issue, but she has new insights gained from experience and the situation would not have prevented itself had it been all sky; it has been offered because those in the position to realize her talents are able to perceive its far-reaching effects (sky) and its grounded aspect (land).

Two items fell beyond the border of the glyph and were disregarded. To look at the whole picture, the indication was that Beth has been overanxious and has some fears of changing the ebb and flow of her life, yet she is excited about the changes. All indications are in favor of her taking this new project and making a calculated risk that will no doubt pay off in the long run.

30

"Preiddeu Annwn" (The Spoils of Annwn) from the Book of Taliesin

To provide you with further background into the source material, here I will present my own translation of the poem that inspired the divination system described. It is immensely difficult to understand without further reference, visualization, and meditation. You will note that the poem starts with a praise to the Christian god and ends with a similar praise; it seems at odds with the theme of the poem, and it is believed that the Celtic poems most replete with Pagan themes all start and end with a praise to the Christian God. There are two possible reasons for this; on one hand it may indicate a manner by which future readers could identify the most relevant mystery material by hiding it in plain view. On the other hand it is possible that the early Christian scribes placed these words at the beginning and end as a way of containing their power. Perhaps we will never truly know.

There is great mystery here; read the poem, read the attributions, memorize the sigils and meanings and journey by means of the Goddess—who in this poem is referred to as Prydwen—and descend into the mysteries in search of the cauldron.

◆ ◆ ◆

I praise the Lord, sovereign of the kingly realm
Who extends his leadership across the entire world
In order was the prison of Gweir in Caer Siddi
Through the course of the tale of Pwyll and Pryderi
None before him went into it
By the heavy blue-grey chain restraining the loyal lad
And before the spoils of Annwn, bitterly he sang
And until judgment day our Bardic invocation shall persist
Three full loads of Prydwen, we went into it
Except seven, none came back from Caer Siddi.

I am splendid in praise, my song is heard
In Caer Pedryfan fully revolving
My first words were spoken concerning the cauldron
Which is kindled by the breath of nine maidens
The cauldron of the head of Annwn; what is its form?
With a dark ridge and pearls around its edge
It will not boil the food of a coward; it is not destined to do so
The flashing sword of Lleawg was thrust into it
And in the hand of Lleminawg it was left
And before the door of hell lanterns burned
And when we went with Arthur, resplendent toil
Except for seven, none came back from Caer Feddwit.

I am splendid in praise, my song greatly heard
In Caer Pedryfan, island of the radiant door
Fresh water and jet are mixed

Sparkling wine the spirit laid before their host
Three full loads of Prydwen, we went by sea
Except for seven, none returned from Caer Rigor.

Those little men of the Lord's scriptures are undeserving of me
Beyond the walls of Caer Wydr none saw Arthur's valor
Six thousand men stood upon its turrets
It was difficult to discourse with their watchman
Three full loads of Prydwen we went with Arthur
Except for seven, none returned from Caer Goludd.

Those pathetic men who trail their shields are undeserving of me
They know not who was created on what day
When at midday the god was born
He who made the one who did not go to the meadows of Defwy
They do not know the brindled ox and his stout collar
Seven-score links in its fastening
And when we went with Arthur, a sad journey
Except for seven, none returned from Caer Vandwy.

Those pathetic men with no go in them are undeserving of me
They know not on what day the lord was created
What hour of the day the ruler was born
What beast is it they guard with its silver head
When we went with Arthur, a sorrowful conflict
Except for seven, none returned from Caer Ochren.

Monks howl like a pack of dogs
From a clash with the masters who know
Is there one course to the wind? Is the sea but one water?
Is fire an invincible tumult, made of a single spark?
Monks gather in packs like wolves
From an encounter with the masters who know
They know not when the darkness and light divide
Nor wind, what is its course, what is its onrush

What place it ravages, what land it strikes
How many saints are lost in the void, and how many altars
I praise the Lord, the great sovereign
I shall not be sad; Christ will reward me.

Glossary

Please note that the Welsh letters *ll*, *ch*, *dd*, and *rh* in italics remain in their original form with no phonetic equivalent provided. Refer to the pronunciation guide for guidance. Note that the letter y has various sounds depending on its position within a word. Its phonetic description below is the nearest sound applicable within that word. Many terms in this glossary can be heard on YouTube: http://www.youtube.com/watch?v=T2cRWP-E8Vs or from http://angleseydruidorder.co.uk, then click on "explore" on the top menu bar, and finally "myths & story."

Afallach **(av-AHLL-*ach*)**—Mythological father of Modron.

Aicme **(AYKH-muh)**—The divisions of the ogam group into distinct groups of trees.

Ailm **(Ae-luhm)**—Irish Celtic name for pine.

Alban Arthan **(AL-Bann ARTH-ann)**—The festival of the winter solstice.

Alban Eilir **(AL-Bann AYE-leer)**—The festival of the spring equinox.

Alban Elfed **(AL-Bann ELL-ved)**—The festival of the autumn equinox.

Alban Hefin **(AL-Bann HEV-een)**—The festival of the summer solstice.

Amaethon **(am-AYETH-onn)**—Agricultural god.

Angar Kyfundawt (ANG-garr KUV-in-doubt)—A poem from the Book of Taliesin.

Annwn **(ANN-oon)**—The indigenous Celtic otherworld/underworld.

***Anyan* (ANN-eeann)**—The inherent nature of an object, animal, plant, or human.

***Ap* (APP)**—A designation to mean "son of."

***Aranrhod* (arh-ANN-rod)**—Sister of Gwydion, the mother of Lleu and Dylan.

***Arawn* (AR-ow-n)**—A king of Annwn.

***Awen* (AH-when)**—The flowing, unifying spirit of Celtica; divine inspiration.

***Barddas* (BARR-*ddas*)**—Compilation of Druidic theology attributed to Iolo Morganwg.

***Beith* (Bayh)**—Irish Celtic name for birch.

***Beli Mawr* (BELL-ee MA-oor)**—Ancestor deity of the British pantheon; literally means big fire or light.

***Bendith y Mamau* (BEN-deeth UGH MAM-aye)**—A race of otherworldly spirits akin to fairies.

***Bleiddwn* (BLAY-*dd*oon)**—Wolf cub offspring of Gwydion and Gilfaethwy.

***Blodeuedd* (blod-AY-e*dd*)**—A woman created from flowers in the fourth branch of the Mabinogi by the magicians Math and Gwydion as a bride for Lleu Llaw Gyffes.

***Blodeuwedd* (blod-AY-We*dd*)**—As above but in owl form.

***Blodyn* (BLOD-in)**—A flower.

***Braint* (BRR-aeent)**—A locality-specific deity on the Isle of Anglesey who shares a common etymological root with Brig/Briganti.

***Brân* (BRA-nn)**—Son of Llŷr, brother of Branwen and Manawydan.

***Branwen* (BRAN-wen)**—Sister of Brân and Manawydan, demigoddess of birds.

***Brenin* (BREN-een)**—A king.

***Cadwallon ap Cadfan* (kad-WALL-onn APP KAD-van)**—A sixth-century king of Gwynedd in North Wales.

***Cadwgan* (kad-OO-gann)**—One of the reputed physicians of Myddvai.

***Caer Fandwy* (VAN-doo-ee)**—A fortification in the poem "The Spoils of Annwn."

***Caer Feddwit* (FEDD-wit)**—A fortification in the poem "The Spoils of Annwn."

***Caer Goludd* (GOL-eedd)**—A fortification in the poem "The Spoils of Annwn."

***Caer Ochren* (OCH-wren)**—A fortification in the poem "The Spoils of Annwn."

***Caer Pedryfan* (ped-RUV-ann)**—The four-walled enclosure synonymous with the island of Britain. A fortification in the poem "The Spoils of Annwn."

***Caer Rigor* (REE-gor)**—A fortification in the poem "The Spoils of Annwn."

***Caer Siddi* (SIDD-ee)**—A fortification in the poem "The Spoils of Annwn."

***Caer Wydr* (WID-hr)**—A fortification in the poem "The Spoils of Annwn."

***Calan Gaeaf* (kal-ANN-Gay-av)**—The feast of Samhain/Halloween; literally translates as the calends of winter.

***Calan Mai* (kal-ANN-My)**—The feast of Beltane/May Day, literally translates as the calends of May.

***Cawlwyd* (cow-LOO-id)**—A valley presided over by the oldest owl in the world.

***Celtica* (KELTEE-KA)**—The name given to the combined cultures of the six Celtic nations and the unifying spirit of Celticness that unites them.

***Cerridwen* (kerr-ID-wen)**—The witch goddess and primary guardian of the cauldron of inspiration.

***Cigfa* (KEEG-va)**—Wife of Pryderi.

***Cilgwri* (kill-GOO-ree)**—A region presided over by the blackbird of Cilgwri, one of the world's oldest animals.

***Coblynau* (kob-LUNN-aye)**—A form of pixie.

***Coll* (Kuhl)**—Irish Celtic name for hazel.

***Creiddylad* (kray-*DD*Ul add)**—One of the fairest maidens to have lived. Two male deities fight for her hand in marriage every May Day until the end of time. She appears in the epic tale of how Culhwch won Olwen.

***Culhwch* (KILL-Hoo-ch)**—Tutelary hero of the Mabinogi tale *Culhwch ac Olwen.*

***Cwn Annwn* (KOON ANN-oon)**—Mythical dogs reputed to belong to Arawn and Gwyn ap Nudd. They are described as white with red-tipped ears.

***Derw* (DARE-oo)**—The oak.

***Derwydd* (DARE-with)**—A Druid.

***Dinas* (DEAN-ass)**—A city.

***Dôn* (DAWN)**—Celtic mother goddess.

***Duir* (Dehr)**—Irish Celtic name for oak.

***Dyfed* (DUV-ed)**—A county in South Wales.

***Dylan* (DULL-ann)**—Zoomorphic demigod of the sea who is birthed by Aranrhod in the fourth branch of the Mabinogi.

***Eadad* (Eh-duth)**—Irish Celtic name for poplar.

***Efnysien* (ev-NIS-ee-en)**—Half brother to the children of Llŷr. Shadow aspect found in the second branch of the Mabinogi.

***Einion* (AYNN-eeonn)**—One of the reputed physicians of Myddvai.

***Ellyll* (EHll-eell)**—A nature spirit akin to fairy.

***Englyn* (ENG-lyn)**—A poetic spell or incantation spoken in rhyming verse.

***Englynion* (eng-LUN-eeon)**—Plural of *englyn*.

***Euroswydd* (ay-ROSS-widd)**—Father of Efnysien and Nisien whose name means golden enemy.

***Fearn* (Fyarn)**—Irish Celtic name for alder.

***Gilfaethwy* (gill-VAYTH-wee)**—Son of Dôn, brother of Gwydion.

***Goewin* (GOY-ween)**—Virgin foot-holder of Math, the king of Gwynedd.

***Gorsedd Arberth* (GORR-sedd arr-BERR-th)**—A mound in South Wales from which miracles and wonders are seen.

***Gort* (Gohrd)**—Irish Celtic name for ivy.

***Govannon* (gov-ANN-onn)**—Smith demigod, a son of Dôn.

***Gronw* (GRONN-oo)**—Secret lover of Blodeuedd.

***Gruddieu* (GREEDD-ee-ay)**—One of the seven survivors to return from Ireland at the end of the second branch of the Mabinogi.

***Gryffydd* (GRIFF-eedd)**—One of the reputed physicians of Myddvai.

***Gwales* (GWAL-ess)**—An island in the Bristol Channel where the company of Brân rested after the war with Ireland.

***Gweir* (GWAY-rrh)**—Mythical exalted prisoner and an aspect of the divine child.

***Gwern* (GOO-errn)**—Son of Branwen, his name means Alder.

***Gwernabwy* (goo-errn-ABB-wee)**—Region presided over by the eagle of Gwernabwy, one of the oldest animals in the world.

***Gwialen* (gwee-AL-en)**—Wand; also cognate with penis.

***Gwion Bach* (GWEE-on BA-ch)**—The innocent employed to tend Cerridwen's cauldron.

***Gwybodaeth* (gwee-BOD-ay*th*)**—Welsh word meaning knowledge.

***Gwydd* (GOO-ee*dd*)**—Welsh word that refers to trees and magic.

***Gwyddon* (goo-WI*DD*-onn)**—A practitioner of magic.

***Gwyddoniaeth* (goo-WI*DD*ON-eay*th*)**—Welsh word for science and the language of Gwydd.

***Gwyddoniaid* (goo-WI*DD*ON-ee-ayd)**—Practitioners of magic.

***Gwyddor* (goo-WI*DD*-orr)**—Welsh word meaning alphabet.

***Gwydion* (GWEED-eeon)**—A magician who appears in the fourth branch of the Mabinogi and is mentioned by name in several of the Taliesin poems; renowned for his skills in magic.

***Gwyl Awst* (GOO-eel OUST)**—The festival of the first harvest, Lammas.

***Gwyl Ffraid* (GOO-eel F-Ride)**—The festival of Imbolc.

***Gwyn ap Nudd* (GWIN ap NI-*dd*)**—Celtic deity reputedly the king of the fairies, he leads the wild hunt on Samhain eve to gather the spirits of the dead. He fights with Gwythyr every May Day for the hand of Creiddylad.

***Gwynedd* (GOO-in-e*dd*)**—One of the largest counties in the North West of Wales.

***Gwythyr ap Greidol* (GWEE-thr ap GRAY-dol)**—A Celtic deity who fights Gwyn ap Nudd for the hand of Creiddylad.

***Hafgan* (HAV-gan)**—A king of Annwn whose name translates as summer song.

***Hafren* (HAV-ren)**—Old Welsh name for Sabrina, goddess of the river Severn.

***Heilyn* (HAY-lin)**—One of the seven survivors at the end of the second branch of the Mabinogi.

***Huath* (Hoo-uh)**—Irish Celtic name for hawthorn.

***Hudlath* (HID-lath)**—Literally a yard of magic; Welsh word for wand.

***Hychdwn* (HUH-*ch*-doon)**—Wild boar offspring of Gwydion and Gilfaethwy.

***Hyddwn* (HUH-*dd*-oon)**—Fawn offspring of Gwydion and Gilfaethwy.

***Idad* (Ih-duth)**—Irish Celtic name for yew.

***Imbas* (IM-bus)**—Irish equivalent to Awen.

***Iolo Morganwg* (YOLO More-GAN-oog)**—Poet genius and recorder of Druidic wisdom and theology, some of which are believed to have been forged.

Kat Godeu (KAT GOD-ay)—Literally means the battle of the trees. A poem from the Book of Taliesin.

***Llediaith* (LLED-eeay*th*)**—Welsh word meaning half or indistinct speech, attributed to the sea god Llŷr.

***Lleu Llaw Gyffes* (ll-ay ll-aw GUFF-ess)**—Abandoned son of Aranrhod and a central figure in the fourth branch of the Mabinogi. His name literally means light of skilful hand.

***Llwyd Cil Coed* (LLOO-wid KIL KO-eed)**—Character from the first and third branches of the Mabinogi who is responsible for the wasteland curse placed on Dyfed.

***Llyn Lliw* (LL-in LL-eeoo)**—The lake of the oldest salmon in the world.

***Llyn Y Fan Fach* (*LL*-in UGH Van VA-*ch*)**—The lake which features in the legend of the physicians of Myddvai.

***Llŷr* (LL-ir)**—Celtic god of the sea whose offspring play significant roles in the Mabinogi tales. He was one of the three exalted prisoners of the islands of Britain.

***Luis* (Loo-shuh)**—Irish Celtic name for rowan.

***Mabinogi* (mab-INN-Og-ee)**—Small tales, or tales of youth, the collective name given to a series of native Welsh tales, the most famed being the four branches of the Mabinogi.

***Mabinogion* (mab-inn-OGG-eeon)**—Incorrect yet common title attributed to the Mabinogi collection.

***Mabon* (MABB-onn)**—Son of the great goddess Modron; the divine child.

***Manawydan* (man-ah-WID-ann)**—Primary character in the third branch of the Mabinogi.

***Maponos* (MAPP-on-oss)**—Earlier Celtic term from which Mabon is derived.

***Mari Lwyd* (MAREE LOO-id)**—A peculiar folk tradition that involved a horse's skull, singing, and drinking alcohol. Attributed to the dark half of the year and believed to have psychopompic attributions.

***Math* (MA-th)**—High king of Gwynedd and a powerful Druid magician who features in the fourth branch of the Mabinogi.

***Matholwch* (math-ALL-oo-*ch*)**—A king of Ireland who marries Branwen, the daughter of Llŷr.

***Matrona* (MAT-rona)**—Earlier Celtic name from which Modron is derived.

***Meddwi* (ME*DD*-wee)**—Literally to be filled with mead; a euphemism for being intoxicated.

Modron **(MOD-ron)**—The great mother goddess.

Morfyd **(MORR-vid)**—Daughter of Modron and King Urien Rheged.

Muin **(Mooin)**—Irish Celtic name for bramble.

Myddvai **(MUDD-vai)**—The region reputed to home the legendary physicians of Myddvai.

Neidr **(NEIGH-dur)**—Welsh word for snake.

Ngetal **(Nyay-tuhl)**—Irish Celtic name for reed or broom.

Nisien **(NIS-ee-en)**—Meaning peaceful; the brother of Efnysien.

Nuinn **(Noo-hin)**—Irish Celtic name for ash.

Olwen **(OLL- wen)**—Female character from the Mabinogi tale *Culhwch ac Olwen*.

Onn **(On)**—Irish Celtic name for gorse.

Owain **(OH-wine)**—Son of King Urien Rheged and Modron.

Penarddun **(pen-ARR-ddin)**—Derived from *pen*, meaning head/chief, and *arddun*, meaning beautiful. She is the mother of the children of Llŷr and Efnysien and Nisien.

Pheryllt **(FAIR-ee-llt)**—The unknown caste of magicians that Cerridwen consulted; also synonymous with the magician Virgil.

Pryderi **(PRUD-erry)**—The kidnapped son of Rhiannon who is the main protagonist in the first, third, and fourth branches of the Mabinogi.

Prydwen **(PRUD-wen)**—The divine feminine figure in the poem "The Spoils of Annwn," she is represented as a ship that carries Arthur, Taliesin, and their explorers on a quest in search of the cauldron.

Pwca **(POO-ka)**—A mischievous Welsh nature spirit.

Pwyll **(PWEE-ll)**—The main character of the first branch of the Mabinogi who trades places with the king of Annwn. He is Rhiannon's husband.

Quert **(Kooert)**—Irish Celtic name for apple.

Rhedynfre **(*rhed*-INN-vre)**—Region presided over by one of the oldest stags in the world.

Rhiannon **(rhee- ANN-onn)**—A goddess, also known as Epona in Celto-Romano culture, and a main character in the first and third branches of the Mabinogi. She was the otherworld wife of Pwyll and the mother of Pryderi.

Rhiwallon **(*rheeoo*-A*LL*-onn)**—Reputed physician and father of the physicians of Myddvai.

Rhys Grug **(*RH*-ees GREEG)**—Employer of Rhiwallon.

Rith **(REETH)**—The assumed shape or form of any object, animate or inanimate.

Ruis **(Roosh)**—Irish Celtic name for elder.

Saille **(Sol-yeh)**—Irish Celtic name for willow.

Straif **(Strayf)**—Irish Celtic name for blackthorn.

Swyngyfaredd **(zooeen-GUVAR-e*dd*)**—A practitioner of folkloric magic.

Taliesin **(tal-YES-inn)**—The prophetic spirit, poet, he with the radiant brow; Gwion Bach becomes Taliesin.

Taran **(TARR-ann)**—Welsh word for thunder.

Tinne **(Tinn-yuh)**—Irish Celtic name for holly.

Trioedd Ynys Prydein **(TREE-OHee*dd* UN-iss PRUD-aeen)**—The Triads of the Islands of Britain, a collection of wisdom written down in the form of triadic verse.

Twrch Trwyth **(TOOR-*ch* TROO-with)**—A mythological boar that features in the challenges of Culhwch in the tale *Culhwch ac Olwen*.

Tylwyth Teg **(TUL-with TEG)**—The Welsh word commonly ascribed to the fairy race.

Ur **(Oor)**—Irish Celtic name for heather.

Urien Rheged **(OORR-ee-en RHEG-ed)**—A king of Britain who mated with Modron.

Ynawg **(UN-aoog)**—One of the seven survivors at the end of the second branch of the Mabinogi.

Yspaddaden **(us-PADDAD-en)**—Primary antagonist in the tale *Culhwch ac Olwen*; in old Welsh it literally means hawthorn.

Ystoria **(us-TORR-eeah)**—Old Welsh term that means story or histories.

A Guide to Welsh Pronunciation

The stress of any word almost exclusively stands on the penultimate syllable.

A vowel is elongated if it appears with a circumflex above it, commonly called a "To Bach" in Welsh, meaning a little roof. For example—Don without the circumflex would be pronounced as *Donn*. With the addition of a circumflex, Dôn would be pronounced *Dawn*.

The Welsh Alphabet

a, b, c, ch, d, dd, e, f, ff, g, ng, h, i, l, ll, m, n, o, p, ph, r, rh, s, t, th, u, w, y

Welsh Vowels

a -	Short as in *mat*	long as in *farmer*
e-	Short as in *let*	long as in *bear*
i-	Short as in *pit*	long as in *meet*
o-	Short as in *lot*	long as in *lore*
u-	Short as in *ill*	long as in *limb*
w-	Short as in *look*	long as in *fool*
y-	Short as in *up*	long as in *under*

Welsh Consonants

Some may be similar in sound to their English counterparts but with emphasis on heavy aspiration of sound.

b-	as in *bin*
c-	as in *cat*
ch-	as in *loch*, never as in *chin*
d-	as in *dad*

dd-	as in *them*, never as in *thin*
e-	as in *elephant*
f-	as in *van*
ff-	as in *off*
g-	as in *gate*, never as in *gem*
ng-	as in *song*, never as in *linger*
h-	as in *hit*; it is never silent
l-	as in *lit*
ll-	no counterpart; voice by placing tip of tongue in *L* position and exhaling voicelessly through the sides of the mouth
m-	as in *mat*
n-	as in *nit*
p-	as in *part*
ph-	as in *phrase*
r-	trilled by the tip of the tongue, as *ravioli* in Italian
rh-	no counterpart; voice by placing tongue in *R* position and exhaling quickly and harshly but voicelessly through the narrow gap the lips form
s-	as in *sit*, never as in *kiss*
t-	as in *tap*
th-	as in *thick*, never as in *them*

Bibliography

Manuscripts Consulted

Peniarth MS 2. Llyfr Taliesin (Book of Taliesin). Fourteenth Century. National Library of Wales.

Peniarth MS 1. Llyfr Du Caerfyrddin (Black Book of Carmarthen). Thirteenth Century. National Library of Wales.

Peniarth MS 4. Llyfr Gwyn Rhydderch (White Book of Rhydderch). Fourteenth Century. National Library of Wales.

These manuscripts can be viewed by means of the National Library of Wales website, which can be found at www.llgc.org.uk; follow the links to "Digital Mirror."

Jesus College MS 111. Llyfr Coch Hergest (The Red Book of Hergest). Fourteenth Century. Bodleian Library, Oxford. This MS can be viewed by following this link: http://image.ox.ac.uk/show?collection=jesus&manuscript=ms111

◆ ◆ ◆

Ab Ithel, Williams J., trans. *The Barddas of Iolo Morganwg*. Boston: Weiser Books, 2004 (original 1862).

Aldhouse-Green, Miranda. *Dying for the Gods*. Stroud, Gloucestershire: Tempus Publishing, 2002.

———. *The Quest for the Shaman*. London: Thames & Hudson, 2005.

———. *Seeing the Woods for the Trees: The Symbolism of Trees and Wood in Ancient Gaul and Britain*. Aberystwyth: University of Wales Center for Advanced Welsh and Celtic Studies, 2000.

Anwyl, E. *The Poetry of the Gogynfeirdd*. Denbigh: Gee and Son, MDCCCCIX [sic].

Barnhart, Robert K., ed. *Chambers Dictionary of Etymology*. Edinburgh: Chambers, 1988.

Bevan, Gareth, and Patrick Donovan, eds. *Geiriadur Prifysgol Cymru (A Dictionary of the Welsh Language)*. Cardiff: University of Wales Press, 2004.

Billington, Penny. *The Path of Druidry*. Woodbury, MN: Llewellyn Publications, 2011.

Bown, Deni. *The Royal Horticultural Society New Encyclopaedia of Herbs and Their Uses*. London: Dorling Kindersley, 1995.

Breeze, Andrew. *Medieval Welsh Literature*. Dublin: Four Courts Press, 1997.

Brickell, Christopher, ed. *The Royal Horticultural Society Gardeners" Encyclopaedia of Plants and Flowers*. London: Dorling Kindersley, 1989.

Bromwich, Rachel, and Simon D. Evans. *Culhwch ac Olwen*. Cardiff: Gwasg Prifysgol Cymru, 1997.

Bromwich, Rachel, ed. *Trioedd Ynys Prydein: The Triads of the Island of Britain*. Cardiff: University of Wales Press, 2006.

Carr-Gomm, Philip, and Stephanie Carr-Gomm. *The Druid Plant Oracle*. London: Connections, 2007.

Cunliffe, Barry. *The Ancient Celts*. Oxford: Oxford University Press, 1997.

Cunningham, Scott. *Encyclopedia of Magical Herbs*. St. Paul, MN: Llewellyn, 2000.

Daniel, Iestyn R. *A Medieval Welsh Mystical Treatise*. Aberystwyth: University of Wales Center for Advanced Welsh and Celtic Studies, 1997.

Davies, Edward. *The Mythology and Rites of the British Druids*. London: J. Booth, 1809.

Davies, Sioned. *The Mabinogion*. Oxford: Oxford University Press, 2007.

Day, Christian. *The Witches Book of the Dead*. San Francisco, CA: Red Wheel/Weiser, 2011.

Dugan, Ellen. *Practical Protection Magick*. Woodbury, MN: Llewellyn Publications, 2011.

Durdin-Robertson, Lawrence. *The Year of the Goddess*. Wellingborough: Aquarian Press,1990.

Enright, Michael. *The Sutton Hoo Sceptre and the Roots of Celtic Kingship*. Dublin: Four Courts Press, 2006.

Evans, J. Gwenogvryn. *The Black Book of Carmarthen*. Pwllheli: Evans, 1910.

———. *Facsimile and Text of the Book of Taliesin*. Llanbedrog: Evans, 1915.

———. *The Text of the Book of Aneirin*. Pwllheli: Evans, 1922.

———. *The White Book of Mabinogion (Llyfr Gwyn Rhydderch)*. Pwllheli: Evans, 1909.

Evans, William. *The Bards of the Isle of Britain*. Red Wharf Bay: Evans, 1915.

Farrar, Janet, and Stewart Farrar. *The Witches' Goddess*. Washington: Phoenix Publishing, 1987.

Ferguson, Anna-Marie. *The Llewellyn Tarot*. Woodbury, MN: Llewellyn Publications, 2010.

Ford, Patrick K. *The Celtic Poets*. Belmont: Ford & Bailie, 1999.

———. *Ystoria Taliesin*. Cardiff: University of Wales Press, 1992.

———, ed. *Math uab Mathonwy*. Belmont: Ford & Bailie, 1999.

———, trans. *The Mabinogi and Other Medieval Welsh Tales*. Los Angeles, CA: University of California Press, 1977.

Fortune, Dion. *Psychic Self-Defense*. York Beach: Weiser Books, 1992.

———. *The Secrets of Doctor Taverner*. York Beach: Weiser Books, 2011.

Frazer, Sir James. *The Golden Bough*. Ware: Wordsworth Reference, 1993.

French, Claire. *The Celtic Goddess*. Edinburgh: Floris Books, 2001.

Fries, Jan. *Cauldron of the Gods: A Manual of Celtic Magick*. Oxford: Mandrake Press, 2003.

Garner, Alan. *The Owl Service*. London: Harper Collins, 2005.

Graham, Mark, and Heather Buchan. *The Celtic Tree Ogham*. Milverton: Cappall Bann, 2006.

Graves, Robert. *The White Goddess*. London: Faber and Faber, 1961.

Green, Miranda J. *Exploring the World of the Druids*. London: Thames & Hudson, 1997.

———. *The Gods of the Celts*. Gloucester: Allan Sutton, 1986.

Griggs, Barbara. *The Green Witch*. London: Vermilion, 1993.

Gruffydd, W. J. *Math Vab Mathonwy: An Inquiry into the Origins and Development of the Fourth Branch of the Mabinogi*. Cardiff: University of Wales Press, 1928.

———. *Rhiannon: An Inquiry into the Origins of the First and Third Branches of the Mabinogi*. Cardiff: University of Wales Press, 1953.

Guest, Charlotte, trans. *Mabinogion, the Four Branches*. Felin Fach: Llannerch Publications, 1990.

———. *Mabinogion Legends* (facsimile reprint of 1849 edition). Felin Fach: Llannerch Publications, 1992.

Gwyndaf, Robin. *Welsh Folk Tales*. Cardiff: National Museums and Galleries of Wales, 1999.

Haycock, Marged, ed. and trans. *Legendary Poems from the Book of Taliesin*. Aberystwyth: CMCS, 2007.

———. *Llyfr Taliesin, Cylchgrawn Llyfrgell Genedlaethol Cymru Cyf XXV*. Aberystwyth: Rhif 4, 1988.

———. "Preiddeu Annwn and the Figure of Taliesin." *Studia Celtica*, vol. XVIII/XIX. Cardiff: University of Wales Press, 1983/84.

Hoffman, David. *Welsh Herbal Medicine*. Abercastle: Abercastle Publications, 1978.

Hole, Christina. *A Dictionary of British Folk Customs*. St. Albans: Granada Publishing, 1979.

Hope, Murray. *Practical Celtic Magic*. London: The Aquarian Press, 1987.

Hughes, H. Brython. *Tlysau Ynys Prydein*. Wrexham: Hughes a'i fab, 1902.

Hughes, Kristoffer. *From the Cauldron Born: Exploring the Magic of Welsh Legend and Lore*. Woodbury, MN: Llewellyn Publications, 2012.

———. "Magical Transformation in the Book of Taliesin and the Spoils of Annwn" (essay, unpublished). http://www.druidry.org/events-projects/mount-haemus-award/thirteenth-mt-haemus-lecture

Hutton, Ronald. *Blood and Mistletoe*. New Haven: Yale University Press, 2009.

———. *The Druids*. London: Hambledon Continuum, 2007.

———. *The Pagan Religions of the Ancient British Isles*. London: BCA, 1991.

Ifans, Rhiannon. *Gwerthfawrogi'r Chwedlau*. Aberystwyth: Y Ganolfan Astudiaethau Addysg, 1999.

Isaac, Evan. *Coelion Cymru*. Aberystwyth: Y Clwb Llyfrau Cymreig, 1938.

Jones, Gwilym T. *The Rivers of Anglesey*. Bangor: Research Center Wales, 1989.

Jones, Gwyn, and Thomas Jones, trans. *The Mabinogion*. London: Everyman's Library, 1949.

Jones, Owen, Iolo Morganwg, and William Owen Pughe, eds. *The Myvyrian Archaiology of Wales*. Denbigh: Thomas Gee, 1870.

Koch, John T., ed. *The Celtic Heroic Age*. Aberystwyth: Celtic Studies Publications, 2000.

Kondratiev, Alexei. *Celtic Rituals*. Dublin: New Celtic Publishing, 1998.

———. "Lugus: The Many Gifted Lord," http://www.imbas.org/articles/lugus.html

Lindahl, Carl (et al). *Medieval Folklore*. Oxford: Oxford University Press, 2002.

Loomis, Roger Sherman. *Celtic Myth and Arthurian Romance*. London: Constable, 1926.

MacCulloch, J. A. *The Religion of the Ancient Celts*. London: Constable, 1911.

Markale, Jean. *The Druids*. Rochester, NY: Inner Traditions, 1999.

Matthews, Caitlín. *Mabon and the Guardians of Celtic Britain*. Rochester, NY: Inner Traditions, 2002.

Matthews, John. *Taliesin: The Last Celtic Shaman*. Rochester, NY: Inner Traditions, 2002.

Matthews, John, and Caitlín Matthews. *British and Irish Mythology*. London: Diamond Books, 1995.

Monmouth, Geoffrey of. *The History of the Kings of Britain*. London: Penguin Classics, 1966.

———, translated by John J. Parry. *The Life of Merlin: Vita Merlini*. Marston Gate: Forgotten Books, 2008.

Morris-Jones, John. *Taliesin*. Cardiff: Y Cymrodor, 1918.

Mountfort, Paul Rhys. *Ogam: The Celtic Oracle of the Trees*. Rochester: Destiny Books, 2001.

Nash, D. W. *Taliesin, or Bards and Druids of Britain*. London: John Russell Smith, 1858.

Newman, Paul. *Lost Gods of Albion*. New York: Sutton Publishing, 1999.

Nichols, Ross. *The Book of Druidry*. New York: Castle Books, 2009.

Nimmo, Jenny. *The Snow Spider*. London: Egmont, 1986.

Owen, Elias. *Welsh Folklore* (facsimile). Felinfach: Llanerch Publishers, 1996.

Parker, Will. *The Four Branches of the Mabinogi*. California: Bardic Press, 2005.

Pughe, John. *The Physicians of Myddvai* (facsimile reprint of 1861 edition). Felinfach: Llanerch Publications, 1993.

Rees, Alwyn, and Brinley Rees. *Celtic Heritage*. London: Thames & Hudson, 1961.

Ross, Anne. *Druids: Preachers of Immortality*. Stroud: Tempus, 1999.

———. *Pagan Celtic Britain*. London: Constable, 1967.

Rudgley, Richard. *Pagan Resurrection: A Force for Evil or the Future of Western Spirituality?* London: Arrow Books, 2006.

Sikes, Wirt. *British Goblins: Welsh Folklore, Fairy Mythology, Legends and Traditions*. London: Sampson Low, Marston, Searle & Rivington, 1880.

Skene, W. F. *The Four Ancient Books of Wales*. Edinburgh: Edmonston & Douglas, 1868.

Smith, Steven R. *Wylundt's Book of Incense*. York Beach, ME: Samuel Weiser, 1996.

Steel, Susannah. *Neal's Yard Remedies*. London: Dorling Kindersley, 2011.

Sugget, Richard. *A History of Magic and Witchcraft in Wales*. Stroud: The History Press, 2008.

Thomson, Derick S. *Branwen Uerch Lyr.* Dublin: The Dublin Institute for Advanced Studies, 1986.

Tolstoy, Nikolai. *The Quest for Merlin*. London: Hamish Hamilton, 1985.

Vickery, Roy. *Oxford Dictionary of Plant-Lore*. Oxford: Oxford University Press, 1995.

Williams, John. *Gomer*. London: Hughes and Butler, 1854.

Williams, Sir Ifor. *Chwedl Taliesin*. Cardiff: Gwasg Prifysgol Cymru, 1957.

Williams, Taliesin. *Iolo Manuscripts*. Liverpool: Welsh Manuscripts Society, 1848.

INDEX

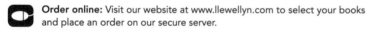

Kristoffer Hughes
from the
Cauldron Born
Exploring the Magic
of Welsh Legend & Lore

From the Cauldron Born

Exploring the Magic of Welsh Legend & Lore

Kristoffer Hughes

This exploration of the Welsh-Celtic myth of the prophet/poet Taliesin and the witch/goddess Cerridwen takes the reader on a transformative journey. It introduces them to core Celtic philosophy and magic, then embarks on a powerful, experiential foray into one of Wales' most profound legends. Readers will gain a deep understanding of the myth that is the heart of Celtic mystery and become well-versed in a magical ritual for successfully working with one of Celtica's most esteemed goddesses: Cerridwen.

Author Kristoffer Hughes, a practicing Druid and scholar, examines the historical development of the Taliesin myth, provides an engaging in-depth analysis of each character's archetypal role in the story, and presents practical applications, including a year-long magic ritual. As lyrical as it is practical, this unique guide offers readers the tools and understanding to fully immerse themselves into the mysteries of Celtic magic.

978-0-7387-3349-4 • 6 x 9 • 312 pp.

the Journey into Spirit
A PAGAN'S PERSPECTIVE ON
DEATH, DYING & BEREAVEMENT
KRISTOFFER HUGHES

The Journey Into Spirit

A Pagan's Perspective on Death, Dying & Bereavement

Kristoffer Hughes

Death is not the end, and neither is it the beginning; it is one step along a perpetual, never-ending road of being.

Move beyond the fear that surrounds death. Explore your own attitudes toward a profound but often taboo subject. Discover within yourself life-affirming beliefs about every state of existence. Written by a Druid priest who has worked in the mortuary profession for over two decades, *The Journey Into Spirit* illuminates the three realms of existence—physical, spirit, and soul/source—meditating upon each realm with stories from the author's close work with death and his deeply personal spiritual experiences.

Discover powerful rituals to honor family and friends in spirit as you join author Kristoffer Hughes in this beautiful journey of insight and practical guidance.

978-0-7387-4075-1 • 6 x 9 • 312 pp.

"Respectful to tradition and relevant to the present . . .
An engaging and readable introduction to Druidry for today."
JOHN MICHAEL GREER,
Grand Archdruid of the Ancient Order of Druids in America and the author of The Druidry Handbook
Penny Billington
THE PATH OF DRUIDRY
Walking the Ancient Green Way

Practical
Protection
Magick
Guarding & Reclaiming
Your Power
Ellen
Dugan

Practical Protection Magick

Guarding & Reclaiming Your Power

Ellen Dugan

Embrace your inner warrior to safeguard your personal power. Use protection magick and psychic self-defense to stay strong, healthy, and happy.

With honesty and humor, best-selling author Ellen Dugan teaches how to weave safe and sensible protection magick into your practice and daily life. This unique practical guide reveals how to pinpoint your psychic strengths, set boundaries, diagnose a problem with divination, and maintain health on physical, psychic, and magickal levels. You'll also find simple and potent spells, rituals, and warding techniques to defend against psychic attacks, emotional and psychic vampires, hexes, unwanted ghosts, and other forms of negativity threatening your home and your well-being.

978-0-7387-2168-2 • 6 x 9 • 240 PP.

To Write to the Author

If you wish to contact the author or would like more information about this book, please write to the author in care of Llewellyn Worldwide and we will forward your request. Both the author and the publisher appreciate hearing from you and learning of your enjoyment of this book and how it has helped you. Llewellyn Worldwide cannot guarantee that every letter written to the author can be answered, but all will be forwarded. Please write to:

Kristoffer Hughes
c/o Llewellyn Worldwide
2143 Wooddale Drive
Woodbury, MN 55125-2989

Please enclose a self-addressed stamped envelope for reply or $1.00 to cover costs. If outside the USA, enclose an international postal reply coupon.

Many of Llewellyn's authors have websites with additional information and resources. For more information, please visit our website:

WWW.LLEWELLYN.COM